Leading Innovation and Entrepreneurship in Healthcare

This book is dedicated to the memory of Syl Kearney, a wonderful, loving, kind and supportive Dad who sadly lost his battle with cancer in 2015. Dad, you always made a difference and you inspired me to write this book. You are a void that will never be filled, forever loved and deeply missed.

Leading Innovation and Entrepreneurship in Healthcare

A Global Perspective

Claudine Kearney

Assistant Professor of Entrepreneurship and Strategy, Graduate School of Healthcare Management, RCSI University of Medicine and Health Sciences, Ireland

Edward Elgar
PUBLISHING

Cheltenham, UK • Northampton, MA, USA

Published by
Edward Elgar Publishing Limited
The Lypiatts
15 Lansdown Road
Cheltenham
Glos GL50 2JA
UK

Edward Elgar Publishing, Inc.
William Pratt House
9 Dewey Court
Northampton
Massachusetts 01060
USA

Paperback edition 2022

A catalogue record for this book
is available from the British Library

Library of Congress Control Number: 2021952127

This book is available electronically in the **Elgar**online
Business subject collection
http://dx.doi.org/10.4337/9781839104282

ISBN 978 1 83910 427 5 (cased)
ISBN 978 1 83910 428 2 (eBook)
ISBN 978 1 0353 0028 0 (paperback)

Printed and bound in Great Britain by TJ Books Ltd, Padstow

Contents

Preface

The nature of healthcare has changed significantly over the last few decades with unimaginable advances in medicine, science and medical devices becoming the norm. Healthcare organizations must continue to survive the unprecedented challenges they are currently facing and likely to face in the future. Such challenges, while having a greater impact on some countries, are not restricted to any one culture or nation. Globally, healthcare is challenged with aging populations and an increasing number of people living with long-term morbidity and multiple comorbidities requiring continuous medical treatment – these challenges have been further escalated as a result of the global Covid-19 pandemic. Healthcare leaders need to embrace opportunities for innovation and entrepreneurship that will enhance the delivery of care, save lives and serve multiple stakeholders and society, in the ultimate goal that leads us all to better health, healthcare and well-being. Such innovation is challenging in a sector that is so overwhelmed by having to do more with less; however, it is through this entrepreneurial spirit that clinicians, healthcare professionals, key staff and experts are motivated to create new innovative ideas. Leaders need to drive this entrepreneurial spirit and vision that accomplishes the imaginable; they need to make it happen and keep making it happen!

This book is timely given the current global healthcare challenges. It provides a framework for understanding the critical elements for Leading Innovation and Entrepreneurship in Healthcare. This book is composed of ten chapters divided into four key sections that are systematically organized around the nature, development, leadership and future of innovation and entrepreneurship in healthcare, as follows.

Part I of the book, "Meaning and Nature of Innovation and Entrepreneurship in Healthcare," comprises one chapter. Chapter 1, "Understanding Creativity, Innovation and Entrepreneurship in Healthcare," lays the foundation for understanding the nature of innovation and entrepreneurship in a healthcare setting. Creativity, innovation and entrepreneurship are important concepts and critical for the global advancement of healthcare. Within healthcare it is important to recognize that creativity is the first step for innovation, which can emerge anywhere and at any level within the organization. Innovation is a necessity for healthcare now and in the future, particularly with the growing demand on the healthcare system driven by an aging population, an increasing prevalence of chronic disease and illnesses, and changes in patient needs with requirements for more personalized patient care. Scientific and technological advances are at the center of healthcare innovation. Therefore leaders of healthcare organizations need to develop a climate that supports and empowers individuals and teams to be creative and innovative and in doing so nurture the entrepreneurial spirit and apply core business principles to bring new ideas into commercially viable medical innovations that will change the world of healthcare.

Once the foundation of innovation and entrepreneurship is understood the question is how it can be developed within healthcare. This is examined in Part II, "Developing Innovation and Entrepreneurship in Healthcare: A Strategic Perspective," comprising three chapters. Chapter 2 focuses on "Developing Innovation in Healthcare." Over recent decades the field of healthcare has experienced significant innovations developed to enhance life expectancy and quality of life. The development of innovation in healthcare is a response to the critical needs of patients that can emerge over time or as a result of certain unprecedented circumstances that quickly emerge and need to be addressed urgently. This can be a result of the aging population and growing needs to address certain chronic diseases or the unprecedented Covid-19 global pandemic. Understanding innovation, different types of innovation and the opportunities for innovation is significant for the field of healthcare. Healthcare organizations that support and nurture the innovative capability of their individuals and engage in open innovation can lead to an effective process of innovation that will result in new products, services, processes, technologies and delivery methods that generate patient value and enhance the healthcare system. It is the effective link between scientific and technological advances and meeting the diverse needs of stakeholders that leads to successful innovations that generate value in healthcare.

Major organizational elements must be aligned to effectively drive innovation and entrepreneurship. Chapter 3, "Strategic Perspective: Integration of Innovation and Entrepreneurship in Healthcare," examines how innovation and entrepreneurship are central to the field of healthcare, and need to be integrated into an organizational strategy to lead to greater and more timely scientific and technological advancements in healthcare. At a time when healthcare systems globally are under severe pressure innovation becomes a necessity to address the challenges and global crises. While there are major advancements in the field of healthcare, it can take many years for an innovation to get to market. More could be accomplished in recognizing how best to overcome time and resource limitations. New strategies are necessary and can be achieved by effectively integrating innovation and entrepreneurship with strategy.

Chapter 4, "Corporate Entrepreneurship, Well-Being, Resilience and Positive Psychology in Healthcare," focuses on the value of corporate entrepreneurship to staff. Psychological well-being and resilience is an integral part of our personal and professional life and has become particularly challenging within the field of healthcare, impacting organizational outcomes, employee productivity, and quality and delivery of patient care. In this context, corporate entrepreneurship and strategic entrepreneurship within healthcare organizations can engender personal satisfaction, motivation, well-being, resilience and a positive psychological mindset by supporting and facilitating healthcare professionals in their innovative and entrepreneurial endeavors. This can bring about positive change among individual healthcare professionals, patients, organizations, citizens and society at large.

Leadership that motivates, supports and encourages innovation and entrepreneurial behavior among individuals and teams is imperative to successful innovative outcomes. Part III, "Leading Innovation, Entrepreneurship and Design Thinking in Healthcare," comprises three chapters. Chapter 5, "Leadership and its Impact on Innovation and Entrepreneurship in Healthcare" examines leadership that is no longer focused on formal senior positions, but the role of all healthcare professionals throughout the healthcare organization. Traditional hierarchical practices have more recently given way to recognition of leaders as part of a group and leadership as a more interactive process. Leadership style and practices have a significant impact on healthcare organizations and their engagement in innovation and entrepreneurship. Therefore, it is paramount to ensure the right leadership practices that will improve patient experience and care; reduce medical errors, infection and mortality; increase staff retention and morale; and decrease staff turnover, absenteeism, stress and burnout. On this premise the integration of entrepreneurship and leadership to achieve entrepreneurial leadership can make a major contribution to the field of healthcare.

Innovation and entrepreneurship do not happen without individuals and teams who are supported to think beyond the normal and make the impossible possible. Chapter 6 explores "Innovation and Entrepreneurship among Individuals and Teams in Healthcare." The challenges facing many healthcare organizations in today's complex and unprecedented environment is how to effectively develop creativity and innovation among individuals and teams. Healthcare organizations need to meet the demands of a diverse group of stakeholders but most importantly address patient needs. The ability of the organization to address daily healthcare needs while at the same time having a futuristic approach to innovation is challenging yet imperative. Innovation and entrepreneurship requires people. Therefore healthcare organizations need to utilize the competencies and creativity of their people to work together to identify opportunities for the betterment of healthcare. This requires leadership that drives innovation and entrepreneurship, and facilitates continuous engagement, collaboration, teamwork and effective communication.

The role and benefits of design thinking is being recognized within the field of healthcare. Chapter 7, "Understanding and Leading Design Thinking in Healthcare," examines design thinking which is important to the field of healthcare with its emphasis on empathy, collaboration and prototyping to find the best innovative patient-centered solutions that will transform the delivery of care. Within healthcare, leaders need to embrace design thinking so they can gain an in-depth understanding of patients' needs and support their teams to generate innovation to address those needs, achieving better patient outcomes, improving patient experience and satisfaction, and delivering higher standards of care. Effective leadership is paramount to the success of design thinking in healthcare.

Part IV, "Making It All Happen: A Future-oriented Mindset", comprises three chapters. Chapter 8 examines "Women in Leadership, Innovation and Entrepreneurship in Healthcare." In the 21st century, women represent 70 percent of the healthcare workforce, yet globally leadership roles, particularly at more senior levels, continue to be highly skewed toward men. This continuous underrepresentation of women in leadership roles in the healthcare sector is a global norm that needs to change. Women in innovation and entrepreneurship in healthcare are also experiencing gender bias. Healthcare organizations are not adequately addressing the disparity of gender equality in leadership, innovation and entrepreneurship. To transform healthcare, innovation and entrepreneurship need to start with patient needs at the forefront. This can be best achieved when there is supportive leadership and equal opportunities for all qualified healthcare professionals to hold leadership roles and engage in the innovation process utilizing competencies and experiences and addressing fundamental gaps and deficiencies in healthcare delivery.

The right human capital is critical for healthcare organizations seeking a pathway for innovation and entrepreneurship that will positively impact key stakeholders. This is taken up in Chapter 9, "Human Capital and the Future Impact of Innovation and Entrepreneurship on Key Stakeholders." Human capital is central for future medical, scientific and technological innovations in healthcare that are imperative for the health and well-being of individuals in society, economic growth and development. Over the last two decades, the field of healthcare has been transformed with major innovations across every aspect of clinical care that has positively impacted and provides opportunity for key stakeholders including patients, clinicians and healthcare professionals, healthcare organizations and governments. While different stakeholders have distinct views, goals and objectives regarding innovation and entrepreneurship, as well as different levels of knowledge and expertise, they share a common goal and passion to improve healthcare provision. Future innovations need to further advance the field of healthcare and in doing so ensure that the delivery of care and patient data is protected at all times through sophisticated cybersecurity.

Finally, we have accomplished more than we imagined and we can continue to do so as we strive to further advance and develop the field of healthcare. Chapter 10 explores the "Future of Innovation and Entrepreneurship in Healthcare." Innovations in healthcare products, assessment procedures, diagnoses, treatments, and delivery of care have been significantly developed in recent decades. Such innovations increase patient quality of life and life expectancy, and enhance the delivery of high quality and safe care for all patients. The development of innovations in healthcare also increases efficiency, effectiveness and accessibility, and reduces medical errors and costs. The growing emphasis on the importance of innovation and entrepreneurship to healthcare should encourage leaders in healthcare organizations to support and facilitate more innovative ways to generate greater patient value into the future. Innovation and entrepreneurship in healthcare needs to have a future-oriented mindset that understands "one size does not fit all" and a more personalized approach through effective interaction between healthcare professionals, stakeholders and other key experts internally and externally to develop future innovations that will further enhance healthcare and lead the world to better health.

Be the healthcare leader that passionately drives innovation and entrepreneurship among individuals and teams, has a vision that accomplishes the imaginable, and who makes it happen – and keeps it happening! The future is upon us; together we can make a difference!

Acknowledgments

I would like to acknowledge with deep love and appreciation, my wonderful Mum, Patricia Kearney, who is my rock and inspiration, always showing infinite love, kindness, support and encouragement that helped make my dreams a reality.

Special thanks to my family, friends, colleagues and the internationally renowned academics who endorsed this book, I am honoured and appreciate your support and encouragement.

Thank you to all my colleagues at RCSI, University of Medicine and Health Sciences; it is a pleasure to work with you all and together make a difference to the field of healthcare.

Thank you to all the clinicians and healthcare professionals globally that have passion and compassion and who make a real difference to their patients' lives everyday.

Thank you to the editors and the excellent team at Edward Elgar Publishing who believed in this book and supported me in making it become a reality.

'This book distills today and tomorrow's complex challenges into a practical decision-making framework that informs thinking about innovation and entrepreneurship in healthcare. I am particularly impressed by the range of insights spanning strategy, leadership, team management, challenges facing women, and human capital. The coverage is pragmatic and comprehensive, helping the reader to recognize and avoid their own common biases, and takes them by the hand to make better decisions. I highly recommend this book for all health care professionals!'
Donald Bergh, University of Denver, USA

'For anyone interested in engaging in change, leadership and creating value in health care, this book is a must read. Claudine Kearney provides a thoughtful, interesting focused innovative approach to a most relevant topic today how to implement innovative leadership and an organizational approach to better healthcare all over the world.'
Robert D. Hisrich, Kent State University, Ohio, USA

'This book provides a thorough, scientific discussion of innovation and entrepreneurship, and then applies it in new and important ways to the healthcare industry. It will help both healthcare scholars and professionals to understand the ways in which the industry can and should be managed, to optimally deal with 21st century challenges.'
Killian J. McCarthy, University of Groningen, the Netherlands

PART I

Meaning and nature of innovation and entrepreneurship in healthcare

1. Understanding creativity, innovation and entrepreneurship in healthcare

QUESTIONS

What do you understand by the term creativity? What role does creativity play in your healthcare organization? Why is creativity important? What is innovation and what does it mean in the context of healthcare? What is the link between creativity and innovation? Is creativity important for innovation to emerge and develop within healthcare organizations? Why? What is entrepreneurship in healthcare? In terms of creativity, innovation and entrepreneurship, what is the future for healthcare?

INTRODUCTION

Creativity, innovation and entrepreneurship research has been developed over decades across many disciplines and is of major importance to the field of healthcare. Given the global healthcare challenges its importance has increased significantly among researchers and practitioners. Globally, healthcare is experiencing major challenges as a result of, for example, aging populations, rising costs, regulations, long waiting lists, inequitable care, inaccessible care, medical errors, and challenges in staff recruitment and retention, all of which impact the timing and response to patient diagnosis, quality and safety. Current approaches are short term, focusing on a single issue with no overarching solution to fully address the challenges. However, there are significant opportunities to address these challenges through creativity, innovation and entrepreneurship.

The terms creativity and innovation are not always differentiated. There are, however, important differences between the two concepts that need to be acknowledged. Effective creativity results in the generation of novel and valued ideas. There is no innovation without creativity because creativity is the foundation on which innovation emerges, develops and grows. Creativity focuses on the generation of ideas, processes or concepts, while innovation focuses on the practical viability of those ideas, processes or concepts. Creativity can result in new inventions; however, innovation is the commercialization of such inventions, that is, putting the creative idea into action. To achieve this, healthcare organizations must utilize their resources and the creative abilities of their people. Creativity and innovation cannot happen without people who have core competencies, drive, motivation and passion to make a difference. It is the creativity among individuals that develops innovation; however, this must be supported and encouraged by appropriate leadership within the healthcare organization. From a healthcare organizational perspective, developing creativity in individuals throughout the organization will generate greater patient value. From an individual perspective, when individuals are creative they are more confident, motivated and feel part of the organization. This results in higher productivity among staff and potentially more innovative ideas and a more entrepreneurial mindset.

Entrepreneurship is a universal concept that can be applied to new ventures, small- to medium-size enterprises, large national and multi-national organizations, and public sector organizations including healthcare. Within healthcare, entrepreneurship requires strong commitment, perseverance and research to develop something novel that will generate patient value. The entrepreneurial spirit needs to be engendered and nurtured to successfully bring medical innovations to fruition.

The purpose of this chapter is to develop an understanding of creativity, innovation and entrepreneurship in healthcare organizations and examine how healthcare can prosper through creativity, innovation and entrepreneurship. The chapter provides an understanding of the meaning and importance of creativity, innovation and entrepreneurship to healthcare. Following this, the link between creativity, innovation and entrepreneurship is discussed. The chapter concludes by providing an overall framework for *Leading Entrepreneurship and Innovation in Healthcare: A Global Perspective* that will serve as the foundation for the structure of this book.

CREATIVITY: MEANING AND IMPORTANCE IN HEALTHCARE

What is Creativity?

Creativity is a core component of innovation and fundamental for the development and generation of innovative ideas. Creativity can be defined as an individual's ability to recognize and develop new ideas, processes or concepts in novel ways – thus creating something new, useful and valuable. In healthcare, creativity is originality that is realistic, viable and novel that will enhance healthcare in order to generate real patient value. Creativity is critical to healthcare to allow us to re-think the current approach, by looking at things in new ways and facilitating the generation of ideas and creative solutions to address the challenges faced by patients, healthcare professionals, stakeholders and society at large.

Creativity is not just a revolutionary changing product or service that comes from globally recognized innovators like Professor Alexander Fleming who discovered penicillin in 1928 and Dr. Raymond Damadian known as the "father of the MRI" (Magnetic Resonance Imaging) in 1969. Creativity in healthcare requires cognitive and non-cognitive skills, curiosity, intuitiveness, perseverance, passion and commitment. To generate patient value in healthcare, individuals need to utilize their creativity despite potential barriers within internal and external environments. Individual and team creativity requires the following:

- An open and objective mindset
- Perseverance and commitment to generate novel ideas
- Passion to generate patient value
- Moderate risk taking
- Resilience to overcome obstacles
- Ability to recognize existing ideas in other industries that could be effectively utilized within healthcare.

Creativity is demonstrated by innovative organizations in healthcare such as: One Medical (affordable and convenient primary care); Apple (mining data to build health apps); Alivecor (mobilizing heart monitoring); and GE Healthcare (reducing pain points at healthcare facilities). Furthermore, technological advancement and development is rapidly changing healthcare as a result of the significant developments in creativity and innovation, for example, artificial intelligence (AI), 3D printing, robotics, telemedicine, wearable monitors, stem cells, gene therapy, mobile device applications. Therefore, effective utilization of creative behaviors among individuals with diverse competencies can lead to successful innovations in healthcare.

Why is Creativity Important?

There is a continuous need to enhance and develop healthcare and generate greater patient value. Creativity is the important first step for innovation. Healthcare continues to be a highly complex sector with healthcare professionals required to provide more creative solutions in their care practices. Creativity that is supported and facilitated can encourage engagement from staff at all levels and show that their creative ideas generate patient value and are core factors in the success of the healthcare organization and the field of healthcare. Creativity is essential for the growth and development of healthcare staff. To achieve this growth, staff must be open to evaluating the gaps and limitations in the current system, and exploring new areas and ways to achieve desirable goals and objectives. In doing this, healthcare professionals need to manage the needs of a diverse group of patients in terms of, for example, age, current and pre-existing health conditions, lifestyle, and making creativity a fundamental element of their day-to-day work. Therefore it is critical that staff are given the time and support to engage in creativity to address these growing demands. The integration of creativity into patient care can generate significant benefits such as decreasing costs, increasing efficiency and effectiveness, ensuring greater utilization of resources, and improve quality and safety.

Creative Techniques

Creative techniques must be utilized in order to generate creative ideas and concepts. There are many techniques that can be used to generate them, including:

1. *Brainstorming:* 6 to 12 team members generate a number of ideas without any negative criticism and then evaluate each idea.
2. *E-Brainstorming:* a form of e-collaboration.
3. *Brainwriting:* a silent version of brainstorming where the generated ideas are recorded individually on a piece of paper and submitted anonymously to the group. The ideas are exchanged a number of times with each person building on the previously generated ideas.
4. *Focus groups:* individuals providing information in a structured format.
5. *Free association:* writing down a word or phrase related to the problem, followed by another and another, with the goal that each new word will add something new to the ongoing thought processes and thereby generate a chain of ideas, finishing with the emergence of a new product idea.
6. *Mind mapping:* allows an individual or team to generate numerous ideas by dividing each idea into many more detailed ideas.
7. *Collection notebook method:* individuals or teams consider the problem and potential solutions, recording ideas at least once but ideally three times daily. After a week, the best ideas are listed, as well as any suggestions.
8. *Problem inventory analysis:* a method for generating new ideas and opportunities by focusing on existing problems.

The value of these techniques depends on the individual's thinking process, problem-solving ability, and decision-making. The thinking process is usually better if participants have diverse perspectives, backgrounds, experiences, skills, and expertise; this avoids *groupthink* and enhances "out-of-the-box" thinking. The goal of creative techniques is to manage creativity in a more systematic way and improve the quality of the creative output, resulting in a high-quality concept or solution.

INNOVATION: MEANING AND IMPORTANCE IN HEALTHCARE

What is Innovation?

Innovation is a process that begins with an idea; proceeds with the development of an invention; and results in the development or enhancement of products, processes, services, or technological advancement as part of organizational/ industry innovativeness (Hisrich and Kearney, 2013). Innovation in healthcare begins with a new idea or concept leading to the development of a product, service, process, technology or delivery method with the ultimate goal of generating patient value and an enhanced healthcare system. The World Health Organization (WHO) recognizes that innovation in healthcare adds value in achieving greater efficiency, effectiveness, quality, sustainability, safety and/ or affordability (World Health Organization, 2016).

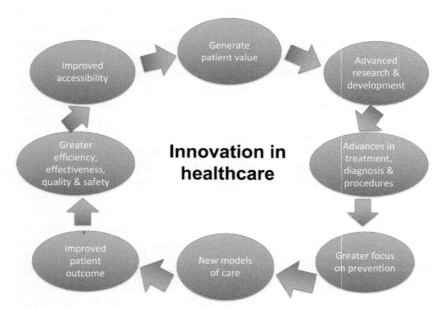

Figure 1.1   Value of innovation in healthcare

The value of innovation in healthcare is recognized through, for example, the generation of patient value; advanced research and development (R&D); advances in treatment, diagnosis and procedures; greater focus on prevention; new models of care that result in, for example, improved patient outcomes, greater efficiency, effectiveness, quality and safety; and improved accessibility for all patients (Figure 1.1).

Innovation in healthcare needs to continuously work toward addressing the unmet needs of patients who are at their most vulnerable. This also includes making existing innovations available to individuals that previously had no access to such treatment and care. This is particularly important in developing countries, because in order to improve access and equity and decrease costs there is a need to leverage existing technologies, for example mobile phone and genomics that are at the core of innovation in healthcare. Furthermore, innovation needs to focus on ways of prevention as well as cure for the well-being of all in society. While the medical profession focuses on early detection of specific illnesses that increases survival, there is a need to go a step further and identify ways individuals at particular risk of certain illnesses can prevent or reduce their risk.

Healthcare organizations in today's complex and dynamic market need to be innovative and support new creative ideas. Innovative healthcare organizations encourage and facilitate new ideas. They are creative with a willingness to take risks as they seek new improved processes, practices and technologies. The most successful innovative healthcare organizations are those that utilize knowledge gained from previous innovations within and outside their sector to develop future innovations. By reviewing innovations in other industries there is an opportunity for potential solutions to healthcare services that otherwise may not be recognized. For example, the rigidity of safety checks in aviation could be adopted in hospitals to work toward a reduction in medical errors. While innovation in healthcare requires new innovations for unmet and unsolved healthcare needs, it also needs novel approaches for addressing existing needs.

Why is Innovation Important?

The healthcare sector needs innovation. Healthcare providers, life science companies, health insurance companies and governments are facing increasing costs and pressures to generate patient value. Innovation is a core focus as healthcare organizations face unprecedented challenges. The continuous need for more innovation in healthcare has escalated as a result of the growth in demand due to aging populations, increasing prevalence of chronic diseases, an increase in unmet medical needs, more people living an unhealthy lifestyle, and an increase in patient demands for quality, safety and accessibility.

Innovations in healthcare should improve patient care, enhance quality and safety, reduce harm and errors, increase accessibility, increase efficiency and effectiveness, eliminate waste, and lower costs. As a result of greater innovations in diagnostics and therapeutic options, healthcare has developed many innovations designed to enhance life expectancy and quality of life. Innovation in terms of new products, processes, services, technologies or delivery method is central to address these needs and achieve a more effective and sustainable healthcare system.

Technological innovations brought about by robotics, virtual reality (VR), automation, AI, 3D printing and drones have the potential to disrupt and transform healthcare. These technological advancements are used in some countries, yet others lag behind; for example, Ireland needs to recognize the opportunities such technological advancement can create and consider exploiting these technologies to transform the delivery of healthcare to patients, including more timely diagnosis, greater precision in surgery and improvement in the accuracy and administration of drugs. However, in time these rapidly developing technologies, such as AI, crowd-sourced health data, gene therapy, genomic sequencing, mobile phone applications, 3D printing, robotics, smart pills, stem cells, synthetic biology, telemedicine and wearable monitors, will continue to be further advanced and developed and will have a significant impact on the future of healthcare for patients, healthcare professionals, healthcare providers, payers, policymakers and all stakeholders.

The healthcare sector is changing as a result of, for example, innovations such as rapid growth of machine learning; genomics and precision medicine; digital technologies; a focus on patients at the center of their own care; and AI that can spot lung tumors more accurately than medical experts. These innovations are transforming medicine and create both opportunities to be recognized and achieved as well as challenges to address for the healthcare sector. The recognition of these opportunities and challenges is critical for the development of successful innovations to meet important unmet needs of patients, providers and payers.

Characteristics of Innovation in Healthcare

Innovation represents something new; this can result in a new product, process, service, technology, or delivery method. Whether innovation is a modification of an existing innovation or a transformational breakthrough offering something unique, it still results in a new way of doing and modifies the thought process to generate a new way of thinking about things.

Innovation in healthcare needs to engage in the following:

1. Develop new products, services, processes, technologies or delivery methods in healthcare;
2. Develop new, more efficient and effective diagnostics, procedures, and treatment pathways;
3. Identify new approaches to promote health, prevent disease, and provide patient care and cures;
4. Extend patient care beyond existing methods so they are tailored for the specific setting, for example homecare.

Innovation in healthcare must deliver patient value by providing diagnostics and treatments that are timely, efficient and effective, with as little invasiveness and as few side-effects as possible in an approach that does not just meet but exceeds patients' needs, wants and expectations, and with dignity and respect. Innovations are not always planned, with some of the most successful being unplanned, for example penicillin. Therefore, the field of healthcare needs to be open to potential innovations beyond and in contrast to what they are aiming to achieve.

CREATIVITY AND INNOVATION IN HEALTHCARE

Creativity without innovation does not create any real value. Likewise, creative ideas are necessary to commence the innovation so it can develop and grow. Creativity and innovation do not just happen; it requires both general knowledge and field-specific knowledge, because creative individuals cannot know what is novel without an understanding of existing knowledge in any specific area. Within healthcare this also requires looking beyond the field of healthcare to discover how innovations in other areas may play a significant role in healthcare. We need to think differently if we want a different outcome. Creative people are always willing to challenge the way we think and not accept the status quo, because doing what is always done will achieve the same results. If those results are not favorable, we need to address this to develop creative ideas and implement innovations that achieve more desirable results and address current limitations within the system.

Healthcare leaders need to recognize the importance of creativity and innovation in their day-to-day operational activities and take action to foster this within their organizational setting. It is the most viable and effective solution to address the increasing challenges across every aspect of the healthcare system. This can only be achieved through strong leadership that supports and empowers staff to be creative and pursue innovation that will contribute to enhance healthcare services and generate patient value. To achieve this the leader needs to spend time listening to followers and patients to find out what goes wrong and then discover how to fix the problems as a team. They must empower staff to use their creativity to identify innovation(s) that will generate patient value and ensure the delivery of quality and safety while utilizing resources and decreasing waste that occurs within the healthcare delivery system. Creativity and innovation as a healthcare management goal can further enhance the organization of healthcare services and result in novel solutions to address challenges, such as increasing efficiency and effectiveness in communication and coordination across different departments, and ensuring appropriate processes for patient discharge that result in enhancing patient outcomes.

Barriers to Creativity and Innovation in Healthcare

Barriers to creativity and innovation in healthcare include:

- *Regulation, rules, and policies.* While it is necessary to enforce strict regulations and guidelines on healthcare innovations to ensure patients are always at the center of care and treatment, innovators must recognize and understand the regulations that affect their innovations from the outset, otherwise they can inhibit "out-of-the-box" thinking and slow down the innovation process.
- *Bureaucratic environment.* Rigidity, red tape, centralization and top-down communication can be typical of some healthcare organizations. These inhibit creativity and innovation becoming embedded within the organization.
- *Culture of risk aversion.* The healthcare sector can be risk adverse with primary concerns of accountability, quality and safety. Medical professionals are trained to determine the most proven method for treating disease, and to adopt that unless a more effective method was tried, tested and proven. This impedes creativity and innovation in finding and proving better ways of doing things.
- *Pressured work environment.* There is limited time to dedicate to creativity and innovation given highly stressed work environments and long working hours. Medical professionals are committed to the delivery of quality patient care, but the pressure to do more with limited resources can make it difficult to engage in creativity and implement innovations.

Healthcare is a highly dynamic complex sector and a healthcare delivery ecosystem can be under intense pressure as a result of increasing costs and patient needs. These challenges, combined with the complexity of the sector, make innovation in healthcare more complicated. To address these challenges and develop creativity and innovation in healthcare, these barriers must be overcome.

Ways of Overcoming Barriers to Creativity and Innovation

- Compliance and knowledge of regulations, rules and policies throughout the creative and innovative process.
- An organic organizational structure, decentralized decision-making and open channels of communication that facilitate creativity and innovation.
- A culture that encourages and supports creativity and innovation with a focus on delivering better healthcare.
- Utilization of resources for creativity and the implementation of innovation that will generate patient value.

ENTREPRENEURSHIP: MEANING AND IMPORTANCE IN HEALTHCARE

What is Entrepreneurship?

Within the literature there is no universally accepted definition of entrepreneurship. There are different forms of entrepreneurship, such as private sector entrepreneurship, public sector entrepreneurship, corporate entrepreneurship (also known as corporate venturing, organizational entrepreneurship, and intrapreneurship), governpreneurship, and social entrepreneurship. Entrepreneurs can be found in all professions, such as education, medicine, research, law, finance, architecture, engineering, technology, social work, and government. Entrepreneurs are recognized as individuals who are innovative and proactive, and who effectively manage risk. They have the ability to get things done despite the challenges or obstacles they may experience. Entrepreneurship in healthcare creates novel interventions, products, processes, services technologies or delivery methods that address health problems. There is a continued need for entrepreneurs and entrepreneurship within healthcare to bring about further needed innovations that will generate patient value.

The term *entrepreneurship* can be traced back almost three centuries with one of the earliest definitions from Richard Cantillion (written in the 1730s but not published until 1755), an economist, who refers to the entrepreneur as a rational decision-maker who assumes the risk and manages the organization. The classical contributors of the term *entrepreneurship* are recognized to be Cantillon, Say, Schumpeter, Knight and Kirzner. Some definitions focus on the creation of a new business, some on the exploration and exploitation of opportunities, while others focus on the generation of wealth and ownership, and the creation of value. Others focus on corporate entrepreneurship, which is a term used to describe entrepreneurial behavior within existing medium to large organizations including healthcare. However, as discussed by Drucker (1985):

> The all but universal belief that large businesses do not and cannot innovate is not even a half-truth; rather, it is a misunderstanding (135). It takes special effort for the existing business to become entrepreneurial and innovative. ... The temptation in the existing business is always to feed yesterday and to starve tomorrow. It is, of course, a deadly temptation. The enterprise that does not innovate ages and declines. And in a period of rapid change such as the present, an entrepreneurial period, the decline will be fast (137).

The value of corporate entrepreneurship in healthcare is the degree to which it becomes part of the strategy to engage in entrepreneurship to generate patient value. While there is variation among the forms and professions, they do, however, incorporate similar concepts such as the exploration and exploitation of opportunities, creativity, innovation, risk taking, and generating value. A broad definition of *entrepreneurship* and *corporate entrepreneurship* "is the process of creativity and innovation by committing the necessary time and energy, taking responsibility for all the risks and uncertainties, and taking personal satisfaction (Hisrich and Kearney, 2013: 9). Understanding the importance of entrepreneurship in healthcare, the following definition recognizing critical factors is proposed:

> Entrepreneurship in healthcare is a dynamic and challenging process of creativity and innovation that identifies and exploits previously unexploited opportunities. It requires energy, passion and commitment toward the creation and implementation of new ideas and creative solutions in light of the challenges and obstacles within healthcare. Essentially it requires the willingness to take calculated risks, formulate an effective team of experts with diverse competencies, ability to access and utilize resources, with the core goal to generate patient value.

Four key elements of this definition for healthcare are:

1. Entrepreneurship is a step-by-step ongoing process that can be applied to healthcare;
2. It exploits opportunities to address unmet healthcare needs;
3. It demonstrates passion and drive to pursue the opportunity despite the challenges healthcare professionals experience in their organizations;
4. It focuses on generating patient value and leading the world to better health.

In healthcare, entrepreneurship involves the process of bringing commercially viable innovations to the market or applying them within the organization, despite potential barriers. However, unlike other sectors, entrepreneurship in healthcare is more challenging as it is dealing with patients' lives. Therefore, all healthcare innovations need to be rigorously tried and tested, comply with all regulations, and demonstrate effectiveness and be recognized as being innovative. Entrepreneurship in healthcare needs to be driven by innovation while also being risk conscious; this requires high levels of creativity to be successful. Finding the balance in being innovative while operating in a risk-averse sector is challenging.

Why is Entrepreneurship Important?

There is a growing global importance for entrepreneurship in healthcare with the increasing needs of society to address more illnesses, diseases and conditions. The impact of an increase in chronic diseases places a major burden on a challenged healthcare system. Furthermore, the majority of countries are dealing with a shortage of doctors and medical professionals, and are experiencing challenges in the recruitment and retention of medical professionals. Staff shortages combined with healthcare system challenges create a major need for healthcare to promote entrepreneurial activities to drive innovation and generate patient value. The growth of entrepreneurship is disrupting the way healthcare is being practiced and is significantly and positively affecting the sector.

LINKING CREATIVITY, INNOVATION AND ENTREPRENEURSHIP

Integration of Creativity, Innovation and Entrepreneurship to Healthcare

How can patient value be created in healthcare through the integration of creativity, innovation and entrepreneurship? This requires looking outside of healthcare and reviewing the value generative approach of highly innovative and sucessful entrepreneurs and their organizations, such as Richard Branson (Virgin), Patrick Collison and John Collison (Stripe), Reid Hastings and Marc Randolph (Netflix), the late Steve Jobs (Apple) (whose legacy continues with Tim Cooks), Larry Page and Sergey Brin (Google), and Mark Zuckerberg (Facebook). They are highly creative, innovative and entrepreneurial, and they support and facilitate their staff to be the same. It is their competencies combined with curiosity, intuitiveness, perseverance, passion and commitment as well as a team to engender this passion for innovation that has resulted in this success. These competencies are needed in healthcare if we are to achieve the potential of the healthcare system and lead the world to better health.

There is technological disruption globally within the field of healthcare and creativity; innovation and entrepreneurship are the catalysts. However, healthcare organizations find it challenging to incorporate the right strategies to initiate creative activity among their staff. To drive creativity, innovation and entrepreneurship within the sector, healthcare professionals must be empowered to utilize their creativity to identify innovative ways to deliver healthcare. The role of patients in the creative and innovative journey is fundamental as they are the key drivers of opportunity generation within healthcare organizations to generate patient value. Healthcare leaders and staff need to meet and engage with patients as part of the innovation process to gain greater knowledge and understanding of their specific experience.

Benefits of Creativity, Innovation and Entrepreneurship

Globally, healthcare professionals and providers are engaging in creativity, innovation and entrepreneurial activities driven by the desire to generate patient value. This has significantly contributed to healthcare over recent decades as a result of innovations such as advanced diagnostic and therapeutic options developed to improve life expectancy and quality of life.

The benefits of creativity, innovation and entrepreneurship are evident at three levels: individual, organizational and societal. From the individual perspective this instills strong passion, drive and motivation. At the organizational level, engaging in this process generates greater synergy and creates a positive and collaborative work environment. Hence, when an organization is more entrepreneurially oriented it creates the opportunity to develop new possibilities and ways of delivering that are characterized by innovation, risk-taking and proactivity. Within the field of healthcare, the link between individual and organizational goals can exceed the boundaries of the organization because of the "fit" between the altruistic nature of the organizational goals and the motivation and commitment healthcare professionals have to work to help others and benefit society (Kearney et al., 2020). For society this leads to better diagnostics, enhanced quality and safety, cost savings, and greater patient engagement and outcomes.

For continued benefits to the field of healthcare creativity, innovation and entrepreneurship need to accelerate further to develop where they are most needed, in areas such as prevention as well as cure, personalized care aligned to the patient's specific needs and genetic profile, and more technologically enhanced care models. This is required at individual and organizational level to benefit society and transform healthcare to have real-world impact and value.

Significance to Healthcare

Patients are assuming greater responsibility for their health and well-being. Therefore the focus of healthcare is changing from managing illness to improving health and ensuring greater engagement in medical decisions. Through the advancement and development of digital technology there is an opportunity to bring more outpatient procedures out of overcrowded hospitals and back into the community. Patients do not have to physically attend a doctor's surgery when they are unwell as they can see a doctor through video conferencing from their own home. Additionally, technological innovations such as smart devices, smartwatches and medical apps facilitate doctors to remotely assess and monitor patients, thus increasing efficiency and decreasing surgery appointments.

Patients do not always need to go to hospital for a surgical procedure but can now have certain surgical procedures performed as an out-patient, for example a colonoscopy. Nursing homes are now one of a number of options for end-of-life care as home-care options and assisted living is providing more choices for those with palliative care needs.

Globally there is a transition toward personalized healthcare that empowers the patient. For example, TickerFit, an Irish company, developed a product used in cardiac rehabilitation that allows clinical teams to prescribe, educate and monitor a patient's recovery from a distance through a wearable device. This type of approach could result in taking patient care out of the hospital and increasing community care, thus reducing pressure on hospitals and offering more personalized treatment plans for patients. This is a timely and much needed approach to a pressured healthcare system.

Helping to Save and Extend Lives

Innovation in healthcare will continue to significantly increase life expectancy and quality of life, improve healthcare outcomes and reduce the cost of healthcare, leading the world to better health. Innovation is crucial to delivering high-quality, safe and affordable healthcare. The rapid advancement in digital technology and AI is revolutionizing healthcare with faster diagnosis and treatments, and potentially supports prevention rather than cure. For example, medical image diagnosis is critical to radiology due to the error rate (caused because radiological images include organs, bones and overlapping tissue, which makes it difficult for the radiologist to accurately identify problems), particularly at earlier stages of development. Additionally, technological advancement can reduce costs and increase efficiency and effectiveness through the development of more advanced, accurate and affordable diagnoses and treatments.

Leading the Way to the Future of Healthcare

Healthcare organizations are leading great efforts to transform healthcare to make it more efficient, effective, accessible, affordable, convenient and patient-centered. Healthcare organizations must be innovative in terms of diagnostics, treatments and models of patient care. Like all industries the future is unpredictable but what is clear is the need to decrease the cost and increase the value of healthcare by delivering superior performance in terms of patient value through the creation of new innovative products, processes, services, technologies or delivery models, and appropriate strategic alliances. There is a change within the healthcare landscape therefore to manage this effectively; it is imperative to influence where it is going by harnessing innovation and entrepreneurship that will result in better patient care and lead healthcare into the future.

A Framework for *Leading Innovation and Entrepreneurship in Healthcare: A Global Perspective*

Leading innovation and entrepreneurship in healthcare has generated interest in recent years by academics, entrepreneurs, healthcare professionals, healthcare organizations and policymakers. While innovation is fundamental for organizational success it is one of the most difficult aspects of corporate activity to effectively manage and plan. When we reflect on the healthcare sector, this challenge is even more extensive due to the intense pressure on the healthcare market to "do more with fewer resources" and at the same time ensure the highest standards of quality, safety and patient care. Globally there is a pressing need for healthcare organizations to become more innovative and engage in entrepreneurial activities to stay ahead. In order to develop and grow an organization, and respond to the increasing and diverse needs of patients, leaders and healthcare professionals need to have innovation and entrepreneurship embedded in their organizational strategy. This requires the creation of an organizational strategy, structure, culture, rules, regulations, policies and procedures that encourages innovative behavior and rewards staff for such behavior. With increasing challenges facing healthcare there is a desperate need for the generation of new ideas and new innovative solutions to address deeply embedded problems on a global scale. Harnessing innovation, through the development of new products, processes, services, technologies or delivery models, will significantly contribute to better healthcare.

This book focuses on the important topic of leading innovation and entrepreneurship in healthcare from a global perspective. To be creative, engender innovation and facilitate an entrepreneurial spirit in healthcare requires knowledge of the process from idea generation to commercialization; additionally, knowledge on how to lead and develop an organization to emerge within this process is required. To guide the readers through this journey an integrative framework for leading innovation and entrepreneurship has been developed. As indicated in Figure 1.2, the framework has four major components:

1. Meaning and nature of innovation and entrepreneurship in healthcare;
2. Developing innovation and entrepreneurship in healthcare: a strategic perspective;
3. Leading innovation, entrepreneurship and design thinking in healthcare;
4. Making it all happen: a future-oriented mindset.

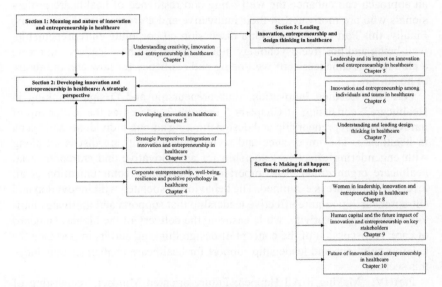

Figure 1.2   *A framework for leading innovation and entrepreneurship in healthcare: a global perspective*

Part I of this book, "Meaning and Nature of Innovation and Entrepreneurship in Healthcare," comprising this chapter, demonstrates an understanding of creativity, innovation and entrepreneurship in healthcare. It has provided the foundation for this book by giving an understanding of the meaning, nature, importance and links between creativity, innovation and entrepreneurship in leading the way to the future of healthcare.

Part II, "Developing Innovation and Entrepreneurship in Healthcare: A Strategic Perspective," consisting of Chapters 2 through 4, adopts a strategic focus on the advancement of innovation and entrepreneurship within a healthcare setting. Innovation is examined by investigating the forms, types and opportunities for innovation in healthcare. The steps in the process of innovation are examined and the value of innovation in healthcare presented. Innovation and entrepreneurship need to be effectively integrated into the organizational strategy. A system for monitoring, assessing and evaluating the external and internal environment, to ensure the right strategic innovative and entrepreneurial decisions are made and actions taken, is discussed with the objective of building a patient-centered innovative entrepreneurial strategy. An innovative and entrepreneurial healthcare organization is one that allows staff to recognize and act on their creative and innovative potential. Such an approach can enhance the well-being and resilience of healthcare professionals who are motivated in their innovative and entrepreneurial endeavors. Finally, this Part concludes with a discussion on corporate entrepreneurship, well-being and positive psychology in healthcare, and how leaders can create a climate that enhances staff well-being and resilience for now and the future of healthcare.

Part III, "Leading Innovation, Entrepreneurship and Design Thinking in Healthcare," consisting of Chapters 5 through 7, addresses the leadership of innovation, entrepreneurship and design thinking among individuals and teams in healthcare. The importance and styles of leadership are discussed along with engendering effective leadership for an innovative and entrepreneurial healthcare organization. The importance of effective communication at all levels in healthcare is examined. The behaviors associated with innovation and entrepreneurship require effective leadership that supports and motivates individual and team creativity, while ensuring the delivery of the highest standard of care. A discussion of the concept of design thinking and its importance for creative solutions and leadership support for healthcare challenges concludes this section.

Part IV, "Making it All Happen: Future-oriented Mindset," consisting of Chapters 8 through 10, focuses on innovation and entrepreneurship in healthcare in the future. Women in leadership, innovation and entrepreneurship in healthcare and the importance of inclusivity in healthcare organizations are discussed. Innovation and entrepreneurship does not happen without the right human capital that can drive and excel at future innovations in healthcare. Innovation and entrepreneurship have a different impact on a diverse group of stakeholders. Therefore, this requires a comprehensive understanding of the effects that innovation and entrepreneurship have on patients, clinicians and healthcare professionals, healthcare organizations, and government and other key stakeholders. Future innovations in medical devices need to be mindful of potential cybercrime vulnerability and ensure that security is built into such devices. An understanding of past and present innovations is required in order to develop and effectively lead innovations for the future of healthcare. The future of innovation and entrepreneurship in healthcare is upon us and *together we can make a difference!*

SUMMARY

The development of creativity, innovation and entrepreneurship across every aspect of the healthcare sector is the most viable solution to the global healthcare crisis, although this is a challenge given bureaucratic organizational structures, risk aversion and management teams who may resist such a transition. The driver of creativity, innovation and entrepreneurship in an organization is the responsibility of the CEO and senior management team who need to lead the way to the future of healthcare, that requires changing the status quo.

Innovation in healthcare needs to ensure more accurate, efficient and timely diagnoses and treatment plans, prevention as well as cure, patient engagement in the process of innovation, training and education, and research in innovation and commercialization, with the long-term focus on generating patient value. The benefits of such innovations will result in a more efficient and effective healthcare organization and enhanced medical solutions for addressing the needs of each patient.

More than ever, healthcare organizations globally must address the growing challenges and this requires leaders who can lead the world to better health by driving creative, innovative, and entrepreneurial behavior among all individuals responsible for delivering healthcare.

REFERENCES

Drucker, P.F. (1985). *Innovation and Entrepreneurship: Practices and Principles* (New York: Harper & Row).
Hisrich, R.D. and Kearney, C. (2013). *Managing Innovation and Entrepreneurship: A Global Perspective* (Thousand Oaks, CA: SAGE Publications).
Kearney, C., Dunne, P.J. and Wales, W. (2020). Entrepreneurial orientation and burnout among healthcare professionals. *Journal of Health Organization and Management* 34(1), 16–22.
World Health Organization (2016). Innovation. Available at http://www.who.int/topics/innovation/en/ (last accessed September 13, 2016).

Suggested Reading

Ciani, O., Armeni, P., Boscolo, P.R., Cavazza, M., Jommi, C. and Tarricone, R. (2016). De innovatione: the concept of innovation for medical technologies and its implications for healthcare policy-making. *Health Policy and Technology* 5, 47–64.

In this article, the authors undertake a systematic review of the academic literature to summarize definitions of innovation in relation to medical devices which they classified according to the source of innovation, to the degree of discontinuity introduced and to the impact associated to the technology. Additionally, they have been compared with definitions adopted for drugs by main healthcare reimbursement agencies.

Patterson, F. and Zibarras, L.D. (2017). Selecting for creativity and innovation potential: implications for practice in healthcare education. *Advances in Health Science Education* 22, 417–28. https://link.springer.com/article/10.1007/s10459-016-9731 -4.

In this article, the authors explore the use of a trait-based measure of creativity and innovation potential, and evaluate its efficacy for use in selection for healthcare education. The authors use a sample of 188 postgraduate physicians applying for education and training in UK general practice. Their research clarifies the associations between personality, and creativity and innovation. In particular, their study highlights the importance of motivation in the creativity and innovation process.

Pillay, R. and Morris, M.H. (2015). Changing healthcare by changing the education of its leaders: an innovation competence model. *Journal of Health Administration Education* 33(3), 393–410.

In this article, the authors draw a distinction between traditional managerial competencies and innovation competencies, and argue that the latter help define the domain of innovation education. The authors employ a multistage Delphi methodology, and provide evidence of a core set of 19 innovation competencies. They also provide evidence for a more experiential and immersion-based approach to innovation education.

Raadabadi, M., Fayaz-Bakhsh, A., Nazari, A., Mousavi, S. M. and Fayaz-Bakhsh, M. (2014). Organizational entrepreneurship and administrators of hospitals: case study of Iran. *Global Journal of Health Science* 6(3), 249–55.

In this article, the authors examine the entrepreneurial activities within the hospitals affiliated to Tehran University of Medical Sciences, Iran. Using a questionnaire containing 29 items, their analysis showed that the majority of the managers agreed with all five areas of entrepreneurship, namely the existence of innovation and innovative behavior, flexibility, decision-making, a rewarding and encouraging system, and a management system supportive of personnel's new ideas. The authors assert that entrepreneurial activities in healthcare can be improved through providing a suitable environment, adjusting reward and encouragement systems, giving more authority to subordinates, promoting awareness and education, and mobilizing managers to attract appropriate opportunities for the organization.

Ratten, V. (2015). Healthcare organisations' innovation management systems: implications for hospitals, primary care providers and community health practitioners. *International Journal of Social Entrepreneurship and Innovation* 3(4), 313–22.

In this article, the author discusses the role of innovation and entrepreneurship for healthcare organizations as a way of adapting to change. The author highlights the importance of creativity in healthcare organizations. Managerial implications for healthcare organizations highlight the evolution of hospitals, primary care providers and community practitioners in utilizing innovative and entrepreneurial techniques.

Weintraub, P. and McKee, M. (2019). Leadership for innovation in healthcare: an exploration. *International Journal of Health Policy Management* 8(3), 138–44.

This article is written for those seeking to foster innovation in the health sector. The authors offer a narrative synthesis approach of eight theories and concepts that have been empirically shown to support innovation through all phases of the innovation process.

PART II

Developing innovation and entrepreneurship in
healthcare: a strategic perspective

2. Developing innovation in healthcare

QUESTIONS

What is innovation in the context of healthcare organizations? What is the process of innovation? Does this process differ between those pursuing break-through innovations and those pursuing incremental innovations in healthcare? How does a pandemic impact the development of innovation in healthcare? What does the term *open innovation* mean? How can open innovation be effectively pursued? How does an effective link between scientific and technological advances and stakeholder needs lead to successful innovations in healthcare?

INTRODUCTION

Innovation is a phenomenon that is increasingly important in the field of healthcare given the highly dynamic, complex and unprecedented global healthcare environment of the 21st century. It is a fundamental feature of healthcare and central to generating patient value and leading the world to better health. It is not just large healthcare organizations that need to be innovative and entrepreneurial but all types of organizations in the field of healthcare. Within healthcare and science there are new business start-ups, university spin-offs, and small, highly innovative and entrepreneurial organizations that are addressing the needs of healthcare, such as new advances in drugs, therapies, surgical procedures, diagnostics and medical devices. Healthcare organizations that are committed and focused on innovation can take advantage of opportunities to innovate during more stable economic times and have the drive and resilience to engage in innovation during times of necessity (e.g., Covid-19). In times of healthcare challenges and more significantly a global pandemic, innovation and entrepreneurship are required more than ever in order to develop, for example, new drugs, vaccines and technologies that can save lives and protect society from the emerging crisis. The field of healthcare cannot stand still but must be able to adapt to the challenges through innovations that can respond to the needs of patients and society at large. While this can be a challenging process particularly in healthcare as patients' lives are at stake, those that can successfully integrate innovation and entrepreneurship as part of the day-to-day philosophy achieve significant benefits and save lives.

Innovation and entrepreneurship are particularly important in the emergence of what is becoming the new normal environment as a result of Covid-19. This pandemic has not only been of high risk to those that contracted the illness, but it has affected the lives and lifestyles of everyone, given the high risk and speed of transmission. This has resulted in social distancing; restricted movement with limitations for medical appointments, pharmacy and grocery shopping; and remote working and business closures that have had an outstanding impact on healthcare systems, individual health and well-being, and the economy. These changes have created a new normal environment for healthcare systems and individuals with major implications for healthcare professionals, patients, government, policymakers, scientists and society at large. It has resulted in a global healthcare environment with major challenges that necessitates the need to address not only the pandemic but also a global economic crisis where jobs are being lost and millions are instantly becoming unemployed having a detrimental impact on the economy. The environment of 2020 and beyond is significantly different to that of 2019, with the greatest need to be innovative to address this pandemic.

In examining the new normal, it is important to acknowledge that this is a global pandemic and innovations on one side of the globe can have a major impact on the other side of the globe. Recognizing the value and importance of what is termed *open innovation and ecosystems* can generate greater results at a faster pace to address this pandemic. Now more than ever healthcare organizations globally need to be the driving force of innovation in the development of scientific and technological advances to find ways to overcome this pandemic and save lives.

The objective of this chapter is to examine innovation in healthcare. Innovation is discussed to provide an understanding of its importance in healthcare. Following a discussion on the forms and opportunities for innovation, it then discusses the meaning and importance of open innovation and ecosystems. A detailed understanding of the process of innovation is discussed. This is followed by a discussion on the important link between scientific and technological advances and stakeholder needs that result in successful innovations in healthcare. The chapter concludes with a discussion on the societal value of innovation in healthcare.

UNDERSTANDING INNOVATION IN HEALTHCARE

Innovation in healthcare is dynamic and complex and needs to address the existing and at times unprecedented needs of society. It is a rare occasion that innovations just emerge. The majority of successful innovations occur as a result of a meticulous search for opportunities having identified a "gap in the market" and most significantly a "market in the gap." Having an open and objective mindset can generate numerous innovations beyond and in contrast to what was planned. Innovations do not have to be "breakthrough" to make a major contribution; many "simple" and "focused" innovations are making a significant difference to healthcare. There is a continuous need for innovation to address the healthcare needs of society. These innovations should further enhance and provide solutions in healthcare products, services, processes, technologies and delivery methods in order to improve the healthcare system.

There are also unprecedented innovation needs that create such an unknown territory, the obvious example being the Covid-19 variant of Coronavirus. This crisis only emerged in Wuhan, China in late 2019 and in early 2020 became a global pandemic that requires urgent innovation in terms of a vaccine or an effective antiviral medicine to save lives. While some innovations like AI, data analytics, robotics or drug development for certain diseases take years to develop and perfect, other healthcare innovative needs can be unexpected and are a race against time to find ways to save lives. These unexpected urgent innovations require making decisions that were never made before at a speed that was never experienced, without clear funding or pilot testing.

In addition to recognizing the internal and external challenges to innovation the key is to understand what is actually innovative and what is not innovative, so that we can identify what gaps need to be addressed in ordinary and crisis times in order to bring about greater advancements and developments for increased efficiency and effectiveness in healthcare systems. Despite the fact that there has been significant innovation in the field of healthcare, major challenges remain as there are many inefficiencies that need to be overcome by being more innovative. Furthermore, for innovation to be achieved in an organization it needs to be supported and facilitated at all levels, because innovation comes from people. The ability to leverage the competencies of people in their innovative endeavors will determine the level to which innovation can be disseminated within a healthcare organization.

Innovation in healthcare can take many forms, such as drugs, therapies, surgical procedures, diagnostic advancement, advancement in health professional training and development, patient engagement and education, leadership, management, funding and financing, and new business models. Over the last few decades, the majority of healthcare innovations have focused on the development of new diagnostic procedures, therapies, drugs, or medical devices. These innovations include new procedures, from stents to more accurate diagnostic scanners and surgical robots for example. Other examples include immunotherapy (with the potential to extend the survival rate of cancer patients without the negative side effects and related healthcare costs of traditional chemotherapy) and biosensors and trackers (technology-enabled trackers, monitors and sensors incorporated into clothing, accessories and devices that allow consumers and clinicians to easily monitor patients' health). Furthermore, innovative healthcare systems are moving toward cloud-based data management systems. This allows programs to combine patient information into a single system that can be accessed and shared among healthcare providers in real time. Technology is generating major innovations in healthcare, for example Seattle Children's Hospital uses big data analytics to diagnose patients more accurately and in a more timely fashion. Big data analytics allows medical professionals to provide more customized treatments that are supported by statistics and research. New innovative ideas and technology can significantly enhance a patient's experience. The growing technological development will generate further innovations in healthcare. More advancement is required in the areas such as prevention rather than cure, more personalized care plans targeting patients' specific genetic risks and requirements, and more technology-driven care models. Technological advancement and development is non-linear and creates major opportunities for disruptive innovation in healthcare.

TYPES OF INNOVATION IN HEALTHCARE

The degree of risk assumed by an organization will depend on the type of innovation being proposed. Innovation is a process that can lead to (a) breakthrough innovation, (b) technological innovation and (c) incremental innovation. *Breakthrough innovations* are also known as radical, discontinuous, revolutionary or transformational and are by far the most disruptive. Breakthrough innovations significantly disrupt the old way of doing things by creating dramatic new value opportunities that revolutionize healthcare. *Technological innovations* are also recognized as dynamically continuous innovation and are not as disruptive as breakthrough innovations. Breakthrough and technological innovations are generally more costly, require more research and expertise, and take time to bring to fruition (breakthrough innovation generates a paradigm shift as it is the invention of new knowledge and technological innovation is the innovative extension and development of an existing innovation). *Incremental innovations* are also referred to as continuous innovation, ordinary innovation or evolutionary innovation, and are non-disruptive. Incremental innovation further improves an existing innovation and generates new incremental opportunities to address existing issues. Incremental innovation is more focused on small and continuous improvements to existing innovations. Each of the three types can vary in the degree of risk, cost, uniqueness and value. A distinction can be drawn between the three types of innovation as follows:

- *Breakthrough innovations* are characterized by their scientific novelty. Generally, they result in a product or service that addresses a need that was not previously addressed. They are less frequent in occurrence and globally recognized in the way they change healthcare. Examples of such innovations when first introduced include penicillin and MRI. More recently, AI in healthcare is providing applications in decision support, image analysis and patient triage, helping physicians to make more accurate decisions at the point of care, providing greater precision in assessing patient scans (e.g., machine learning algorithms can identify problem areas on images), and supporting the screening process. Innovation in robotic surgery has resulted in shorter and less invasive surgery (e.g., the Da Vinci for prostate cancer). Robots can provide surgeons with guidance for extreme surgical precision. Surgical platforms have become extremely well advanced and are used in many procedures (e.g., endovascular and spine).
- *Technological innovations* occur more frequently than breakthrough innovations. Technology is increasingly generating significant innovations in healthcare. Clinical (drug-coated stents), pharmaceutical (bio-engineered pharmaceuticals), medical surgeries and procedures (miniature laparoscopic cameras), information technology (integrated electronic patient records) are continuously advancing and transforming healthcare. As a result of technological innovation there has been an increase in day surgery through laparoscopic interventions that decrease inpatient requirements and surgical complications, thus reducing costs.
- *Incremental innovations* occur most frequently as they extend a technological innovation into a more advanced product or service. Products can, for example, be smaller, easier to use, or more cost effective without making any changes to the functionality of the product. Services can be made more efficient and effective through continuous enhancement. Therefore, incremental innovation can include revisions to medicines which are similar to the originally developed medicines but differ in terms of features, such as dosage schedule, reduction in potential adverse side effects, or improved formulation. For example, the first developed medicines for antihistamines had anticholinergic (e.g., dry mouth) and drowsiness effects; however, incremental innovation to antihistamines, such as Allegra, have the same impact as previous compounds but have less adverse side effects and are safer. In terms of cardiovascular therapy, controlled-release formulations of anti-hypertension drugs has created significant benefits in terms of safety, efficacy and compliance. For patients with Type-1 diabetes, the advancement of administering insulin through an inhaler has demonstrated

faster action time compared to injected insulin. Incremental innovation can also include new use of existing products; for example, Beta-blockers have over 20 different uses, and Infliximab was first approved to treat rheumatoid arthritis, but later recognized as a treatment for Crohn's disease. Incremental innovation that improves the use of existing products is not as costly as a breakthrough or technological innovation; however, it is still a time-consuming, risky and expensive process that requires incentives. The development of existing innovations through incremental innovation can create significant value for patients (e.g., providing a range of therapeutic options), healthcare professionals (e.g., flexibility to address the diverse needs of patients with greater precision and reduce adverse side-effects), and the overall healthcare system (more choice is more competition among suppliers thus generating greater savings), and should not be underestimated.

OPPORTUNITIES FOR HEALTHCARE INNOVATION

In light of the global healthcare challenges and the global pandemic, the need for innovation in healthcare is greater than ever. The key internal source of innovation is individuals and teams at all levels within an organization. The recognition and utilization of the core competencies of these individuals at every level of the organization is a major source of creative ideas. Organizations need to support the innovative process and allow individuals and teams to engage in this process throughout the organization. Creative ideas do not emerge in any planned sequence; furthermore, innovation is not a rational activity and cannot be predicted. Innovation can be embedded in the organizational culture where individuals are motivated and supported to be creative and innovative. For this to be achieved successfully, healthcare leaders at all levels need to ensure they embrace viable opportunities.

Organizations must have an understanding of the desired innovation prior to engaging in the process of innovation. This will provide greater clarity in the "'need" and "opportunity" for innovation when engaging in the process. Organizations can have both formal and informal approaches in their recognition of opportunities for innovation. Within healthcare, formal approaches require a strong R&D department together with links to universities, particularly for the generation of more advanced breakthrough or technological innovations. For example, medical consultants link with academics, medical device experts and industry experts to brainstorm so together they can address a specific healthcare challenge. Incremental innovations once supported are more informal and emerge in-house through the recognition of specific gaps that need to be addressed.

Opportunities for Healthcare Innovation in a Global Pandemic

Opportunities can emerge for innovation out of necessity and emergency. The urgency of innovations due to a pandemic has consultants, scientists, medical device specialists and engineers working globally to address the unprecedented challenges and work on innovations to address the pandemic and save lives. This was evident during the tuberculosis (TB), AIDS, SARS, MERS, Swine Flu and Zika virus pandemics. In 2019–20, the world faced another unprecedented pandemic with Covid-19 and was experiencing an increasing death toll. No healthcare system could prepare for such a pandemic that has spread rapidly around the world and resulted in a continuous and substantial increase in the number of people with severe, critical symptoms and tragically a significant number of deaths. To add to this crisis there was a shortage of ventilators. Even in times of crisis we can try and learn from some of the worst affected countries and be innovative. For example, in Italy, medical professionals had to make the most difficult and heartbreaking decisions about whom to provide with life-support measures, given the shortage of ventilators. To address the situation that could likely follow in Ireland, Professor John Laffey of NUI Galway and consultant in anesthesia and intensive care medicine at University Hospital Galway together with a team of academics, industry representatives and medical device specialists set themselves a task to get each ventilator to ventilate two patients at the same time. The objective of the team is to globally replicate this in response to the ventilator shortage. While Professor Laffey recognized this as a challenging task it is possible and had been used in mass casualty circumstances such as shootings in the United States where a person has normal lung function. However, the circumstances surrounding Covid-19 are vastly different because the individual has a compromised lung function. To advance this to address Covid-19 they also require more advanced technology, because this is a significant engineering and technological challenge. Furthermore, global recognition of the limited number of life-saving ventilators generated an initiative called Open Ventilator Project that emerged on Facebook to design and develop a 3D printed ventilator. Sapien Innovation in Ireland, specialist in applied innovation, creativity and design thinking quickly produced a prototype that it aims to have validated by Irish Health Authorities to be used in the fight against Covid-19.

Globally, many organizations are developing innovations in the fight against Covid-19. Among these there are new developments emerging from Ireland, with one of the leading medtech hubs being used to help combat this virus. One such organization includes HiberGene Diagnostics, an Irish based company that develops and manufactures molecular diagnostic tests for human infectious diseases. Recognizing the urgent need, it is currently developing a new test for the novel coronavirus with the objective of being the fastest molecular diagnostic test that can diagnose positive Covid-19 results in approximately 20 minutes. It will potentially have clinical evaluation in China, Italy and Ireland and aims to be on the market thereafter. Furthermore, an Irish biotech company, Aalto Bio Reagents, has put in motion a new protein to fight Covid-19 through diagnosis, vaccines and research.

The continuous global emphasis from world leaders and healthcare professionals on the importance of proper, regular hand-washing to prevent the spread of Covid-19 has generated further opportunities for innovation. A new augmented reality hand-washing app called SureWash provides correct hand hygiene training to healthcare workers, patients and visitors worldwide. This meets the WHO hand hygiene protocol. The app provides real-time feedback with a software system that provides infection control personnel with data that monitors hand hygiene progress. As part of the fight against Covid-19 this app is now available to the general public. This recognizes how existing innovations can extend beyond the initial focus and generate real value.

The search for breakthrough, technological, or incremental innovations requires the integration of internal and external people in R&D with diverse competencies that recognize the need and gap, and have the drive, passion and motivation to work together to generate innovation for the benefit of healthcare. It is the diverse group of people (e.g., patients, healthcare professional, academics, service users, engineers, designers, technology developers) that can devise, develop and disseminate viable innovations in healthcare. However, the majority of healthcare innovations (particularly vaccines, drugs and medical equipment such as ventilators) are highly regulated and require years of rigorous testing and significant levels of funding for each stage of the process before they are fully approved. This rigor is paramount and totally understandable as we are dealing with patients' lives – if a patient is administered medication, or undergoes a treatment or is put on a machine such as a ventilator, it has to work as there is no scope for error that could put the patient at further risk. Therefore innovations within the field of healthcare need to be rigorously tried and tested to ensure they work perfectly, for the greater good of the patient.

OPEN INNOVATION

The world of healthcare is already facing challenges of limited resources; high costs; increasing demand as a result of the growing burden of, for example, aging populations; increasing numbers of patients with communicable and noncommunicable diseases; patients' demands driven by their knowledge of global healthcare options; unhealthy lifestyles; limited resources; and the high cost of some technological and scientific advancements. The inherent features of healthcare services' limited resources, high costs, unlimited demands and pressure on services necessitates extended timelines and delays for patients to be treated. Furthermore, the global Covid-19 pandemic has generated unprecedented challenges that could never have been anticipated. This has created an urgent need to evaluate how healthcare services and systems are managed and how a more open approach to innovation could reduce these pressures.

Healthcare organizations engaging in their own R&D is not sufficient for survival and sustainability but requires new approaches to innovation in order to lead the world to better health. Open innovation is one approach that healthcare organizations can adopt. Originally defined by Henry Chesbrough (2003), open innovation is a paradigm that assumes that organizations can and should use external ideas, as well as internal ideas, and internal and external paths to the market as organizations look to advance their technology.

Open innovation in healthcare extends opportunities for innovation beyond the organizational boundaries and generates internal and external collaborations with patients, healthcare professionals, academics, payers, policymakers and other stakeholders. Open innovation focuses on the notion that there is a breadth of innovative knowledge widely dispersed throughout the environment. Creativity beyond the organizational boundaries is important to generate viable innovations from different perspectives. It is no longer appropriate to suggest that it is only healthcare professionals that can be creative and develop innovative solutions. Rather, the integration of diverse competencies and expertise in R&D for the advancement of healthcare innovations is essential. It is through this integration that novel concepts can be devised, developed and disseminated, and provide innovations leading to better healthcare.

Despite this growing interest in open innovation there is limited focus in the field of healthcare. Open innovation is more prevalent in the pharmaceutical/biotechnology sectors than in healthcare. A study undertaken by Wass and Vimarlund (2016) identified factors that inhibited open innovation in healthcare to include organizational complexity, a focus on routines for capturing knowledge from patients and clinicians, regulations and data laws. Healthcare organizations need to address those inhibiting factors because open innovation can more effectively utilize resources and generate more ideas, which is paramount given the complexity and challenges facing healthcare globally. Open innovation can generate many opportunities for healthcare. Bringing healthcare professionals, researchers and industry experts together in an open innovative partnership can further enhance and develop individual competencies, research focus, products, services and processes within healthcare.

To address the increasing needs for innovation from patients together with scientific and technological advancements, healthcare organizations increasingly incorporate innovation *ecosystems* globally. These innovation networks facilitate organizations to collaborate with individuals, institutions, universities, government agencies, and other worldwide organizations to resolve problems and generate new ideas (Hisrich and Kearney, 2013). In the current challenging healthcare environment, innovation has never been more important for healthcare organizations as they come together to actively engage in networks that can resolve the world's healthcare crisis with the Covid-19 pandemic.

Innovation Ecosystem in Healthcare

There is increased interest in both the theory and practice of open innovation from small group level generating ideas to ecosystem level. An innovation ecosystem can be defined as an "evolving set of actors, activities, and artifacts, and the institutions and relations, including complementary and substitute relations, that are important for the innovative performance of an actor or a population of actors" (Granstranda and Holgerssonb, 2020: 3). Innovation ecosystems are an important source of knowledge sharing, idea generation and diffusion. This is particularly important for the complex field of healthcare where there is a continuous need for innovations to address ever increasing healthcare challenges. A healthcare innovation ecosystem incorporates a specific group of stakeholders required to bring innovation to the healthcare organization and healthcare system. The right group of stakeholders is fundamental to the success of the ecosystem and requires significant communication and collaboration as part of the creativity and innovation process. Partners that form this ecosystem include, for example, other private and public healthcare organizations, patients, medical professionals, academic partners, government and funding agencies. The core objective of a healthcare innovation ecosystem is to improve the health and well-being of patients and increase efficiency and effectiveness through the greater utilization of limited resources among those engaged in the ecosystem. The biggest challenge to achieving a successful and innovative ecosystem in healthcare is ensuring full commitment of such a diverse group of stakeholders and creating a shared vision for innovation.

   An effective ecosystem can achieve synergy so that the "outcome is greater than the sum of its parts." An open innovation ecosystem refers to a network of appropriate relationships where there is shared knowledge and communication for innovation and value. For a greater understanding of an open innovation ecosystem in healthcare, the following definition is proposed:

An innovation ecosystem in healthcare is a group of stakeholders as well as other independent experts across other sectors that is fundamental for the innovative performance of generating patient value through products, processes, services and technologies.

This group openly shares competencies and expertise, and generates ideas for innovation. Those stakeholders can include patients, healthcare professionals, academics, scientists, payers and policymakers, as well as medical device experts, industry experts and other stakeholders.

In an open innovation ecosystem, value is generated from effective integration, collaboration and leveraging core competencies that emerge from a shared vision across the network. It is this shared vision that is generated as a result of specific events, experiences and networks that transforms and strengthens the innovation ecosystem. In the challenging field of healthcare it is imperative that all stakeholders share knowledge and information to drive and accelerate innovations that generate patient value through the open innovation ecosystem. It is focused on the generation of patient value where the outcome of the ecosystem exceeds the sum of its parts.

PROCESS OF INNOVATION

The process of innovation typically begins with the awareness of a problem or need and ends with the implementation of an innovation to address the problem or satisfy the need. The level and depth of analysis at each stage of the process depend on the type of innovation (breakthrough, technological or incremental) and the organizational resources (Figure 2.1).

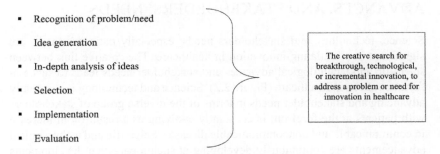

- Recognition of problem/need

- Idea generation

- In-depth analysis of ideas

- Selection

- Implementation

- Evaluation

The creative search for breakthrough, technological, or incremental innovation, to address a problem or need for innovation in healthcare

Figure 2.1   Phases of the innovation process

- *Recognition of Problem/Need* – the process begins with recognition of a problem/need facing the healthcare organization. It is important to clearly identify the problem/need for innovation. This requires probing and asking challenging and frequently controversial questions to a diverse group of stakeholders.

- *Idea Generation* – generating ideas is critical for healthcare organizations. Search the internal and external environment both within and outside the healthcare sector to generate ideas about potential innovations that would respond to the problem/needs of the situation.
- *In-depth Analysis of Ideas* – this requires an in-depth analysis of the ideas generated in order to prioritize and choose from the concepts developed. Improvement can still be made to concepts at this point.
- *Selection* – the best alternative is the one that is most feasible and addresses the problem/need and best fits the overall goals and achieves the desired innovation results.
- *Implementation* – bringing it all together and making it happen.
- *Evaluation* – once the new innovation is implemented it must be closely evaluated to identify any deviations or gaps between the desired and actual innovation.

The phases of the innovation process are complex and have many aspects to them that necessitate an in-depth analysis of each stage. Actively engaging in the acquisition of knowledge that facilitates the creation of new solutions. Additionally, combining new and existing knowledge brings about greater synergy, which helps generate new ideas. This is all crucial for the complex and knowledge-intensive healthcare environment.

INNOVATION, SCIENTIFIC AND TECHNOLOGICAL ADVANCES, AND STAKEHOLDERS' NEEDS

Science, technology and stakeholders needs, especially patients' needs, are significant in stimulating innovation in healthcare. The creative link between scientific and technological advances and stakeholder needs leads to successful innovations in healthcare (Figure 2.2). Science and technology is constantly advancing and stakeholder needs in terms of the diverse group of stakeholders with patients at the forefront is constantly evolving as a result of an increase in communicable and noncommunicable diseases. Scientific and technological advancements are continuously developing at such a pace that developments in, for example, robotics; AI genetic engineering; synthetic biology; nanotechnology; data science; new drug development; new diagnostics methods; advanced, less invasive surgeries; and changes in patient treatment plans that are less expensive, intrusive and have reduced side-effects (all of which were unimaginable a decade ago), are part of today's practice. Likewise, what is unimaginable today may be feasible in a few years' time.

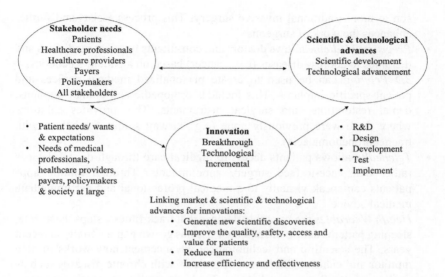

Figure 2.2   Innovation through scientific and technological advances and stakeholder needs in healthcare

The relationship between the development of innovation through scientific and technological advances and stakeholder needs is complex, particularly with today's scientific and technological advancements and changing patient needs. The competencies of the healthcare professionals and academics, healthcare providers, medical device experts and industry experts in collaboration with patients are key to connect scientific and technological advancement to patient needs that are innovative. It is this body of knowledge, skills and abilities that leads to the innovation. These innovations generate new scientific discoveries, which can save and extend patients' lives, improve quality, safety, access and value for patients while reducing harm and increasing efficiency and effectiveness.

This link is evident in many healthcare innovations where scientific and technological advances connect to identify the gaps and address patients' needs. The following are examples of scientific and technological advancements that are truly innovative:

*   *Robotic Surgery* is a minimally invasive surgery where procedures are performed through very small incisions. This form of surgery has now become normal practice and is used in a number of procedures, for example gall bladder, knee and hernia surgery. It allows complex procedures to be undertaken with a greater degree of precision and flexibility in compari-

son to more traditional invasive surgery. This process assists and further enhances the work of surgeons.

- *Precision Medicine* allows doctors and consultants to select medicines and therapies to address diseases (e.g., cancer) based on a patient's genetics.
- *3D Printing* can be used to create personalized medical devices and patient-specific implants. This includes orthopedic and cranial implants, dental restorations and surgical instruments. This provides solutions where there were previously none (e.g., airway splints for babies with tracheobronchomalacia).
- *Telehealth* allows patients access to medical care through digital devices rather than face-to-face surgery appointments. Through mobile apps patients can speak virtually to a medical professional and get immediate medical advice.
- *Health Wearables* are wearable devices that track fitness, steps, heart rate, sleeping patterns and so on, and their use has grown exponentially in recent years. The scientific and technological advancement now works to help monitor and enhance the fitness of patients with chronic diseases such as cardiovascular disease and diabetes. These advancements continue to grow with Apple Series 4 Watch including an integrated ECG to monitor the individual's heart rhythms.

We are now moving in the direction where technology is contributing significantly toward more patient-centered, personalized care where AI, digital health, data analytics and connected medical devices can support patients in their own homes, thus reducing pressure on overstretched hospital systems. Patient-centered care puts patients at the center of their own care, where they are more actively engaged in their own care plans. Patients are therefore engaged in the decision-making and have access and control over their own personal healthcare data.

The link between scientific and technological advancements and stakeholder needs is paramount at every stage of the innovation process from the idea generation through the entire research, design, and development process to the introduction of the new product, service, process, technology or delivery method into healthcare.

SOCIETAL VALUE OF INNOVATION IN HEALTHCARE

Opportunities for innovation need to address healthcare needs in order to create societal value. Innovations need to generate value for patients, healthcare professionals, scientists, service users, policymakers, governments, payers and society at large. Healthcare innovators need to be mindful of the value of the innovation they are proposing. Value means different things to the diverse number of stakeholders; therefore, the different perspectives need to be recognized. Despite differences in how they define value to the patients, healthcare system, economy, society or future of healthcare innovations, they have the passion, drive and commitment to advance the world of healthcare through these innovations that will improve patient outcomes.

Innovations in healthcare can be invaluable in changing the world of healthcare. Such innovations have contributed to increasing the life expectancy of patients, decreasing patients' morbidities, and improving the quality and safety of healthcare. Where possible, innovations are also needed in preventing illnesses and diseases in the first place, rather than being employed as interventions in a pressured system.

While certain innovations can be considered important they may have undesirable outcomes. Objectivity is key in evaluating the proposed innovation and its benefits, as well as recognizing any unintended outcomes. For example, digital health technologies that require patients to have smart phones may create a divide among members of the population that do not have such a device or are not living in a location where there is advanced broadband. Additionally innovations in biosimilars have a low patient uptake as physicians are more favorable toward prescribing biologics and patients are apprehensive about changing from biologics to biosimilars. Despite the potential cost benefits of biosimilars in chronic disease it will take time for their use to establish a more consistent market share because they are competing with more established biologics.

Patients should be at the forefront of innovations in healthcare. The greatest value patients can achieve is not to become a patient by first and foremost looking after their health and well-being and doing what they can to ensure a healthy lifestyle and diet, exercise appropriately and take an active role in their care if they become unwell. However, successful healthcare innovations need to ensure that they focus on five core areas:

1. How long does it take for the patient to be first seen? Patients should receive the most timely and appropriate treatment that is available.
2. How is the patient first seen? Patients should be seen as soon as is reasonably possible by the most appropriate healthcare professional to address their issue without delay.
3. How is the patient listened to? Patients need to be at the center of their own care and treatment and need to be listened to and asked the right questions.
4. How is the patient communicated with? Patients must be clearly and concisely communicated with, with humanity and respect, without using complicated medical terminology.

5. How are the patient's needs being addressed? For value to be generated their needs must be addressed in the most timely way with the most appropriate treatment and care.

While the cost of innovative drugs, treatments and technologies can be extremely high, there needs to be a balance between accessibility for every patient who can benefit from those innovations as well as incentivizing healthcare innovations and investment in R&D. Once this balance is achieved, further life-changing innovations can be delivered to address today's needs while developing tomorrow's breakthroughs of scientific and technological advancement that will continue to deliver a cycle of innovation for the betterment of healthcare to society at large.

With the diverse needs and expectations of stakeholders and society at large, it is impossible for all to agree on the specific value of the innovation. The visions of its value can range from, for example, equitable accessibility, efficiency and effectiveness, enhanced quality and safety, reduction of side effects, to market competition. For innovation to capture true value, its benefits must exceed what already exists and the innovation must be shared and widely accessible to meet the needs of patients and society at large.

SUMMARY

Generating innovative solutions is imperative in the field of healthcare. Within healthcare there are many areas of opportunity for innovations. The main sources of innovation are individuals and teams working within healthcare in cooperation with patients, other healthcare professionals, academics, payers, policymakers, service users, engineers, designers, technology developers and other stakeholders. Healthcare organizations need to utilize the core competencies of their healthcare professionals internally and externally through appropriate approaches to open innovation and the development of ecosystems in order to generate ideas and take appropriate action to develop and implement innovations that will generate patient value. The steps in the innovation process are all well known, but the most important ones are those associated with the creative search for new solutions and new possibilities that will lead the world to better health.

Healthcare is a challenging environment facing unprecedented demands. To develop and grow in such a dynamic, uncertain environment necessitates the creative link between scientific and technological advances with stakeholder needs. Successful innovations are those that are better than what already exists and not only meet but are able to exceed the needs of patients and society at large.

REFERENCES

Chesbrough, H. (2003). *Open Innovation: The New Imperative for Creating and Profiting from Technology* (Boston, MA: Harvard Business Press).

Granstranda, O. and Holgerssonb, M. (2020). Innovation ecosystems: a conceptual review and a new definition. *Technovation* 90–91, 1–12.

Hisrich, R.D. and Kearney, C. (2013). *Managing Innovation and Entrepreneurship: A Global Perspective* (Thousand Oaks, CA: SAGE Publications).

Wass, S. and Vimarlund, V. (2016). Healthcare in the age of open innovation: a literature review. *Health Information Management* 45(3), 121–33.

Suggested Reading

Davies, G.H., Roderick, S. and Huxtable-Thomas, L. (2019). Social commerce open innovation in healthcare management: an exploration from a novel technology transfer approach. *Journal of Strategic Marketing* 27(4), 356–67.

This article presents an Open Innovation approach, *AgorIP*, for commercialization of opportunities within health and social care and life sciences, piloted in south-west Wales. This approach aims to develop new markets and innovations, where all opportunities are rigorously assessed for existing and/or new market potential. The authors offer the *AgorIP* initiative as an interesting space to observe the potential for open innovation of social commerce within the health sector.

Granstranda, O. and Holgerssonb, M. (2020). Innovation ecosystems: a conceptual review and a new definition. *Technovation* 90–91, 1–12.

The authors in this article review received definitions of innovation ecosystems and related concepts, and propose a synthesized definition of an innovation ecosystem.

Lakdawalla, D.N., Doshi, J.A., Garrison, Jr., L.P., Phelps, C.E., Basu, A. and Danzon, P.M. (2018). Defining elements of value in health care: a health economics approach: an ISPOR Special Task Force Report [3], *Value in Health* 21, 131–9. https://www.valueinhealthjournal.com/article/S1098-3015(17)33892-5/pdf.

This article identifies and defines a series of elements that warrant consideration in value assessments of medical technologies. The authors aim to broaden the view of what constitutes value in health care and to spur new research on incorporating additional elements of value into cost-effectiveness analysis (CEA). Twelve potential elements of value are considered.

Kimble, L. and Massoud, R.M. (2016). What do we mean by innovation in healthcare? *European Medical Journal* 1(1), 89–91. https://www.emjreviews.com/innovations/article/what-do-we-mean-by-innovation-in-healthcare/.

This article clarifies what innovation in healthcare truly means. To address this issue, the authors first define innovation as a general term, and then define what innovation means in the context of the healthcare industry. To better understand what may be considered "innovative" in healthcare, they suggest criteria for innovation and identify potential challenges to newly introduced innovations in the field.

Orianaa, C., Patrizioa, A., Robertaa, B.P., Mariannaa, C., Claudioa, J. and Rosannaa, T. (2016). De innovatione: the concept of innovation for medical technologies and its implications for healthcare policy-making. *Health Policy and Technology* 5, 47–64.

In this article, the authors summarize acceptable definitions of innovation in relation to medical devices. Based on the innovation management and economics theory, proposed definitions have been classified according to the source of innovation, to the degree of discontinuity introduced and to the impact associated to the technology.

Secundo, G., Toma, A., Schiuma, G. and Passiante, G. (2019). Knowledge transfer in open innovation: a classification framework for healthcare ecosystems. *Business Process Management Journal* 25(1), 144–63. https://doi.org/10.1108/BPMJ-06 -2017-0173.

This article explores how knowledge is transferred and flows among all the healthcare ecosystems' players in order to support open innovation processes.

3. Strategic perspective: integration of innovation and entrepreneurship in healthcare

QUESTIONS

What is the role of strategy in the development of an innovative and entrepreneurial healthcare organization? What is the link between innovation and entrepreneurship with strategy, and how can this be developed in healthcare? What internal organizational characteristics make some healthcare organizations more innovative and entrepreneurial than others? How can strategy be effectively implemented and evaluated to ensure patient value and sustained competitive advantage? How can healthcare organizations demonstrate that corporate governance, social responsibility and ethical principles are at the core of their healthcare practices?

INTRODUCTION

Healthcare organizations globally are facing challenges due to aging populations, the growing needs of patients with communicable and noncommunicable diseases, technological advancement and development, and most recently the unprecedented Covid-19 global pandemic that has caused a global healthcare tsunami that will shape the future of healthcare. The internal organization needs to be able to adapt to the rapid and at times unprecedented changes taking place. To adapt to these challenges requires a revolutionary patient-centered strategy that maximizes patient value by achieving the best results at the lowest cost through effective utilization of resources. Patient value is generated from how medicine is practiced and how innovation can further develop the practice of medicine. However, the field of healthcare is complex and dynamic and many healthcare organizations are conservative, bureaucratic, with centralized decision-making, substantial red tape and rigidity, and resistance to change. Top management and healthcare professionals are essential for strategic success and any strategy that they are not fully engaged with will not succeed.

Innovation and entrepreneurship are an integral component of an organization's strategy across all sectors. Strategy aims to capture the vision, mission, objectives and values of an organization. The essence of strategy is being true to your vision, mission, objectives and values. Strategy needs to ensure "congruence" between the internal organization and external environment. Globally, healthcare organizations are facing major challenges beyond their normal practices due to the Covid-19 pandemic. As a result there is a greater need to integrate innovation and entrepreneurship with strategy to develop organizational success and generate patient value in healthcare. To achieve this, healthcare organizations need to implement a strategy that ensures top management and leadership support flexible organizational structures, and a culture that is conducive to innovation and entrepreneurship. Within healthcare, all innovative and entrepreneurial endeavors must be patient centered.

This chapter examines the integration of innovation and entrepreneurship with strategy in healthcare. An understanding of strategy and the strategic management perspective in healthcare is provided. The role of innovation, entrepreneurship and strategy in healthcare, along with the challenging healthcare environment and strategic needs for innovation and entrepreneurship, are discussed. Integrating innovation and entrepreneurship with strategy is examined and a model is presented for healthcare. This is followed by an understanding of the importance of corporate governance, social responsibility and ethical principles in strategic development in healthcare. The chapter concludes with a discussion on the need for the integration between innovation and entrepreneurship with strategy to be patient-centered in that it meets and exceeds the unmet needs of patients, stakeholders and society at large.

WHAT IS STRATEGY?

There is no one universal definition of strategy. Strategy is an action plan for achieving the organization's goals. The organization needs to think clearly about its strategy and consider what *unique* position it can sustain, how to achieve *competitive advantage* and *sustain that advantage* over time. Within healthcare, strategy can be defined as focused-directed actions an organization takes to achieve its vision, mission, objectives and values that are patient-centered and will generate patient value. The *Vision* focuses on what the healthcare organization wants to accomplish and captures its core aspirations. The *Mission* focuses on the core purpose of the healthcare organization and how it will achieve its goals. The *Objectives* focus on the end results in pursuit of the achievement of the organization's mission and vision. The *Values* focus on the core principles of internal organizational behavior and the organization's relationship with the external environment ensuring legal and ethical behavior in achieving the healthcare organization's vision and mission.

Developing a strategy in healthcare is a challenging task and requires comprehensive knowledge of the internal and external environment, patient requirements, evaluation of current operations, and quality of service. Strategy is a short-, medium- and long-term plan on *what* is to be achieved and *how* best it can be achieved. The focus is on "how to get from where we are to where we want to be." Strategy needs to be challenging but realistically achievable in light of internal organizational and external environmental factors. The longer the term of the strategy, the more flexible it needs to be to adjust and adapt to unforeseen events and circumstances.

Within healthcare, strategy is the pattern of decision-making that demonstrates the vision, mission, objectives and values. It sets out the policies and plans to achieve those goals and highlights the core focus of the healthcare organization and its contribution to generate value for patients, employees, stakeholders and the wider community. It must be noted that:

- There is no one best strategy;
- Strategies can be both intended and emergent;
- An organization's strategy may need to be changed in light of unexpected factors;
- Successful strategies of the past do not guarantee future success;
- Effective strategic leadership must be demonstrated.

Given the complexity of healthcare, strategists need to have the ability to reflect and learn from the past, have a clear understanding of the present and through their learning can effectively plan for the future. They possess strong awareness, effective analysis and critical thinking skills, are creative and innovative with an ability to incorporate different perspectives, and have the ability to synthesize and reflect.

Strategic Management Perspective

Strategic management in healthcare must capture specific goal-oriented actions undertaken by the organization to achieve patient value and sustain superior performance. Within healthcare, strategic management can be defined as the set of commitments, decisions and actions required for the health-care organization to generate patient value and sustained competitiveness. Sustaining competitive advantage is recognized as an important determinant of organizational performance (Ireland, 2007). The reality is that your competitor is anyone your customer/patient has access to. With globalization, the technological revolution and the development of telemedicine competition has intensified. Global concerns about aging populations, cuts in healthcare funding, and the unprecedented impact and cost of the Covid-19 global pandemic are significantly driving new levels of competitive pressure. The ability to achieve competitive positioning is a key determinant of the organization's ability to create value and wealth for stakeholders and society (Ketchen et al., 2007; Porter, 1980). In light of intensified competition and increased complexity and challenges this positioning is important for healthcare organizations to differentiate themselves in the value they generate for patients and society at large.

Strategic management must continuously work towards the fulfillment of vision, mission, objectives and values in meeting needs of patients and the healthcare system demonstrating innovation, continuous learning, and sustained patient and societal value. Clearly communicated strategies enable management and leaders to view the organization in its entirety and position the organization for superior patient value. This is particularly important in healthcare where the environment is turbulent, complex and unpredictable with increasing pressure to improve quality and safety and reduce costs.

Strategic management needs to develop a strategy that focuses on the best ways for the organization to create and sustain a competitive advantage while simultaneously identifying and developing new opportunities (Hisrich and Kearney, 2013). They need to be patient-centered with strategic plans that focus on medical excellence in all patient care, high quality in all services, and innovative techniques to support excellence, quality and safety. Changes in global healthcare systems and increasing regulation mean that strategy incorporating innovation is increasingly important. Developing a strategy for healthcare organizations requires a comprehensive knowledge of the current market challenges; patient, stakeholder and societal needs; evaluation of patient satisfaction; evaluation of operations; evaluation of quality; and safety of services.

For healthcare organizations the integration of innovation and entrepreneurship into strategy is important in pursuit of competitive advantage and superior performance that focuses on generating patient value. Strategic management requires the ability to maximize the creation of patient value by achieving the best patient outcome at the lowest cost as well as value for citizens and society. Strategic managers' in healthcare organizations must be strategic thinkers, with an ability to evaluate the changes within the healthcare sector, analyze data, question assumptions, and develop new ideas for now and the future of healthcare.

ROLE OF INNOVATION, ENTREPRENEURSHIP AND STRATEGY IN HEALTHCARE

Healthcare organizations that aim to achieve and sustain competitive advantage will develop a strategy that will have innovation and entrepreneurship at its core. This will result in new and novel products, services, processes, technologies and delivery methods that generate patient value and achieve sustainable competitive advantage. The most successful strategies for healthcare are those that are integrated with innovative and entrepreneurial activities that can generate superior patient value. A concept integrating strategic management and entrepreneurship is known as "strategic entrepreneurship," defined as "the integration of entrepreneurial (i.e. opportunity seeking behavior) and strategic (i.e. advantage seeking) perspectives in developing and taking actions designed to create wealth" (Hitt et al., 2001: 481) (see also Chapter 4). More specifically, "strategic entrepreneurship allows the firm to apply its knowledge and capabilities in the current environmental context while exploring for opportunities to exploit in the future by applying new knowledge and new and/or enhanced capabilities" (Hitt et al., 2011: 69). The integration of those two disciplines is supported by the way opportunity and advantage seeking behaviors are seen as complementary. In the current global pandemic this integration is particularly important as there is intense pressure and scrutiny on a healthcare system to address the pandemic while also managing existing and growing global healthcare challenges with limited resources.

Strategy and strategic management define the direction of the healthcare organization. Management needs to develop a strategy that focuses on the best ways for the organization to create and sustain a competitive advantage while simultaneously identifying and developing new innovative approaches that will lead to better patient outcomes. Innovation and entrepreneurship are focused on searching for new opportunities that will generate patient value. At times within the healthcare system the focus is on mitigating risk and while this is core there is also a necessity to generate patient value. We need to be getting better and better at "doing the right thing – right" not "doing the wrong thing – right." Within healthcare it is not that there is a lack of innovative ideas but that these ideas are not properly supported as part of the organizational strategy. Strategy in healthcare is focused on generating greater patient value and sustaining competitive advantage. Simultaneously embracing entrepreneurial philosophies, an entrepreneurial climate and entrepreneurial strategic behaviors increases the likelihood an organization will identify and use its unique capabilities as a pathway to increasing its performance (Ireland et al., 2009). Therefore, the integration of innovation and entrepreneurship for opportunity exploration and exploitation, and a strategy for sustaining competitive advantage, are necessary for generating patient value. Healthcare organizations that can develop competitive advantages today, while using innovation and entrepreneurship to cultivate tomorrow's advantages, increase the opportunity for long-term success.

Challenging Healthcare Environment: Strategic Needs for Innovation and Entrepreneurship

The challenges facing the healthcare environment are at an all-time high: healthcare costs are increasing; there are significant demands on new and existing services; new diseases and conditions are prominent; new treatments are emerging; technological advancement and development is continuing; and there is increased patient engagement and awareness of treatments. Furthermore, toward the end of 2019, the world of healthcare dramatically changed in ways that could never have been envisaged with Covid-19. In many countries, healthcare services were at breaking point prior to the Covid-19 pandemic; now the combined urgency, risk, uncertainty and cost of intervention makes it very challenging to control the infectious disease. As a result, healthcare organizations are operating in the most challenging, unprecedented times where they are competing at every level nationally and internationally for the recruitment and attraction of high-caliber medical professionals, personal protective equipment (PPE) for staff in this high-risk environment where there are extreme levels of transmission, and a race against time to develop a vaccine. As a result of the severity of Covid-19, stringent measures were taken globally with stages of lockdown in many countries. The new level of intensity is characterized by the increasing risk of mortality and pressure beyond the capability of any system, risk of surge until there is a vaccine (which was introduced in late 2020) or an effective antiviral medicine, limited ability to forecast due to the unknown nature of the virus, and more diverse patient demands and expectations. While Covid-19 has taken over the world there is still the ongoing needs' of patients with communicable and noncommunicable diseases that has been put on hold. This will have an astounding impact on patients and healthcare systems as these conditions "do not stand still in a crisis" and can be life-threatening if not addressed, in many cases requiring urgent care and treatment.

The level and pace of change is significantly greater than ever experienced globally within healthcare, which has significant implications for healthcare organizations and their management and leadership. Environmental changes have an impact on the development of products, services, processes, technologies and delivery methods either through opportunity and/or necessity. As external environments become more dynamic, complex and turbulent, there are opportunities to be explored and exploited. The rapid pace of change can emerge from new markets (e.g., alternative treatments), technology (e.g., AI, telemedicine), economic conditions (impacting health and well-being), demographic patterns (e.g., aging populations), globalization (e.g., mobility of patients for treatment), the knowledge economy (e.g., new treatments, inventions and approaches to treatment), and a pandemic like Covid-19 that has instantly changed the world of healthcare and the economy. The need for innovation and entrepreneurship in the world of healthcare is at an all-time high. While environmental changes inhibit the potential of some innovations, they create opportunities for others. New markets can provide new opportunities. New healthcare advancements include new diagnostic procedures, drug development, advances in treatment diagnoses and techniques, and new technologies that can develop new competencies and, for example, more efficient and effective ways of diagnosing patients through AI. The world of healthcare needs to embrace the potential opportunities that can be found as a result of the threat of Covid-19.

In today's healthcare environment, to sustain competitive advantage, healthcare organizations need to recognize that patient groupings are more diverse and there is more competition. Change in one area such as technological advancement and development has resulted in changes in other areas such as the evaluation of the role and development for some healthcare professionals, and more intensified competition as patients have more choice. For example, AI is changing radiology. It is proving to be more reliable than radiologists in identifying pathologies in images such as bone fractures and cancerous lesions. As further AI advancement and development emerge the question is what this will mean for radiologists. While radiologists are fundamental in identifying and addressing complex issues and managing the diagnostic processes, AI will be part of that process. This can be recognized as an opportunity to facilitate radiologists in the delivery of higher quality and more timely services. Other major changes include robotic surgery or robotic-assisted surgery that has been widely adopted across the United States and Europe for a number of procedures. This innovation allows surgeons to perform complex surgeries that were too challenging or risky with traditional surgical approaches. Technology has also resulted in growth and development of telemedicine. Prior to the Covid-19 pandemic, the strict regulations of virtual medicine combined with patients' resistance created major challenges for telemedicine in many countries. As a result of Covid-19 and the restrictions due to social distancing measures and risk of asymptomatic patients, telemedicine has become the normal doctor and patient consultation. This revolution emerged overnight across Europe and the United States due to the urgency to keep patients safe and reduce the spread of Covid-19. The strict regulations have been reduced across Europe and the United States to give patients treatment without leaving their homes. While telemedicine does not replace a physical examination and the testing of more subtle signs of cancer and other noncommunicable diseases, it does allow the treatment of conditions and illnesses that need immediate attention and recognition of those that require further testing and investigation to ensure quality, safety and standard of care.

Telemedicine supports healthcare in being more accessible and cost-effective. The rapid pace of this change emerged out of necessity to address a pandemic and clearly recognizes the strength and resilience of healthcare to make those changes. The core focus on healthcare organizations is to generate patient value and in doing that they need to improve quality and safety, reduce costs, enhance patient services, reduce waiting times, exceed patient expectations, and provide innovations that enhance the world of healthcare.

Healthcare organizations that are focused, adaptable, flexible, responsive, proactive with a propensity to take risks, and engage in R&D are in a more advantageous position to adapt to the challenges of the external environment and achieve competitiveness and potentially sustainable competitive advantage. Innovation and entrepreneurship are central to healthcare organizations achieving sustainable competitive advantage.

Competitive advantage in healthcare organizations requires the following:

- Adaptation to external environmental challenges and changes;
- Being patient-centered;
- Flexible strategies and processes that can address the needs and diverse requirements of patients, stakeholders and society at large;
- Responsiveness to environmental change by exploring and exploiting opportunities as they emerge;
- Being proactive in generating patient value;
- Engaging in R&D to ensure the development of innovation in products, services, processes, technologies and delivery methods.

Strategies that integrate innovation and entrepreneurial activity to generate patient value are the key success factors for healthcare organizations in the challenges of the 21st century to "lead the world to better health."

INTEGRATION OF INNOVATION AND ENTREPRENEURSHIP WITH STRATEGY

"The integration of innovation and entrepreneurship with strategy can be defined as a vision directed strategic analysis with a core focus on innovative and entrepreneurial behaviors that continuously develop the organization through the identification and development of innovative and entrepreneurial opportunities that result in value creation and sustained competitive advantage" (Hisrich and Kearney, 2013: 71). For a healthcare organization to support and facilitate innovative and entrepreneurial behavior it needs to be properly integrated into the organizational strategy. Healthcare organizations like St. Mary's hospital London have a strong history of innovation that goes back to 1928 when bacteriologist Dr. Alexander Fleming discovered penicillin. The Mayo Clinic which focuses on transforming the healthcare experience and the Cleveland Clinic which has achieved major medical breakthroughs in its history are among numerous highly innovative healthcare organizations that capture the true nature of a strategy that is unique, innovative and entrepreneurial in defining and generating patient value.

Ensuring the effective integration of innovation and entrepreneurship with strategy allows top management to develop strategies that focus on new and novel approaches to address patient needs, generate patient value, and sustain competitiveness. This integration facilitates successful innovation that explores and exploits viable opportunities. This requires a supportive internal organizational environment and individual behavior and mindset that embraces new (and strives for better) ways to generate patient value. Hisrich and Kearney's (2013) work identifies three core dimensions for the integration of innovation and entrepreneurship with strategy: "(1) innovation and entrepreneurial strategic analysis, (2) strategic choice for value creation and competitiveness, and (3) strategic implementation for wealth creation and sustained competitive advantage" (Hisrich and Kearney, 2013: 71). Building on Hisrich and Kearney's (2013) model as the foundation, a model is proposed for the integration of innovation and entrepreneurship with strategy in healthcare.

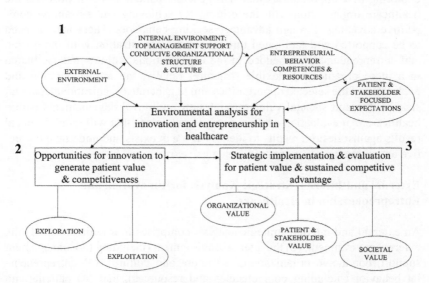

Figure 3.1   *The integration of innovation and entrepreneurship with strategy in healthcare*

The model presented in Figure 3.1 identifies three core dimensions:

1. Environmental analysis for innovation and entrepreneurship in healthcare;
2. Opportunities for innovation to generate patient value and competitiveness;
3. Strategic implementation and evaluation for patient value and sustained competitive advantage.

The first dimension requires an in-depth monitoring and evaluation of the environment. It specifies the key factors influencing the process at different levels, including external and internal environmental factors (top management support, structure and culture), behavior (competencies and resources) and patient and stakeholder expectations. How a healthcare organization evaluates the external and internal environment and coordinates the utilization of resources significantly impacts the plans and achievement of their strategy. The second dimension focuses on choices available from the environmental analysis, specifically focusing on the external environment and internal environmental support, competencies and the utilization of resources from the first dimension that are used to identify current opportunities while simultaneously exploring new opportunities that will generate patient value. It provides the healthcare organization with the criteria for achieving and sustaining competitive advantage through advantage-seeking behaviors. These actions need to be supported and facilitated throughout the organization with innovation and entrepreneurship embedded in the organizational culture and facilitated in a more organic and flexible structure. Finally, the implementation and evaluation of the selected opportunities aim to generate organizational, patient, stakeholder, and societal value through new and novel developments within healthcare. An evaluation process needs to take place that will monitor actual results against desired results to identify if a gap exists and undertake corrective action in a timely manner if such a gap exists.

External and Internal Strategic Analysis for Innovation and Entrepreneurship in Healthcare

An external and internal strategic analysis comprises four main areas: (1) the external environment, (2) the internal environment (including top management support, conducive organizational structure and culture), (3) entrepreneurial behavior (including competencies and resources), and (4) patient- and stakeholder-focused expectations.

External environment

According to Peter Drucker (2005: 9), "The most important task of an organization's leader is to anticipate a crisis. Perhaps not to avert it, but to anticipate it … One has to make the organization capable of anticipating the storm, weathering it, and in fact, being ahead of it. That is called innovation, constant renewal." While some "storms" cannot be anticipated, it is a flexible and adaptable approach that is core to innovation and entrepreneurship. This is one with an organic structure and a culture that embraces and seeks opportunities with distinctive capabilities that is quick to respond to a crisis no matter how catastrophic.

No organization can work in isolation from its external environment. The external environment includes the political, economic, social, technological, regulatory, competitive, supplier, and patient/customer environments, and plays a central role in the field of healthcare to ensure compliance with regulation, legislation, ethics and patient safety. The external environment strongly influences the internal organization and the opportunities for innovation and entrepreneurship. There is a need to continuously monitor and evaluate the external environment to ensure the exploration and exploitation of viable market opportunities so that innovations being proposed are realistic and viable. There needs to be not just a "gap in the market" but most significantly a "market in the gap," otherwise the innovation will fail. External environmental analysis is not a one-time implementation but a continuous process to ensure patient value and sustainable competitive advantage. This analysis requires scanning the healthcare sector's external environment by using appropriate frameworks for analysis, for example PESTEL (political, economic, social, technological, environmental, legal) analysis, used to analyze external environmental factors that have an impact on the organization. The results can be used to identify external opportunities and threats which are used as part of a SWOT (strengths, weaknesses, opportunities, threats) analysis. The analysis facilitates the assessment and evaluation of external opportunities and/or concerns.

As the external environment changes, these changes require a different approach to innovation and entrepreneurship. When the economy is strong and prosperous, innovation and entrepreneurship occur as a result of many forthcoming opportunities. During times of economic recession, health crises and pandemics, innovation and entrepreneurship occur out of urgency. As current healthcare has changed with Covid-19, market conditions have changed significantly, and competition has intensified to find a vaccine or an effective antiviral medicine to address the virus. Due to this urgency and necessity scientists do not have the normal timeframe to develop such a vaccine but are fighting against time to address the pandemic. The extremity of such a pandemic is not just impacting healthcare with the high risk of transmission and impact on those that are Covid-19 positive, but also the catastrophic impact of such a crisis on individuals' mental health and well-being as a result of the inevitable lockdown restrictions that have been enacted. Furthermore, the detrimental impact on economies due to the lockdowns will result in the survival of only the most innovative organizations. Therefore we must be closely aligned to the needs of the external environment as it affects an organization's ability to explore and exploit opportunities and develop those opportunities to generate patient value and achieve sustainable competitive advantage.

Internal environment: top management support, organization structure and culture
The internal environment needs to focus on how best to achieve the organization's vision, mission, objectives and values. This internal environment needs to encourage the pursuit of innovative and entrepreneurial opportunities that can generate patient value and increase competitiveness. In doing so, the organization needs to identify their core strengths and weaknesses and how they can further develop those strengths and minimize those weaknesses to achieve competitive advantage. This in turn links to external opportunities and threats as part of the SWOT analysis. The value of the opportunity is the organization's ability to take advantage of that opportunity and develop ways to reduce the threats. By identifying external opportunities and threats in relation to internal strengths and weaknesses, top management can determine the distinctive competencies of the organization that will give it competitive advantage.

To integrate innovation and entrepreneurship with strategy requires an internal environment that is supported and facilitated by top management with a clear entrepreneurial vision. Top management is responsible for developing an internal environment that is supported by an appropriate flexible structure, adaptable systems and a culture that embraces innovation and entrepreneurship. This environment needs to reward success and accept and learn from failure without fear. In an innovative and entrepreneurial healthcare organization, top management supports and encourages staff to explore and exploit opportunities in search of patient value and competitive advantage.

An appropriate organizational structure is paramount for achieving entrepreneurial and innovative endeavors; this can be seen in the differences between organic and mechanistic structures. Generally an organic organizational structure is more flexible and adaptable, with open channels of communication and more flexible control systems; on the other hand, a mechanistic organizational structure is more bureaucratic and hierarchical with top-down communication and tight control systems. The more hierarchical and bureaucratic the structure the more challenging it is to explore and exploit opportunities, achieve top management support, reallocate resources and take moderate risks.

Bureaucracy that can be most dominant in traditional healthcare organizations and hospitals does not provide flexibility, adaptability, timeliness and motivation for innovation and entrepreneurship. The appropriate structure is paramount as it supports the evaluation, selection and implementation of innovation for the benefit of healthcare. Therefore an organization's innovative and entrepreneurial engagement can be inhibited or it can flourish depending on the organizational structures. Research across sectors has found that organic structures are associated with higher performance among innovative and entrepreneurial organizations.

For innovation and entrepreneurship to develop there needs to be greater flexibility, autonomy and willingness to change with an organic structure, decentralized decision-making and open channels of communication. This flexibility supports the organization in its response to the unpredictable, dynamic, complex healthcare and highly regulated environment. This allows the organization to more readily embrace opportunities that emerge and respond to the immediate and at times unpredictable needs of patients and society at large.

The overall culture of the organization can either support or inhibit innovation. Therefore, innovation needs to be a core element of the culture of any healthcare organization that aspires to be innovative and entrepreneurial. The development of an entrepreneurial strategy in healthcare requires a change in the organizational culture that will support and facilitate the innovative and entrepreneurial mindset. Culture in healthcare influences the values, behaviors and attitudes of people within the organization. It guides individual behavior and provides a shared sense of purpose, value, and behavioral norms with a clear understanding of "who they are" and "what they are trying to accomplish." Culture can be defined as "the way things are done around here." An organizational culture that is guided by a vision, encourages freedom and flexibility, and demonstrates open communication, trust and support in people, generates more creativity and increases the quality and output of innovation. This provides a supportive environment allowing employees to take ownership of their position, own their jobs and to make a difference to the world of healthcare. However, while change is challenging and changing culture is particularly challenging, it is paramount in the realization of integrating innovation and entrepreneurship with strategy.

Structures and culture are necessary for the achievement of the organizational strategy and must be congruent with strategy. Integrating innovation and entrepreneurship with strategy must be embedded in the organizational culture in alignment with top management support and a flexible structure to support this strategy. Structure needs to support the implementation of the overall strategy. It is this internal alignment and integration that will support the organization's efforts to generate patient value and gain and sustain competitive advantage.

Entrepreneurial behavior, competencies and resources

Entrepreneurial behavior, competencies and resources are fundamental for organizations to engage in innovative activities and work toward the development of innovations for the greater good of healthcare. They are central for opportunity exploration and exploitation to generate patient value and in doing so achieve and sustain competitive advantage. The development of an entrepreneurial mindset is generated through numerous actions. At an individual level, alertness, self-efficacy, and effectuation are indicators of entrepreneurial behavior (Hisrich and Kearney, 2013). Entrepreneurial alertness within healthcare is the openness and readiness to recognize opportunities that have not been considered by others and have the potential to generate patient value. Entrepreneurial self-efficacy is the evaluation of capabilities to achieve success in their entrepreneurial task. Healthcare leaders with the drive, passion, commitment and entrepreneurial self-efficacy are more motivated to undertake and lead others to pursue strategic and entrepreneurial goals that are central to the integration of innovation and entrepreneurship with strategy. "Effectuation processes take a set of means as given and focus on selecting between possible effects that can be created with that set of means" (Sarasvathy, 2001: 245). Within healthcare, it is the motivation and passion to generate patient value that drives innovation and entrepreneurship, in addition to the effective utilization of capabilities and resources that create an innovative and entrepreneurial culture in the organization that in time can significantly contribute to patient value and competitiveness.

Patient- and stakeholder-focused expectations

In order to fully utilize the benefit of the effective integration of innovation and entrepreneurship with strategy, the focus needs to be on successfully achieving core objectives that generate patient value and are important to a diverse group of stakeholders. Healthcare organizations must understand the needs of patients, obtain input from patients, and identify what is most important to them and develop innovation in terms of products, services, processes, technologies and delivery methods that address those needs. For this to be achieved effectively they need to fully engage with patients and diverse groups of stakeholders beyond healthcare professionals as part of the process of innovation, so the patients and diverse groups of stakeholders can contribute to the design and development of the innovation. It is the patient that is experiencing the condition, treatment and/or procedure, so they are strongly placed to contribute to the innovation and this provides more control over their own and other similar patients' healthcare needs. When a healthcare organization not only satisfies but also has the ability to exceed the needs of their patients, they are creating an opportunity for sustainable competitive advantage. Healthcare organizations must actively support and engage in exploration and exploitation of opportunities for the greater good of healthcare. An innovative, entrepreneurial healthcare organization will develop a reputation in the value they are generating to their patients.

Opportunities for Innovation to Generate Patient Value and Competitiveness

Emerging from the innovation and environmental analysis, top management needs to drive and support the exploration and exploitation of innovative opportunities that will generate patient value and achieve sustained competitive advantage. They need to be responsible in their innovative endeavors by strategically aligning healthcare innovations with public healthcare needs and objectives. They must effectively synchronize appropriate resources while simultaneously addressing strengths and weaknesses to achieve competitiveness that will support the pursuit of future opportunities resulting in patient value and sustained competitive advantage. Further to our discussion on the phases of the innovation process in Chapter 2, there is a need to link the integration of innovation and entrepreneurship with strategy. The following summarizes the key components for integration to emerge.

Exploration of innovative opportunities
Exploration of innovative opportunities requires an openness to engage in the process and recognition that innovation can emerge from anywhere inside or outside the field of healthcare. Scanning the environment in order to identify potential opportunities is not a one-time process as environments keep evolving and organizations must support and facilitate the engagement in this search process. As previously discussed, the search for opportunities can occur out of either opportunity or necessity. These opportunities are the result of research activities or recognition of gaps that need to be addressed, or necessity due to an urgent pandemic, or a need to conform to regulations and legislation, or intensity of competition within the sector. Whether opportunity or necessity, the organization must drive creativity and innovation in a sector that is so dependent on saving lives and enhancing the quality of life.

Exploitation of viable opportunities
From the potential options identified strategically select the most viable that the organization can commit time and resources to undertaking, and provide the best opportunity to address some of the pressing patient needs and achieve competitiveness. Innovations carry risk and the more innovative the idea the

higher the level of risk. Healthcare organizations by nature are risk-averse. They are dealing with patients' lives and must adhere to strict regulation and compliance but that does not mean they cannot take appropriate levels of risks. They need to identify ways to balance the risk with potential rewards and ensure they are not putting patients' lives at risk. Healthcare organizations need to select strategically how the innovative idea fits their strategy. Does it develop and build on their specialism? Do they have the necessary competencies and resources to bring this to fruition?

Strategic Implementation and Evaluation for Patient Value and Sustained Competitive Advantage

The more aligned the organization's strategy is to its core competencies and resources, and the more it is integrated with internal activities, the easier it will be to implement and evaluate. Forward-thinking leaders recognize that command and control leadership creates mediocrity. For a healthcare organization to succeed and create patient value in today's challenging environment, it needs to effectively implement and evaluate viable innovations to address those unmet needs and add value for the organization, patient, stakeholder, and society. Leadership style strongly influences how the strategy is implemented and evaluated in terms of, for example, the organizational structure, culture, delegation of autonomy and responsibility in decision-making, incentives and rewards. A successful strategy creates value for the organization, patient, stakeholders, and society.

Organizational value

Innovation is critical for healthcare to develop and advance the field of medicine. Innovation does not happen in isolation – it requires collaboration with people within and outside the organization across different disciplines. Hospitals are linked to universities as their academic partner but these relations go beyond education, training and research. These relationships and joint collaborations are fundamental so that hospital groups can work with universities, pharmaceutical companies and medical device companies in the development of effective evidence-based healthcare innovations. Innovation advancement supports the organization in addressing patient needs, wants and expectation by optimizing the diagnoses, treatment and outcome of the service provided by the specific organizational innovation.

Patient and stakeholder value

Effective strategic implementation focuses on generating patient value, stakeholder value, and benefits for society at large. Improving patient value must be the overarching objective for healthcare providers and stakeholders. Patients diagnosed with a disease or a chronic condition are concerned about life expectancy, quality of life, cure and/or treatment options and risk of readmission. Providing the best patient value despite the disease that they are experiencing is paramount for the field of healthcare. Healthcare organizations that generate patient value are more competitive. Successful innovations generate new value for patients and stakeholders in line with public health needs. For example, taking the Covid-19 pandemic and the study of infectious diseases, the benefit of multiple vaccines has extended far beyond the patient being treated. Such treatment limits the spread of the disease to others, significantly benefiting healthcare with the reduced transmission of the virus, the global economy can open again and less restricted normality can resume for society at large.

Innovations do not have to be new inventions to generate value. Healthcare organizations can explore and exploit opportunities created by existing innovations within or outside healthcare and aim to further develop or modify them so they provide patients with products or services that are, for example, more efficient, effective, reliable, accessible or customized, of higher quality and safety, offer better patient service, and come at a lower cost than other competing organizations.

Societal value
Within the field of healthcare, innovation and entrepreneurial activities go beyond economic growth and development, creation of new jobs, and enhancing market value to leading the world to better health through scientific breakthroughs. Innovations can reduce the risks borne by healthy patients that potentially face the likelihood of future disease. It is evident that noncommunicable diseases such as cardiovascular disease, type 2 diabetes, obesity, cancer, lung disease and poor mental health are the leading causes of death globally (WHO, 2020). Through education, lifestyle changes and innovation this can be reduced and have positive impact on society. Over that last five decades there have been advances in global vaccinations, hygiene practices, access to clean water and cheaper food, as well as increases in family incomes which has reduced the number of deaths due to infection and malnutrition (Egger et al., 2017). Reducing the risk to patients results in lives saved and cost reductions for society, as the more severe the illness the more costly it becomes. Additionally, innovation and entrepreneurial activity can contribute toward the development of new economic, social, institutional and cultural environments and thereby provide significant benefits to society at large. The proposed innovation needs to be evaluated to ensure it leads to the betterment of society generally.

CORPORATE GOVERNANCE, SOCIAL RESPONSIBILITY AND ETHICAL PRINCIPLES IN HEALTHCARE

The main drive for change in society has escalated through globalization, the technological revolution, scientific advancement and development, greater access to information, and knowledge of human rights. These changes have provided greater knowledge, and expectation of ensuring corporate governance, social responsibility and ethical principles is central to healthcare practices.

Corporate governance is the system by which an organization is directed and controlled. Social responsibility emphasizes a universally accepted shared vision of common good, ethical principles and respect for human rights among all healthcare professionals and stakeholders in the delivery of healthcare. Corporate social responsibility in healthcare means that organizations have an obligation to deliver quality healthcare in compliance with legal, ethical and societal expectations. Ensuring socially responsible conduct and ethical principles contributes to the stronger reputation and competitiveness of the healthcare organization. Ethical principles in healthcare ensure codes of conduct and behavior, and morally good decisions in medical treatment based on well-researched practices. Healthcare organizations need to ensure the adoption of ethical, moral and social objectives in accordance with legislation, regulations and ethical practices.

Corporate governance, social responsibility and ethical principles should be implemented because it is essential and morally appropriate to the practice of healthcare and human rights. Healthcare organizations should clearly define their mission, social responsibilities and ethical principles in their strategy and this should be embedded in the culture and day-to-day operational activities of the healthcare organization. When integrating innovation and entrepreneurship with strategy there is a need for clear governance, social responsibility and ethical principles to ensure values are embraced and demonstrate compliance, performance, responsibility, transparency and accountability in all practices as the organization strives for operational excellence.

IMPORTANCE OF A PATIENT-CENTERED INNOVATIVE AND ENTREPRENEURIAL STRATEGY

Patient treatment needs to be at the forefront of healthcare delivery. The journey a patient experiences in the process of such treatment is as important as the outcome, as the treatment should not be worse than the actual disease. According to WHO findings, surgery globally results in high rates of illness, disease and death with almost seven million surgical patients suffering significant complications annually, and one million dying during or immediately following surgery (WHO, 2009). While the focus is on saving lives this should not mean almost killing the patient in the process.

The number of avoidable medical errors globally each year is astonishing – while the figures are not available consistently, those we can identify are shocking. A 2016 study by Johns Hopkins that analyzed medical death data over an eight-year timeframe claims over 250,000 people die annually in the U.S.A. due to medical errors. The study suggests that medical errors are the third-leading cause of death after heart disease and cancer.

According to the WHO, strategies to decrease the rate of adverse events in the European Union would result annually in the prevention of over 750,000 harm-inflicting medical errors. This reduction would result in over 3.2 million fewer days of hospitalization, 260,000 fewer incidents of permanent disability, and 95,000 fewer deaths per year (WHO, n.d.).

It is easier to describe a problem than it is to fix it, but it is the patient-centered innovative entrepreneurial strategy that will strive to fix the problems and identify potential problems that need to be addressed before they even emerge. Prevention is better than cure, not just in medical terms but also in the recognition of issues and concerns that are likely to occur based on our aging population, critical illnesses and now risk of further global pandemics like Covid-19.

SUMMARY

Healthcare organizations globally are operating is a very dynamic, complex and competitive environment, which has been exceeded beyond any expectation with the global Covid-19 pandemic. The global healthcare challenges pre-Covid-19 were extreme but this has now moved at an exponential rate with the intense pressure and stress on the system to address this unprecedented crisis and still provide quality and safe healthcare to those with communicable and noncommunicable diseases.

In responding to this dynamic and complex situation, effective strategies that will transform a healthcare organization require the integration of innovation and entrepreneurship with strategy to create a greater opportunity to sustain competitive advantage and the ability to continuously generate patient value. This integration must be supported and facilitated by top management, a supportive organizational structure that is flexible and adaptive, and a culture of core innovative and entrepreneurial activities. Organizations need to continuously explore and exploit opportunities for innovations that address the unmet needs of patients. By doing this, they are putting themselves in a stronger position to provide optimum healthcare services, be the provider of choice for patients, and attract investment.

Patient value is generated through improved overall patient outcomes, including lower costs, greater efficiency, effectiveness, quality, safety and improved accessibility for all patients. When the organization is capable of exceeding patient needs, they are differentiating themselves from competitors and creating greater opportunity for sustainable competitive advantage. It is the role and responsibility of top management to effectively integrate innovation and entrepreneurship with a strategy that inspires and motivates healthcare professionals throughout the organization to fully engage in the process and utilize their creative and innovative mindsets.

REFERENCES

Drucker, P.F. (2005). *Managing the Nonprofit Organization: Principles and Practices* (New York: Collins Business).

Egger, G., Binns, A., Rossner, S. and Sagner, M. (2017). *Lifestyle Medicine* (London: Academic Press).

Hisrich, R.D. and Kearney, C. (2013). *Managing Innovation and Entrepreneurship: A Global Perspective* (Thousand Oaks, CA: SAGE Publications).

Hitt, M.A., Ireland, R.D., Camp, S.M. and Sexton, D.L. (2001). Strategic entrepreneurship: entrepreneurial strategies for wealth creation. *Strategic Management Journal* 22 (Special Issue), 479–91.

Hitt, M.A., Ireland, R.D. and Hoskisson, R.E. (2011). *Strategic Management: Competitiveness and Globalization* (9th edn.) (Mason, OH: Thomson South-Western).

Ireland, R.D. (2007). Strategy vs. entrepreneurship. *Strategic Entrepreneurship Journal* 1, 7–10.

Ireland, R.D., Covin, J.G. and Kuratko, D.F. (2009). Conceptualizing corporate entrepreneurship strategy. *Entrepreneurship Theory and Practice* 33(1), 19–46. https://doi.org/10.1111/j.1540-6520.2008.00279.x.

Ketchen, D.J., Ireland, R.D. and Snow, C.C. (2007). Strategic entrepreneurship, collaborative innovation, and wealth creation. *Strategic Entrepreneurship Journal* 1(3–4), 371–85.

Porter, M.E. (1980). *Competitive Strategy* (New York: Free Press).

Sarasvathy, S.D. (2001). Causation and effectuation: toward a theoretical shift from economic inevitability to entrepreneurial contingency. *Academy of Management Review* 26(2), 243–288.

WHO (2009). Guidelines for safe surgery 2009: safe surgery saves lives. Geneva: World Health Organization. http://apps.who.int/iris/bitstream/handle/10665/44185/9789241598552_eng.pdf?sequence=1.

WHO (2020). The top-10 causes of death. https://www.who.int/news-room/fact-sheets/detail/the-top-10-causes-of-death.

WHO (n.d.). Data and statistics. https://www.euro.who.int/en/health-topics/Health-systems/patient-safety/data-and-statistics.

Suggested Reading

Bhatti, Y., del Castillo, J., Olson, K. and Darzi, A. (2018). Putting humans at the center of healthcare innovation. *Harvard Business Review*, March, 2. https://hbr.org/2018/03/putting-humans-at-the-center-of-health-care-innovation.

In this article, the authors conclude that alternatives emerging at healthcare institutions worldwide are human-centered design and co-creation, a set of approaches that can accelerate and humanize healthcare innovation. The authors studied three models: the Helix Centre at Imperial College London, the Center for Innovation at the Mayo Clinic, and the Consortium for Medical Technologies at Massachusetts General Hospital. Each locates interdisciplinary innovation labs within or near hospital environments; involves diverse stakeholders beyond clinicians (designers, engineers, business professionals and patients) early in the innovation process; and engages end-users in customizing solutions for their own needs. All have related missions, types of successes, and common challenges.

Brown, A. (2019). Understanding corporate governance of healthcare quality: a comparative case study of eight Australian public hospitals. *BMC Health Services Research* 19, 725. https://doi.org/10.1186/s12913-019-4593-0

In this article, the authors present evidence of a comprehensive range of processes related to governing healthcare quality undertaken at the corporate governance level. The authors provide a detailed picture of how corporate governance of healthcare quality is enacted by boards and management. This study provides practical guidance in outlining processes for effective corporate governance of healthcare quality and highlights areas for further examination.

Ferreira, J.M., Fernandes, C.I., Alves, H. and Raposo, M.L. (2015). Drivers of innovation strategies: testing the Tidd and Bessant (2009) model. *Journal of Business Research* 68(7), 1395–403.

The authors in this study focus on two innovation management issues: identification of determinants of the innovation management process and the implications of these determinants for firm innovation performance. The authors build on Tidd and Bessant's (2009) conceptual model, and examine innovation capacity constructs within innovation management structures.

Kash, B.A., Spaulding, A., Gamm, L.D. and Johnson, C.E. (2014). Healthcare strategic management and the resource-based view. *Journal of Strategy and Management* 7(3), 251–64. https://doi.org/10.1108/JSMA-06-2013-0040.

This article examines how two large health systems formulate and implement strategy with a specific focus on differences and similarities in the nature of strategic initiatives across systems. The aim of this article is to gain a better understanding of the role of resource dependency theory (RDT) and resource-based view (RBV) in healthcare strategic management.

Porter, M.E. and Lee, T.H. (2013). The strategy that will fix healthcare. *Harvard Business Review* 91(10), 50–70. https://hbr.org/2013/10/the-strategy-that-will-fix -health-care.

The authors in this article discuss a strategy for moving to a high-value health-care delivery system that comprises six interdependent components: organizing around patients' medical conditions rather than physicians' medical specialties, measuring costs and outcomes for each patient, developing bundled prices for the full care cycle, integrating care across separate facilities, expanding geographic reach, and building an enabling IT platform.

Govindarajan, V. and Ramamurti, R. (2018). Transforming healthcare from the ground up: top-down solutions alone can't fix the system. *Harvard Business Review* July–August, 2–11. http://www.hbsab.org/s/1738/images/gid8/editor _documents/2018-2019/pdflib_ttg/20200114_healthcare/20191023c_curing_health _care_hbr_threearticles.pdf?gid=8&pgid=61&sessionid=8ea05fdd-93ee-412c-bb2f -ef782621c0ff&cc=1.

In this article, the authors look at two examples of bottom-up innovation involving a radical transformation of healthcare delivery. The University of Mississippi Medical Center (UMMC) created a homegrown telehealth network to increase patient access to care; Iora Health developed a new business model that doubled down on primary care to reap large savings in secondary and tertiary care. To understand the strategies that drove each effort, the authors interviewed the organizations' principals, investors and employees, along with other industry leaders, as part of a six-year study of innovations in healthcare delivery around the world. The results of these two initiatives were astonishing. These successful initiatives demonstrate the potential of creative leaders to reshape the U.S. health system.

4. Corporate entrepreneurship, well-being, resilience and positive psychology in healthcare

QUESTIONS

What does corporate entrepreneurship mean for healthcare organizations? How can strategic entrepreneurship be effectively achieved in healthcare? What impact does entrepreneurship have on the well-being of healthcare professionals? How can we develop resilience among healthcare professionals? What is positive psychology and how does it benefit healthcare professionals? What impact does leadership have on corporate entrepreneurship in healthcare and the well-being and resilience of healthcare professionals?

INTRODUCTION

Our health and well-being is fundamental to how we function as individuals. A leading cause of death in the modern world is diseases due to lifestyle. According to the World Health Organization (WHO, 2018), cardiovascular diseases (17.9 million deaths annually), cancers (9.0 million deaths annually), respiratory diseases (3.9 million deaths annually) and diabetes (1.6 million deaths annually) account for over 80 percent of all premature noncommunicable disease (NCD) deaths. Lifestyle plays a significant part in all these diseases. As individuals we need to take care of our physical and mental health and well-being, know our core values and priorities, and effectively manage the stresses in our lives.

Well-being is fundamental for personal and professional satisfaction and is associated with an individual's ability to work, achieve positive relationships and experience positive emotions (e.g., Seligman, 2012). Resilience is the ability to positively adjust to adversity. Furthermore, positive psychology focuses on character strengths (e.g., justice, humanity) and behaviors that allow individuals to build a flourishing life which in turn develops their well-being. For much of the 20th century, the field of psychology focused on alleviating disease states. Using an arbitrary scale as an analogy, psychology was focused on bringing impacted individuals from −8 to 0; an acceptable neutral state. Although this was an admirable endeavor that has helped many people, it does not address all of our psychological needs as humans. Positive psychology was developed in an attempt to develop interventions and practices that encourage humans to flourish in all areas of life. To continue the scale analogy – positive psychology is about bringing the person from 0 to +8. Globally, health systems have been facing the same challenges of increased demand on services with limited resources. As previously discussed, this pressure has been extenuated further with the global Covid-19 pandemic. This puts further pressure on healthcare systems to preserve psychological well-being and resilience among all staff.

Through crisis there is opportunity. Covid-19 creates such unprecedented times in that it creates an opportunity to make significant changes to the world of healthcare – it is a catalyst for monumental change. The urgency to address this pandemic means that there can be a fundamental rethink of the way healthcare is delivered. There is now opportunity to make permanent changes that will develop innovative and entrepreneurial activity for the benefit of healthcare while also enhancing the well-being, resilience and positive psychology of healthcare professionals in the delivery of healthcare. Creativity and innovation can increase well-being and happiness, giving a sense of value and achievement that skills are being used to their full potential. Entrepreneurial activity has been described as a potential source of personal development, growth, and well-being (e.g., Stephan, 2018). Engaging in entrepreneurial activity has been found to be strongly associated with well-being (Shir et al., 2019). In this respect, through leadership support and facilitation of both corporate and strategic entrepreneurship, healthcare organizations can play a major role in psychological well-being, resilience and positive psychology that can motivate and energize healthcare professionals to persevere in the pursuit of innovations that become a force for positive change and benefit to patients, stakeholders and society at large. The benefits of these innovations must be shared, be sustainable and aim to exceed the needs of patients and society at large.

The objective of this chapter is to examine both corporate and strategic entrepreneurship in healthcare organizations and the positive impact they place on well-being, resilience and positive psychology among healthcare staff when supported by appropriate leadership. Corporate entrepreneurship and strategic entrepreneurship are discussed to provide an understanding of their importance for healthcare organizations. The link between well-being and entrepreneurship in healthcare is examined as well as the importance of resilience and positive psychology among healthcare staff. The chapter concludes with a discussion on the importance of leadership for the well-being, resilience and positive psychology of staff, and leadership approaches to drive successful corporate entrepreneurship in healthcare.

CORPORATE ENTREPRENEURSHIP IN HEALTHCARE

Corporate entrepreneurship can be defined as the pursuit of entrepreneurial opportunities within an established organization. It can be viewed as a system that supports and facilitates individuals to be innovative and entrepreneurial within the existing organization. The term corporate entrepreneurship is also known as intrapreneurship, corporate venturing, intra-corporate entrepreneurship, and internal corporate entrepreneurship. More specifically, within healthcare it is the process of creating value for patients and society at large by bringing together unique combinations of resources to explore and exploit healthcare opportunities that will enhance the lives of patients.

There is significant entrepreneurial response to the changes that have emerged in the scientific and social underpinnings of healthcare service delivery in addition to the immediate changes necessitated with Covid-19. As a result of the technological revolution, healthcare has changed with major innovations in, for example, digital health, big data, telemedicine, advanced analytics and machine learning, all of which have radicalized the health sector and created new possibilities. Healthcare innovations are driven by the need to lower the cost of care and keep patients healthy. The openness of healthcare organizations to recognizing the talent within healthcare and other industries that can be utilized to address the biggest challenges facing the sector is a necessity. It is through that openness and diverse knowledge and competencies that stakeholders across the healthcare ecosystem can identify opportunities and develop innovations that will lead the world to better health. Technological advancements are providing direct access to patients and giving them more empowerment and access to their own data. The growth of wearable devices from companies like Fitbit provide major changes in how patients have greater control and can monitor their own health. Digital tools are significantly changing the landscape of healthcare beyond reducing costs and waiting times. Digital tools are now designed and developed for many uses including, consultation purposes, diagnoses and prevention. These continuous technological advancements will provide major opportunities and infinite possibilities for innovation in the delivery of healthcare. Therefore healthcare organizations need to embrace these opportunities through corporate entrepreneurship.

For innovation within healthcare settings to continue to grow and develop, it needs to be supported within the internal organization. Therefore to successfully engage in corporate entrepreneurship healthcare professionals at all levels must be encouraged to be entrepreneurial in their endeavors and be given the flexibility and support to pursue opportunities and not be inhibited by rigidity and bureaucratic inertia, which can be present in some healthcare organizations. The effective pursuit of opportunities requires the generation of innovation from motivated individuals and teams, which is supported by a conducive internal environment and leadership. Innovative and entrepreneurial leadership in healthcare needs leaders that will set the goals and direction but allows the individuals that are engaged in the day-to-day issue, problem, concern and/or opportunity to make the decisions and drive the innovation.

Due to scientific and technological advancements and developments in health systems and the urgent need for fast and effective planning, particularly during the Covid-19 pandemic, corporate entrepreneurship is a crucial element to respond to the unprecedented needs of patients and society at large. Corporate entrepreneurship is not only beneficial to organizations and patients but also to society, as it can impact healthcare by increasing productivity, improving best practices, creating new innovations to diagnose and treat patients, and enhance national and international competitiveness.

Corporate entrepreneurship is an organization's strategic choice. For corporate entrepreneurship to succeed it is paramount that there is organizational and management support for entrepreneurial activity. This support can include championing innovative ideas, providing appropriate resources and/or expertise, and engendering the entrepreneurial activity within the organization's system and processes. This support needs to ensure that individuals and teams will not be penalized or have their career inhibited if the innovation fails. Organizations that plan to engage in corporate entrepreneurship need to ensure leadership support in pursuit of such activity. It is important for healthcare leaders to understand and embrace the fact that failure is part of the innovation journey, and that failure can be dealt with. Innovation is not a linear process and there are numerous unexpected factors outside the control of the organization that need to be managed along the process. Breakthrough and technological innovations are more unpredictable, and due to the innovative nature have a higher risk of failure in comparison to more incremental innovations. Failure can occur at any stage and at many stages of the process and it provides an invaluable learning experience. The most innovative healthcare organizations are the ones that embrace opportunities for corporate entrepreneurship, integrate entrepreneurship and strategy, and have an innovative culture that can learn and grow from failure focusing on what they can do differently next time.

STRATEGIC ENTREPRENEURSHIP IN HEALTHCARE

As discussed in Chapter 3, the integration of strategic management and entrepreneurship is known as "strategic entrepreneurship." Strategic entrepreneurship is concerned with an organization's ability to better perform current activities or operations while at the same time seeking new opportunities

(Ireland et al., 2009), resulting in individual, organizational and/or societal value. The pursuit of strategic entrepreneurship allows the organization to orientate itself toward the recognition and exploitation of opportunities. In the context of healthcare, the integration of strategic (advantage seeking) and entrepreneurial (opportunity seeking) needs to focus on the development of innovations that will generate patient value and address the most pressing needs within healthcare. It is this integration that increases the possibility of innovation resulting in organizational effectiveness and success.

Strategic entrepreneurship is particularly important for healthcare organizations in today's dynamic and challenging environment. The challenges affecting the healthcare sector include, for example, global aging populations, changes in the delivery of healthcare, payment of care, rising prevalence in chronic disease, and increase in the demand for certain services. The most recent turbulence affecting the field of healthcare globally is Covid-19; this crisis comes in addition to an already challenged healthcare system that was at breaking point in many countries. Healthcare providers have demonstrated entrepreneurship in how they have addressed these challenges; for example, technological advancement and development has resulted in online consultations to reduce the number of patients visiting GP offices and hospital appointments during Covid-19. This immediate change in GP service and consultants in private practice and in hospitals was to protect patients and staff from risk and the rapid spread of Covid-19 and follow the protocols of social distancing, hand-washing and hygiene, and quarantine for those with Covid-19 symptoms. This rapid redesign of care has been innovative and this evolution in patient experience will redefine the future of healthcare. Therefore, healthcare organizations that can work toward addressing today's problems even when at crisis point, while also exploring and exploiting opportunities to cultivate tomorrow's advantages, increase their chances of generating patient, stakeholder and societal value in the long term.

Strategic entrepreneurship is a necessity for the continued development and advancement of healthcare. It is the healthcare professionals that have the competencies to seek opportunities, engage with other innovators and lead the world to better healthcare. There have been significant innovations in healthcare including the accelerating growth of genomics and precision medicine, digital technologies, the reimagining of digital surgery and pathology through AI, and a renewed focus on patient-centered care. Hospitals are dedicating growing attention and resources to innovation and increasingly beginning to create rather than just adopt novelty (Salge and Vera, 2009). It is through innovation that there are now opportunities for less invasive surgical procedures, reduction in waiting times and more day-care procedures, all of which can more effectively utilize limited healthcare resources and enhance patient satisfaction and recovery.

Strategic entrepreneurship must be supported and encouraged by the internal environment and management team at all levels. This can be assessed using the Corporate Entrepreneurship Assessment Instrument (CEAI) that was designed to measure the key internal organizational dimensions that influence an organization's entrepreneurial activities and outcomes (Hornsby et al., 2013). The CEAI identified specific organizational antecedents of managers' entrepreneurial behavior, including senior management support, work discretion/autonomy, rewards/reinforcement, time availability, and organizational boundaries (e.g., Goodale et al., 2011; Hornsby et al., 2009). These dimensions determine the level of interest and support for entrepreneurial activities in an organization and are important to the field of healthcare (Kearney et al., 2020), particularly during such challenging times where innovation is a necessity. By creating an internal environment that is conducive to innovation and entrepreneurship, the senior management team will have the opportunity to transform healthcare through strategic entrepreneurship and thereby contribute to the well-being of healthcare professionals. Strategic entrepreneurship facilitates freedom and autonomy to engage in opportunity-seeking innovations that can provide healthcare professionals with a sense of personal fulfillment, motivation, passion and commitment that in turn will contribute to their well-being.

WELL-BEING AND ENTREPRENEURSHIP IN HEALTHCARE

Well-being is an integral part of our personal and professional life and is fundamental for individual satisfaction and performance. Well-being is paramount for healthcare professionals where patient's lives are at the forefront of healthcare delivery. There is no universal definition or measurement for well-being. Psychologists usually refer to two theoretical perspectives of well-being, hedonic (in terms of life satisfaction, happiness, positive affect) and eudaimonic (e.g., realization of personal potential, self-acceptance). Hedonic well-being is concerned with pleasure attainment through psychological, physical, social and cultural means, as well as what might be termed as "happiness" (Ryan and Deci, 2001). According to Wiklund et al. (2019) psychological well-being occurs when an individual (1) attains a sense of self-awareness and actualization through meaning and purpose in life, and (2) acquires the capacity to limit suffering, whilst simultaneously developing positive emotions and behavior, resulting in happiness. Well-being improves physical and mental health and promotes positive personal and professional relationships. This in turn can result in motivations to be creative and innovative resulting in greater organizational success and patient outcomes.

An intensified workload can result in stress which has an adverse affect on an individual's well-being. Healthcare professionals work in highly stressful environments, are constantly being challenged and are exposed to numerous occupational stressors that, if persistent, can result in burnout. It is estimated that 68 percent of doctors in the U.S.A. (Shanafelt et al., 2012) and 31 percent of Irish hospital doctors (Hayes et al., 2017) meet the criteria for burnout. By 2017, the total cost of burnout for all physicians practicing in Canada and the U.S.A. was estimated to be $213 million (Dewa et al., 2014) and $3 billion (Shanafelt et al., 2017), respectively. The negative impact of stress and burnout has significant implications on individuals' physical and psychosocial functioning. Such negative implications can result in a reduction in professional functioning, higher absenteeism, and higher staff turnover. This in turn can result in poor healthcare delivery and medical errors. The risk of burnout is now at an all-time high in addressing the existing challenges in addition to the unprecedented global Covid-19 pandemic. This has a more significant impact on the well-being of healthcare professionals, and needs to be managed effectively and in a timely manner to reduce the risk of long-term implications for their well-being. Improving the well-being of healthcare professionals has positive outcomes for staff and patients as poor well-being has implications for the delivery of patient care.

At Mayo Clinic, leaders recognize the importance of both healthcare providers and patients. If the physical and mental well-being of healthcare professionals is not good this will impact the quality of care and put the patient at risk. Mayo Clinic developed the "Well-being Index" to measure the risk of distress among their healthcare professionals, monitor organizational well-being, and support staff with appropriate resources to enhance their mental health and well-being. The "Well-being Index" is available to organizations globally and is used by leading hospitals, for example Toronto General (University Health Network); the Johns Hopkins Hospital; the Alfred; Weill Cornell at New York Presbyterian Hospital-Columbia and Cornell; and Hospital of the University of Pennsylvania-Penn Presbyterian. This demonstrates the importance of taking care of the well-being of healthcare professionals and all involved in the delivery of healthcare to ensure excellence in care for all.

Entrepreneurship is recognized as a source of personal growth and well-being. This entrepreneurial mindset, where there is vision, passion and commitment to make a difference for the greater good of healthcare, can also have a positive impact on staff well-being. It is through innovation and entrepreneurship that the field of healthcare has developed and brought about positive change in society through breakthrough innovations that save and extend lives and contribute to the well-being of society. Furthermore, corporate entrepreneurship in healthcare can develop innovations that address the needs of patients while also facilitating the fulfillment of individual well-being. The important impact of entrepreneurship on eudaimonic well-being has been recognized (Ryff, 2019). To generate greater impact for healthcare organizations and their staff requires a vision for exploration and exploitation and the leadership to drive innovations with clear objectives in terms of rational and sustainable benefits for patients, staff, stakeholders and society at large. Through hedonic and eudaimonic traditions, corporate entrepreneurial well-being in healthcare can be defined as the experience of satisfaction, happiness and positive affect in the realization of reaching one's potential in relation to the exploration and exploitation of innovations that generate patient value. A study undertaken by Shir et al. (2019) shows that there are multiple well-being benefits from engaging in entrepreneurial activities. These benefits result from the opportunity and the freedom allowed to support and facilitate innovations that develop individuals' competencies. Hence, senior management within healthcare organizations who engender corporate entrepreneurship and adopt a strategic entrepreneurial approach to management can potentially enhance the overall well-being of their staff, which should in turn generate patient value.

Resilience in Healthcare

Resilience is key to individual well-being and is associated with hedonic and eudaimonic well-being. The role of many healthcare professionals is both personally and professionally demanding. Stress has adverse physiological effects on individuals such as the immune system and cognitive functioning. Therefore, healthcare professionals need to develop resilience for their personal health and well-being, as well as the sustainability of their position and quality in the delivery of patient care. However, it is not just the individual that is responsible for managing and increasing their own personal resilience so they can address the challenges they experience; the organization needs to take responsibility to ensure that staff are supported in the challenges they encounter. Resilience needs to be developed by individuals in collaboration with strong organizational support and leadership.

Individual and organizational resilience is the ability to positively adapt to adversity with minimal stress or risk of burnout. Healthcare professionals need to be able to cope with the inevitability of adversity that is part of their everyday work experience. Resilience in healthcare refers to the challenges healthcare professionals experience and their personal ability to manage the demands and limitations of their organization. It requires adapting to the challenges and opportunities and learn and develop from them on a personal and professional level, while continuing to sustain high standards of healthcare delivery. Resilience makes a significant contribution to the delivery, quality and safety of patient care. Healthcare professionals need to continuously work to develop their individual resilience, while understanding what impacts their ability to cope and recover from adversity, as well as how teams and the organization influence and support individual resilience. Healthcare professionals need to be resilient particularly in times of adversity and Covid-19 could not have created a more adverse situation for healthcare workers. What is important is how they address this adversity on both a personal and professional level. Resilience helps individuals recover, survive and even flourish as they work through the adversity. Therefore to strengthen their resilience they need to be optimistic, adaptable and flexible, have the ability to work on their own initiative and as part of a team, accept and learn from mistakes, maintain professionalism at all times, and demonstrate confidence and personal values. They need to have the necessary characteristics that can effectively turn a crisis into an opportunity for personal growth and development. Those that have the ability to successfully respond to adversity are deemed to be resilient and have an ability to recover more quickly from stressors.

Individuals have the ability to increase their resilience and learn to better respond to adversity. Resilience can be developed through the following:

- Be open and objective and maintain a realistic perspective.
- Take small steps that are challenging but realistic in addressing problems and/or opportunities.
- Do not procrastinate; be action-oriented as problems that are not addressed will only get worse.
- Embrace the opportunity for change for the greater good of healthcare.
- Do not take things personally.
- Take care of your mental and physical health and well-being.
- Seek opportunities for innovation, learning from past experiences and mistakes.
- Develop a network of open communication, collaboration, trust and support throughout the organization for the benefit of all.

In developing our resilience it is important that adverse events are put into the right perspective. Individuals that blame themselves for negative things that happen, believe one negative event filters into all aspects of life, and/or feel there is no way out, become overwhelmed, lose perspective and inhibit their ability to be resilient. At an individual level it is important to recognize how our mindset and beliefs impact our reaction to events. By understanding ourselves and our ability to put things in perspective and respond positively, we can become more resilient in coping with life's challenges both personally and professionally.

It is important that healthcare professionals develop strategies that will help them become more resilient. Such strategies must include those that foster total health, impacting positively on physical, mental and social aspects of life. Lifestyle practices that foster and sustain resilience include a balanced diet, regular physical exercise, practices for mental health (meditation, counseling and self-development courses), sleep hygiene, substance control (alcohol in moderation, avoiding tobacco and drug use) and positive relationships with strong social connections. Additionally, the appropriate organizational structure, culture and leadership are paramount in supporting individuals to become more resilient in light of the challenges and adversity they experience within their healthcare environment. Organizations must make it easy for staff to adopt these practices for sustainable resilience, through incentives and accessible infrastructure. Developing resilience among healthcare professionals is an integral part of ensuring the highest quality and standard of patient care.

Positive Psychology in Healthcare

Positive psychology is a science that is having a significant effect on individuals' ability to increase their well-being and happiness and obtain their desired goals. Professor Martin Seligman is known as one of the founders of positive psychology. It emphasizes positive psychological states (e.g., happiness), traits (e.g., strengths), relationships (personal and professional) and institutions (e.g., work organizations). The field of positive psychology concentrates on strengths, happiness, satisfaction, well-being, resilience, gratitude, compassion for self and others, confidence and hope. It focuses on the application of individual strengths to successfully achieve desirable goals and a healthy and flourishing life. There is growing evidence that psychological factors play a major role in optimizing health and well-being.

While psychology as a field of study has worked on the diagnoses, treatment and prevention of disorders such as anxiety and depression, Seligman recognized this as too much emphasis on the negative, such as mental health disorders, pain and suffering and minimal attention on strengths, happiness and well-being. Positive psychology goes beyond overcoming problems. Just because an individual does not have an illness or disease does not mean they are living a good life. Positive psychology places attention on both strengths and weaknesses, developing good and overcoming bad, enhancing the lives of those that are well and addressing the problems of those that are unwell. It is about improving the lives of normal, untroubled people, making them happier, more fulfilled and more productive, getting people to know their greatest strengths and use those strengths to be part of something larger.

Seligman created the PERMA Model of well-being as a template to explore optimal human functioning and happiness. This model is for those individuals that are focused on achieving balance and fulfillment and incorporates five building blocks to facilitate flourishing. There is variation among individuals in how they attain well-being. What one person considers positive another may not; furthermore, people differ in what they consider to be a flourishing life. Therefore the PERMA Model can support people in making better informed decisions on how to achieve fulfillment that meets their core values and objectives. Each of the five building blocks is undertaken for its own reason, is independently measured and contributes to well-being. PERMA refers to:

P – **P**ositive Emotion – this focus on well-being is hedonic. It is about feeling good, pleasure and joy. To some extent positive affectivity is heritable. However, we can enhance our positive emotions about the past, present and future, for example through gratitude and forgiveness about the past, mindfulness for the present, and hope and optimism for the future.

E – **E**ngagement – utilization of strengths to fulfill a challenging task. Achieving "flow" in which time stops when in the flow of the moment, thus rewarded by undertaking the task. Flow can be achieved in any number of ways, such as a specific work, sport, or social activity.

R – **R**elationships – an integral part of well-being is our relationship with others and the sense of belonging it provides. Our social connections, love, and emotional and physical interactions can give life purpose and meaning. Previous research has shown that showing kindness toward others increases well-being.

M – **M**eaning – having a meaning and purpose in life, with a sense of belonging. This can be achieved through, for example, religion, family, work, community, justice, and environmental rights.

A – **A**ccomplishment – people have certain ambitions, goals or achievements, which they aim to pursue for a variety of reasons.

Positive psychology and well-being is paramount in healthcare for the development of a happy and fulfilled workforce that will be motivated to be innovative and entrepreneurial and perform to the highest standards in the delivery of patient care. This positive mindset will develop conducive relationships and effective teamwork. Leaders need to know the core character strengths of staff and maximize their engagement to instill motivation and creativity that in turn will result in innovation. Within healthcare, staff are the most important asset for the delivery of high-quality patient care. By encouraging and motivating staff, building on the PERMA model can transform staff and the organization to be more resilient to the challenges they experience and embrace those challenges with a more innovative mindset.

LEADERSHIP FOR WELL-BEING, RESILIENCE AND POSITIVE PSYCHOLOGY

Healthcare leaders need to adopt positive behaviors in light of the exponential challenges they face in today's healthcare environment. Well-being, resilience and positive psychology are not achieved in isolation; the process requires a supportive environment with the right leadership that focuses on the development of positive relationships, creating a sense of belonging, taking on board others' views and opinions, recognizing they do not always have or know the answer, and developing an innovative and entrepreneurial environment enabling organizational success. Leaders that can permeate positive psychology into their leadership through their character strengths are creating a positive psychological work environment that allows staff to engage in innovation. Positive psychology allows leaders to create a more positive culture that in turn develops a more positive psychological state among staff.

Healthcare leaders need to support and facilitate people to flourish, recognize and acknowledge the strengths that staff bring to the organization, and utilize their core competencies while also managing their health and well-being. They need to reinforce positive psychological actions such as encouraging positivity, demonstrating gratitude, utilizing individual and team strengths, being mindful in actions and reactions, nurturing positive interactions, and developing individual and team resilience, thus reducing stress, anxiety and the risk of burnout, which in turn improves the quality and delivery of patient care.

Healthcare professionals have a passion and drive to help people and make a positive change to the world of healthcare. Patient care and generating patient value is at the core of healthcare; to achieve this, the health and well-being of healthcare professionals must be prioritized so they can effectively deliver a high level of patient care. Leaders need to utilize this passion and commitment through innovation and entrepreneurship that will motivate staff to leverage their creativity and capture innovative opportunities. This approach develops a positive culture and work environment where innovation can emerge which generates greater value in the delivery of patient care.

LEADERSHIP APPROACH FOR CORPORATE ENTREPRENEURSHIP IN HEALTHCARE

Recognizing the challenges within healthcare and the unprecedented demands that Covid-19 is adding to an already overly stretched global healthcare system increases the need for healthcare organizations to be more flexible and provide staff with an environment where they are engaged and empowered to utilize their creativity and explore and exploit ideas that generate patient value and develop their well-being and resilience.

Effective leadership is required to develop and grow corporate entrepreneurship in healthcare organizations. Within healthcare, leaders are faced with change that creates many challenges, for example new technologies, globalization, increased regulatory compliance, specialty health systems, telemedicine, virtual patients, out-sourcing and increased competition (Guo,

2009). Healthcare leaders must exert themselves so that they are continuously striving to engender innovations that generate greater patient value. The positive influence of innovation and entrepreneurship within an internal healthcare environment requires:

- Leadership and management support at all levels with a commitment to change and a clear vision for innovation.
- Internal and external collaborations with patients, healthcare professionals, academics, payers, policymakers and other stakeholders involved in the development and implementation of the innovation.
- Dedicated resources including staff, infrastructure, time and funding to bring the innovation to fruition.
- Open transparent communication throughout the organization.
- Continuous monitoring and evaluation of progress and viability.
- Demonstration of the benefits of the innovation with particular focus on an assessment of health benefits and patient value.

Leadership is influential in determining the degree of innovation within an organization. Leaders in healthcare must recognize the importance of developing and supporting a culture through which innovation and entrepreneurship can flourish for the benefit of healthcare and staff. Leaders that drive this corporate entrepreneurial culture in healthcare facilitate and encourage idea generation and creativity, support moderate risk-taking, tolerate failure as part of the innovation process, promote learning, challenge assumptions with the goal of creating greater patient value and care, and embrace innovation across the organization. They are willing to continuously learn and adapt in the dynamic and challenging environment of healthcare. This in turn positively influences the level of satisfaction, motivation, commitment and teamwork among staff, which increases their well-being and resilience.

The organizational culture and leadership style must be congruent for entrepreneurial success. For corporate entrepreneurship to be engendered in healthcare, the leader must motivate their team in their advantage-seeking and opportunity-seeking endeavors, and the organizational culture must positively influence the pursuit of such opportunities. Such leadership practices are paramount in creating a context where innovative and entrepreneurial outcomes can be effectively nurtured and managed. The success of corporate entrepreneurship in healthcare is influenced by leaders; they are the driving force for entrepreneurship within healthcare.

SUMMARY

The world of healthcare has become more uncertain than ever due to Covid-19, which is the worst global health emergency the WHO has ever experienced. However, out of these challenges come phenomenal opportunities to create new value for healthcare. Over the last few decades we have seen major transformations in healthcare; for example, accelerating development of machine learning, genomics and precision medicine, AI, digital technologies, telemedicine, and more concise focus on patient-centered care. These advancements are creating further opportunities for innovations across healthcare.

Corporate entrepreneurship within healthcare organizations is key in order for these innovations to succeed and meet important unmet needs of patients, healthcare providers, healthcare professionals, stakeholders, and society at large. Within this entrepreneurial approach to healthcare, strategic entrepreneurship is the means through which healthcare organizations can integrate "advantage-seeking" and "opportunity-seeking" approaches, allowing them to simultaneously exploit existing advantages while exploring opportunities for future innovations central to the development of healthcare.

The highly demanding and challenging field of healthcare can result in increased levels of stress and risk of burnout. High levels of stress and risk of potential burnout is counterproductive and negatively affects staff potential to be innovative and entrepreneurial. Therefore, it is time for healthcare organizations to ensure that health and well-being of healthcare professionals becomes part of their strategy for the development of healthcare. The well-being, resilience and positive psychology of leaders and healthcare professionals is imperative for the delivery of patient care that is safe, efficient and effective, which leads to a more positive patient experience and outcome. Innovation, entrepreneurship, well-being, resilience and positive psychology must be supported within the internal organizational structures, a culture with leadership that drives innovation and entrepreneurship.

Leadership practices are paramount in creating an environment that supports and facilitates staff well-being, resilience and positive psychology, which in turn are the critical aspects in achieving innovative and entrepreneurial outcomes for the benefit of patients and society at large. Staff well-being, resilience and positive psychology are central to enhancing individuals' creativity and contributing to the delivery of innovative and entrepreneurial outcomes for the benefit of healthcare. The future of healthcare can bring about major changes, and innovators and entrepreneurs within and outside healthcare provide solutions that change how we can prevent, more effectively diagnose, cure and manage diseases and conditions using new innovations.

REFERENCES

Dewa, C.S., Jacobs, P., Thanh, N.X. and Loong, D. (2014). An estimate of the cost of burnout on early retirement and reduction in clinical hours of practicing physicians in Canada. *BMC Health Services Research*, 14, 254.

Goodale, J.C., Kuratko, D.F., Hornsby, J.S. and Covin, J.G. (2011). Operations management and corporate entrepreneurship: the moderating effect of operations control on the antecedents of corporate entrepreneurial activity in relation to innovation performance. *Journal of Operations Management* 29(1–2), 116–27.

Guo, K.L. (2009). Competencies of the entrepreneurial leader in health care organizations. *The Health Care Manager* 28(1), 19–29. https://doi.org/10.1097/HCM.0b013e318196de5c.

Hayes, B., Prihodova, L., Walsh, G., Doyle, F. and Doherty, S. (2017). What's up doc? A national cross-sectional study of psychological wellbeing of hospital doctors in Ireland. *BMJ open* 7(10), e018023.

Hornsby, J.S., Kuratko, D.F., Holt, D.T. and Wales, W.J. (2013). Assessing a measurement of organizational preparedness for corporate entrepreneurship. *Journal of Product Innovation Management* 30(5), 937–55.

Hornsby, J.S., Kuratko, D.F., Shepherd, D.A. and Bott, J.P. (2009). Managers' corporate entrepreneurial actions: examining perception and position. *Journal of Business Venturing* 24(3), 236–47.

Ireland, R.D., Covin, J.G. and Kuratko, D.F. (2009). Conceptualizing corporate entrepreneurship strategy. *Entrepreneurship Theory and Practice* 33(1), 19–46.

Kearney, C., Dunne, P.J. and Wales, W. (2020). Entrepreneurial orientation and burnout among healthcare professionals. *Journal of Health Organization and Management* 34(1), 16–22.

Ryan, R.M. and Deci, E.L. (2001). On happiness and human potentials: a review of research on hedonic and eudaimonic well-being. *Annual Review of Psychology* 52(1), 141–66.

Ryff, C.D. (2019). Entrepreneurship and eudaimonic well-being: five venues for new science. *Journal of Business Venturing* 34, 646–63.

Salge, T.O. and Vera, A. (2009). Hospital innovativeness and organizational performance: evidence from English public acute care. *Health Care Management Review* 34(1), 54–67.

Seligman, M.E. (2012). *Flourish: A Visionary New Understanding of Happiness and Well-being*. New York: Simon and Schuster.

Shanafelt, T.D., Boone, S., Tan, L., Dyrbye, L.N., Sotile, W., Satelem D., West, C.P., Sloan, J. and Oreskovich, M.R. (2012). Burnout and satisfaction with work–life balance among US physicians relative to the general US population. *Archives of Internal Medicine* 172(18), 1377–85.

Shanafelt, T.D., Goh, J. and Sinsky, C. (2017). The business case for investing in physician well-being. *JAMA Internal Medicine* 177(12), 1826–32.

Shir, N., Nikolaev, B. and Wincent, J. (2019). Entrepreneurship and well-being: the role of psychological autonomy, competence, and relatedness. *Journal of Business Venturing* 34(5), 1–17.

Stephan, U. (2018). Entrepreneurs' mental health and well-being: a review and research agenda. *Academy of Management Perspectives* 32, 290–322.

Wiklund, J., Nikolaev, B., Shir, N., Foo, M.-D. and Bradley, S. (2019). Entrepreneurship and well-being: past, present, and future. *Journal of Business Venturing* 34, 579–88.

WHO (2018). Noncommunicable diseases. June 1. https://www.who.int/news-room/fact-sheets/detail/noncommunicable-diseases.

Suggested Reading

Garbuio, M. and Lin, N. (2019). Artificial Intelligence as a growth engine for healthcare startups: emerging business models. *California Management Review* 61(2), 59–83. https://doi.org/10.1177/0008125618811931.

In this article, the authors provide a timely and critical analysis of AI-driven healthcare startups and identify emerging business model archetypes that entrepreneurs from around the world are using to bring AI solutions to the marketplace. It identifies areas of value creation for the application of AI in healthcare and proposes an approach to designing business models for AI healthcare start-ups.

Kearney, C., Dunne, P.J. and Wales, W. (2020). Entrepreneurial orientation and burnout among healthcare professionals. *Journal of Health Organization and Management* 34(1), 16–22.

In this article, the authors propose a conceptual model which considers how entrepreneurial orientation (EO) has the potential to provide an operational context that may negate, lessen, or delay the negative effects of burnout among healthcare professionals. The model is advanced as a useful focal point to foster research exploring connections between organizational orientation and employee well-being. Their research agenda proposes new insights and the need for additional research into how the manifestation of organizational EO may contribute to the field of medicine, influence burnout and enhance well-being among healthcare professionals.

Matheson, C., Robertson, H.D., Elliott, A.M., Iversen, L. and Murchie, P. (2016). Resilience of primary healthcare professionals working in challenging environments: a focus group study. *British Journal of General Practice* 66(648), e507–e515.

In this article, the authors explore what primary health professionals working in challenging environments consider to be characteristics of resilience and what promotes or challenges professional resilience. The authors propose a model of health professional resilience that concurs with existing literature but adds the concept of personal traits being synergistic with workplace features and social networks. These facilitate adaptability and enable individual health professionals to cope with adversity that is inevitably part of the everyday experience of those working in challenging healthcare environments.

Park, N., Peterson, C., Szvarca, D., Vander Molen, R.J., Kim, E.S. and Collon, K. (2016). Positive psychology and physical health: research and application. *American Journal of Lifestyle Medicine* 10(3), 200–206.

In this article, the authors propose that the goal of positive psychology is to complement and extend the traditional problem-focused psychology that has proliferated in recent decades. The authors describe evidence of how topics of positive psychology apply to physical health. Research has shown that psychological health assets (e.g., positive emotions, life satisfaction, optimism, life purpose, social support) are prospectively associated with good health measured in a variety of ways. They conclude that the application of positive psychology to health is promising, although much work remains to be done.

Ryff, C.D. (2019). Entrepreneurship and eudaimonic well-being: Five venues for new science. *Journal of Business Venturing*, 34, 646-663.

In this article, the author examines the relevance of eudaimonic well-being for understanding entrepreneurial experience. The author asserts that the central importance of bringing eudaimonia to the field of entrepreneurial studies is that the essential core of this type of well-being involves the realization of personal talents and potential. Such active pursuit of such personal excellence, in the spirit of Aristotle, is fundamental to entrepreneurship.

Wiklund, J., Nikolaev, B., Shir, N., Foo, M-D. and Bradley, S. (2019). Entrepreneurship and well-being: Past, present, and future. *Journal of Business Venturing*, 34, 579-588. https://www.sciencedirect.com/science/article/pii/S0883902618308942

In this article, the authors provide an overview of the well-being concept, related research, and its connection to entrepreneurship. They define entrepreneurial well-being as the experience of satisfaction, positive affect, infrequent negative affect, and psychological functioning in relation to developing, starting, growing, and running an entrepreneurial venture. They explain this definition of entrepreneurial well-being and review significant developments in the broader field of well-being.

PART III

Leading innovation, entrepreneurship and design thinking in healthcare

5. Leadership and its impact on innovation and entrepreneurship in healthcare

QUESTIONS

Why is leadership so important in the field of healthcare? What is the most appropriate style of leadership for healthcare in today's dynamic and unprecedented environment? What is the role of the leader in developing an innovative and entrepreneurial approach to healthcare? What is entrepreneurial leadership and how can it be further developed in healthcare?

INTRODUCTION

In today's healthcare organizations, leadership and the appropriate style of leadership is a key ingredient for success in healthcare delivery and patient care. Leadership is particularly important in influencing others and attaining organizational goals and objectives. Healthcare is dramatically changing as a result of, for example, technological advancement, globalization, increased regulatory compliance, telemedicine, virtual patients, aging populations and, most significantly, the unprecedented impact of Covid-19. Furthermore, leadership is more challenging during turbulent times, and the turbulence of Covid-19 puts exceptionally high stressors on healthcare globally. This highlights the need to focus on the importance of the right leadership to manage and address the challenges facing healthcare. Healthcare leaders that are authentic and honest, and demonstrate humility, curiosity, optimism, appreciation and compassion, are better equipped to cope with the challenges and engage with their team(s). Healthcare leaders also need to precipitate the need to develop hope, strength, resilience and compassion in how they connect with themselves and their team(s).

A new normal is emerging as a result of Covid-19 with constant shifts as new challenges and demands on an over-stretched system continue to grow exponentially. Therefore, to effectively address those global healthcare challenges, leaders must ensure new strategies are introduced that are innovative, flexible and timely and entrepreneurial in nature. Hence, healthcare leaders must recognize the need for innovation and entrepreneurship as part of their long-term vision. This can be achieved through the effective integration of entrepreneurship and leadership qualities which is termed "entrepreneurial leadership." This is a relatively new concept in the field of healthcare and to achieve this, healthcare professionals need to better understand the qualities of effective leadership and the impact this has on the development of innovation and an entrepreneurial spirit within their organization.

The purpose of this chapter is to provide scholarly discourse on leadership styles for healthcare organizations as well as the effective integration of entrepreneurship and leadership in healthcare. Understanding leadership and leadership competencies is examined, followed by a discussion on leadership styles and what is appropriate for healthcare organizations. Given the challenges facing today's healthcare organizations, an understanding of the authentic leadership approach and leadership with compassion is discussed. Recognizing the need to ensure innovation and entrepreneurship in healthcare, the following section proposes a conceptual model on the importance of entrepreneurship and leadership in the development of entrepreneurial leadership in healthcare. There is a discussion on entrepreneurial leadership and how to achieve a vision for the betterment of healthcare organizations. The leadership style for innovation and entrepreneurship in healthcare is examined with specific focus on authentic, transformational and compassionate leadership through which entrepreneurial leadership is achieved. Following that, the importance of leadership for innovation and entrepreneurship in healthcare is discussed, and a conceptual model is presented of entrepreneurial leadership as a driver for innovation in healthcare.

UNDERSTANDING LEADERSHIP

Research in leadership emerged early in the 20th century, with a more social scientific approach in the 1930s. Scholars across many disciplines have recognized leadership as a core area of research; more recently it has been incorporated into the field of entrepreneurship. Over the decades, scholars have suggested many leadership paradigms. Traditionally, leadership studies focused on individual traits and personalities (Avolio et al., 2009). These "traditional" leadership models, described "leader behavior in terms of leader–follower exchange relationships, providing direction and support, and reinforcement behaviors" (Avolio et al., 2009: 766). Modern leadership paradigms focus on transformational/charismatic leadership (e.g., Bass 1985; Burns 1978) and authentic leadership (e.g., Avolio and Gardner, 2005). Since the early 1990s, transformational/charismatic leadership theories have been the most frequently researched. Transformational/charismatic leadership is recognized as motivating followers to be the best they can which in turn results in better performance outcomes.

There is no universally accepted definition of leadership. How leadership is defined is influenced by the paradigm. Traditionally, definitions of leadership have focused on the individual leader and failed to recognize other significant components such as the follower, context and culture. More recently, leadership has been recognized in various models as dyadic, shared, relational, strategic, global and a complex social dynamic (Avolio, 2007). Leadership is a function of management and is the process of influencing followers to recognize what needs to be achieved and how best it can be achieved. Not every manager is a leader and not every leader is a manager, but every good manager is a leader.

Today, leadership is more of an interactive process, where the leader is part of a group, and attempts to influence followers to work toward organizational goals and objectives and perform successfully. This interactive process, where leaders influence, inspire, motivate and support followers in achieving organizational goals and objectives, is particularly important in the field of healthcare where the focus is on patients' lives and well-being. In healthcare, effective clinical leadership is recognized as being fundamental to ensure quality and safety in the delivery of patient care.

Leadership can be defined as the relationship between the leader and follower, in leading the activities of the team toward achieving the organizational goals and objectives. Within healthcare, leadership is not just focused on the individual leader, but also on followers, peers, work context and culture, including a diverse group of individuals that contribute to the overall organizational goals and objectives. A healthcare leader needs to influence, inspire and motivate staff individually and collectively to achieve goals and objectives, with highest standards and delivery of patient care, that results in the best outcome for patients. Effective leadership is a key requirement for strengthening the quality, standard and delivery of care, and supporting and facilitating the growth and development of innovation and entrepreneurship within healthcare.

Leadership Competencies

Strong leadership competencies are paramount to ensuring health systems respond appropriately to the needs of patients and society at large. The development of leadership competencies should be aligned to the context and leadership needs. There is a growing complexity in healthcare due to increased convergence of technology and expertise:

• Information technology and the "big data" revolution;

- Increased convergence of drugs and diagnostics;
- Increased use of robotics/high-tech equipment complementing the art of medicine and surgery;
- Increased precision of therapies and treatments resulting in price increases.

Therefore, the increased convergence of different areas of expertise (e.g., drugs, IT, diagnostics, use of biomarkers, surgery, robotics) requires leadership that is capable of inspiring and motivating high-caliber experts in healthcare to be more innovative in the delivery of healthcare. Leaders in today's healthcare organizations need to encourage diversity of thought to support innovation and entrepreneurship. A true leader is one that can develop followers into leadership roles. Furthermore, increased cost containment combined with the extreme unprecedented cost of Covid-19 requires more efficient leadership that is capable of balancing cost and delivering effective healthcare in what are the most challenging times.

LEADERSHIP STYLES

Leadership style is the specific behavior pattern of an individual who aims to influence others in achieving organizational goals and objectives. The style of leadership has a significant influence on the internal organization. There are many different styles of leadership with the most dominant being: autocratic, democratic, laissez-faire, transactional, and transformational.

Autocratic (Authoritarian) Leadership Style

- An autocratic leadership style is authoritarian, directive and bureaucratic.
- The core focus of power is with the manager/leader, where authority, autonomy and decision-making is centralized.
- Information and communication is top-down.
- Change can be slow and challenging due to centralization.
- The process to achieve goals and work tasks is determined by the manager/ leader.

Healthcare leaders that adopt an autocratic leadership style make decisions with minimal to no input from their team; this is problematic as their vision is based on their own expertise and may be wrong. They frequently provide limited information on a need-to-know basis only, which is very challenging for any team. This style of leadership is dominant with limited tolerance for mistakes.

Democratic Leadership Style

- A democratic leadership style is participative.
- The core focus of power is with the team, where authority, autonomy and decision-making is decentralized.
- The manager/leader is part of a team.
- There is a strong level of interaction within the team.
- Information and communication is a two-way process.

The democratic leadership style welcomes and encourages input and communication from the team when making decisions. Relationships are highly valued by this type of leader, and it is important to them that their team feels comfortable and willing to voice concerns, opinions and ideas. A democratic leader also sees value in providing feedback to their team, genuinely considering communication as a two-way process.

Laissez-faire Leadership Style

- A laissez-faire leadership style has minimal intervention from the leader.
- The manager/leader observes that the team members are highly skilled and experienced and capable of working well on their own.
- The manager/leader delegates power to the team.
- The team is permitted to do what they think is best.

Laissez-faire leadership in healthcare refers to a "hands-off" approach that demonstrates no leadership and does not take responsibility in decision-making or in addressing key issues. The leader's behavior demonstrates an indifference toward the team and the organizational goals and objectives. It is an ineffective approach as the leaders are passive and do not have a positive impact on the team. This style of leadership seldom provides the team with a sense of direction, feedback or supervision.

Transactional Leadership Style

Transactional leadership focuses on the exchanges that occur between leaders and their followers. The transactional leader aims to build solid exchange relationships with followers that substantially influence outcomes. This style of leadership aims to motivate followers' self-interests by the exchange of rewards for their compliance. Rewards can include, for example, recognition, praise, time off or bonuses. The focus is on followers correctly implementing procedures and completing clearly defined tasks with minimal changes. There are two components of transactional leadership. The first involves the use of *contingent reward* behaviors, that is, the extent that the leader organizes rewards in exchange for meeting expectations. The second is *management by exception*, that is, the extent that the leader takes corrective action based on the outcome of leader–follower transactions. Leaders that are actively engaged throughout the process will monitor followers' behavior, anticipate problems or concerns, and take corrective action before a serious problem occurs. More passive leaders take action when the behavior of the follower has created a problem.

Transformational Leadership Style

Transformational leadership was introduced by James Downton in 1973, extended by James McGregor Burns in 1978 and further developed by Bernard Bass in 1985. Transformational leaders have the ability to inspire, motivate, challenge and develop followers', resulting in enhanced levels of job satisfaction, staff morale and innovation. Transformational leaders build trust among their followers; they take time to get to know people, act with integrity and on a set of values, and frequently make those values explicit. Transformational leaders set out to develop and transform the follower to be the best they can, advancing to higher levels of motivation and increasing morale. Transformational leaders are very active; their leadership is very effective and has a profound impact on others. They lead by example and create an environment where innovative thinking is encouraged, supported, recognized and aligned with the core values and objectives of the organization. Transformational leaders focus on distinctiveness between individual goals, objectives, strengths and values. Recognizing the distinctiveness of the team and developing and synergizing those differences can enhance the performance of the team. Transformational leadership is described as the four I's by Bernard Bass (1985): Idealized Influence; Inspirational Motivation; Intellectual Stimulation; and Individualized Consideration. These are critical elements for the leader to inspire, motivate, challenge and develop their followers.

Four I's of transformational leadership

1. *Idealized Influence* (Inspire): Leaders demonstrate charisma and are strong role models that take responsibility, operate with integrity, and emphasize trust, commitment, pride and the moral and ethical consequences of decisions. Others are inspired to follow the leader's vision.

   Managerial Implication: Leaders can build trust through open communication and commitment to share knowledge and expertise. This leads to greater trust, and provides identification with the leader, and a desire to achieve and demonstrate support.

2. *Inspirational Motivation* (Motivate): Leaders articulate an inspiring vision for the future, challenge followers with high standards, and provide encouragement and meaning for what needs to be done. They align organizational goals with individual goals. They treat problems and mistakes as opportunities.

   Managerial Implication: Leaders create a vision and articulate it with conviction such that followers are encouraged to join the collective effort, providing a willingness to exert extra effort.

3. *Intellectual Stimulation* (Challenge): Leaders question the status quo, traditions and beliefs, thus stimulating in others new perspectives and ways of doing things. They encourage imagination, creativity and innovation. They reward success, learn from mistakes and innovate.

   Managerial Implication: Leaders create a trustful environment through idealized influence that allows them to exploit the cognitive capabilities of their followers, providing followers with a willingness to think.

4. *Individualized Consideration* (Development): Leaders are concerned about individuals and consider the needs, abilities and aspirations of others to further their growth and development. They aim to match challenges to individual abilities, and coach and provide developmental feedback.

   Managerial Implication: Leaders identify the strengths of the team members and motivate each of them according to their motivational needs, providing followers with the desire to improve and learn.

AUTHENTIC LEADERSHIP APPROACH

Oscar Wilde said "Be yourself; everyone else is already taken." In order to be a transformational leader one needs to develop authentic leadership. This is a genuine, ethical, transparent form of leadership. Within organizations, staff want leaders who are "genuine" and invest time and energy into their leadership for the benefit of the organization. Authentic leadership is associated with ethics, integrity and trustworthiness, leading to more positive outcomes for leaders, followers and the organization, which is imperative in the field of healthcare. Authentic leaders are more effective, leading with clear goals and values, and capable of addressing the challenges they experience in their endeavors. Healthcare organizations need authentic leaders to cope with the turbulent and dynamically changing healthcare challenges and help followers find meaning in what they are aiming to achieve. Walumbwa et al. (2008: 94) defined authentic leadership as:

> a pattern of leader behavior that draws upon and promotes both positive psychological capacities and a positive ethical climate, to foster greater self-awareness, an internalized moral perspective, balanced processing of information, and relational transparency on the part of leaders working with followers, fostering positive self-development.

Drawing on the work of Kernis (2003), a modified conception by Walumbwa et al. (2008) shows four key types of behaviors that authentic leaders demonstrate:

1. Self-Awareness (Know yourself): refers to the level to which leaders understand their strengths, weaknesses and values, as well as knowing the impact they have on others.
2. Internalized Moral Perspective (Do the right thing): refers to leader behaviors being guided by internal moral standards and values. They "do the right thing" and are driven by ethics.
3. Relational Transparency (Be genuine): refers to being honest and presenting the authentic self through openly sharing information and feelings as appropriate for the situation.
4. Balanced Processing (Be fair-minded): refers to objectively analyzing all relevant information before making a decision. Plans are well considered with no hidden agenda.

Authentic leadership can be developed through self-awareness, practicing your core values and principles, facilitating and supporting followers, empowering people to be their best and letting them shine. Self-awareness is recognized as a critical component of authentic leadership. In order to build self-awareness an individual must have a clear understanding of their personal values and goals. The Johari Window was developed by Joseph Luft and Harrington Ingram; it is a widely adopted model for gaining a better understanding of oneself and others (Figure 5.1).

The Johari Window is based on a four-square grid – it is like looking through a window with four "panes."

1. What is known by the person about him/herself and is also known by others – Arena (public).
2. What is unknown by the person about him/herself but which others know – Blindspot.
3. What the person knows about him/herself that others do not know – Private/Hidden self.

4. What is unknown by the person about him/herself and is also unknown by others – Unknown self.

The Johari Window is an effective model for supporting leadership development. It provides the opportunity to see yourself and others more clearly through seeking feedback, informing and communication, self-discovery and shared discovery. It supports leaders in identifying issues and concerns, and helps create open honest communication and develop trust.

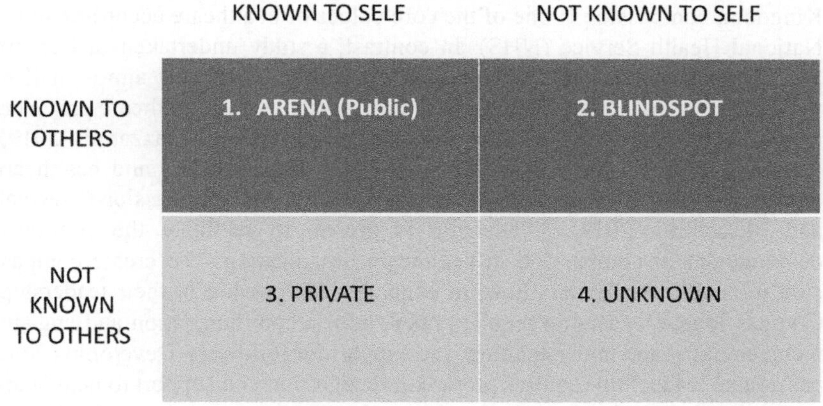

	KNOWN TO SELF	NOT KNOWN TO SELF
KNOWN TO OTHERS	1. ARENA (Public)	2. BLINDSPOT
NOT KNOWN TO OTHERS	3. PRIVATE	4. UNKNOWN

Figure 5.1   The Johari Window model

LEADERSHIP WITH COMPASSION

Compassion can be defined as "the sensitivity to suffering in self and others (engagement), with a commitment to try to alleviate and prevent it (action)" (Gilbert, 2014: 19). Healthcare leaders and healthcare professionals have a duty of care to themselves, each other and patients, and need to embody compassion. Self-compassion is fundamental to undertake challenges and maintain resilience in the demanding world of healthcare. There is a need to understand and be compassionate toward oneself in order to demonstrate compassion toward others. It is therefore important to stay close to your core values that give life meaning. The core values of leading with compassion in healthcare are listening and being present with others, understanding others, demonstrating empathy and care, and providing help and support within your own area and across boundaries. The role of leaders is particularly important in what they focus on and reward; what they demonstrate in their behavior helps inform us of what they value. Compassion has mutual benefits for leaders, healthcare professionals and patients. When healthcare professionals have a compassionate leader they are more likely to demonstrate that compassion toward each other and patients. Healthcare professionals that provide compassionate patient care results in patients being more satisfied and this in turn has an impact on the well-being and commitment of staff.

Being authentic and open, while also demonstrating humility, optimism and support and facilitating staff in the delivery of high-quality compassionate care, is vital. Compassion, empathy, humanity, kindness and respect for all staff and patients are paramount to the delivery of healthcare. In the United Kingdom, compassion is one of the core values of healthcare according to the National Health Service (NHS). In contrast, a study undertaken in Harvard Medical School on 1,300 patients and physicians found that almost half of Americans in each group feel that healthcare systems and healthcare providers in the United States are not compassionate (Trzeciak and Mazzarelli, 2019). However, globally the vast majority of healthcare providers and healthcare leaders would agree that patients should be treated with compassion (Trzeciak and Mazzarelli, 2019). Leadership is pivotal to facilitate the continued development of compassion in healthcare organizations. To create compassion in healthcare, leaders have to engender compassion in their leadership. Compassionate leadership requires open, honest communication and engagement, empathy and understanding, and support for followers. Developing compassionate leadership requires providing recognition and support to healthcare professionals working in a challenging and at times unprecedented healthcare environment. This means providing a trustful, respectful and supportive environment, sharing of competencies, appropriate training and development, thus ensuring retention of staff and their well-being. This facilitates the chance to view mistakes as an opportunity for learning and development. Furthermore, with patients being front and center, it enables staff to engage in innovation without fear or repercussions.

There is growing scientific evidence demonstrating the importance and value of compassion in healthcare. Professors Stephen Trzeciak and Anthony Mazzarelli have highlighted research showing the extraordinary effects of compassion on the giver and receiver in their book *Compassionomics: The Revolutionary Scientific Evidence that Caring Makes a Difference*. Never before have we seen such compassion across healthcare globally as we have during Covid-19. The pandemic has created significant fear, anxiety and uncertainty for patients, healthcare professionals, families and society. Despite the unprecedented challenges frontline healthcare professionals have been selfless in the way they have sacrificed their own self-interests for the benefit of others, which has resulted in many healthcare professionals contracting Covid-19 and, sadly, some have not survived. Reports from many countries and across diverse cultures are recognizing the added impact of Covid-19 on mental health and well-being among healthcare professionals. Within healthcare, staff are usually driven by altruism and a vocational desire to help. Within the challenges of healthcare, and more specifically in the Covid-19 crisis, this is not sustainable. Healthcare leaders need to be compassionate in their support for staff. Compassion needs to be toward oneself, each other and patients.

ENTREPRENEURIAL LEADERSHIP IN HEALTHCARE

Entrepreneurial leadership is the integration of an entrepreneurial mindset and leadership qualities in the management of organizations. It has developed as a field of study since the early 1990s. Entrepreneurial leadership is generally explored in the context of leadership traits and behaviors, integration of an entrepreneurial perspective to leadership with emphasis on the development of creativity and innovation. By its nature, entrepreneurial leadership drives change, creativity and innovation by creating a vision that inspires followers, utilizes competencies to identify opportunities, and successfully exploits opportunities into commercially viable products and/or services. Healthcare leaders need to integrate entrepreneurship in their leadership so they can address the challenges and complexities in the healthcare environment. Entrepreneurial leadership in healthcare can be defined as the leader's ability to be entrepreneurial in exploring and exploiting viable opportunities with their team and demonstrating an open, flexible and strategic approach to work with the team to drive change that will lead to the delivery of better patient care.

Entrepreneurial leadership is not specific to any one industry, and in the current challenging global healthcare environment could make a significant contribution to healthcare organizations. Within healthcare, successful entrepreneurial leaders have vision and passion and work collectively with their team to identify viable opportunities and utilize existing resources to facilitate the exploitation of these opportunities, which in turn should generate greater patient value. Innovation is key in the field of healthcare and entrepreneurial leaders need to drive followers to explore and exploit viable innovative opportunities by allowing the necessary time, resources and support for "out-of-the box" thinking among healthcare professionals at all levels. These innovations benefit society through new medical products and health services that enhance the quality and standard of patients' lives. Successful entrepreneurial leaders influence followers to think and act creatively and innovatively for the benefit of healthcare.

Exploration and exploitation of innovative solutions is imperative for healthcare services globally. Healthcare professionals need to contribute to the generation of innovation to ensure effective healthcare services; however, this needs to be supported and facilitated through appropriate leadership. The conceptual model in Figure 5.2 identifies the importance of entrepreneurship and leadership in the development of entrepreneurial leadership in healthcare. Building on the work of Kearney (2020: 11), the proposed model suggests that successful entrepreneurial leadership in healthcare is achieved through an entrepreneurial vision, drive and passion for the exploration and exploitation of viable innovative opportunities; and the appropriate leadership skills to inspire, motivate and support followers to achieve the entrepreneurial vision for the betterment of healthcare. This model implies that entrepreneurial leadership significantly impacts innovation in healthcare.

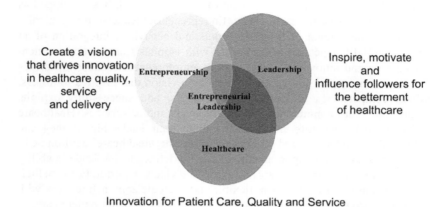

Innovation for Patient Care, Quality and Service

Figure 5.2   Entrepreneurial leadership in healthcare

Healthcare organizations need to engender creativity and innovation to address the needs of patients and therefore this requires entrepreneurial leaders that encourage and support followers in exploring and exploiting new opportunities for the betterment of healthcare. Success is influenced by the entrepreneurial leader's ability to influence and motivate followers to think creatively and innovatively for the benefit of patients. It is the supported integration of entrepreneurship and leadership that drives the exploration and exploitation of viable opportunities that will benefit patients – thus, the concept of entrepreneurial leadership.

LEADERSHIP STYLE FOR INNOVATION AND ENTREPRENEURSHIP IN HEALTHCARE

"Entrepreneurial leadership style is typically characterized as an authentic, charismatic and transformational leadership" (Kearney, 2020: 15).

Furthermore, when the leader demonstrates compassionate behaviors charac-terized by higher levels of cohesion, optimism and a sense of efficacy, there is greater opportunity for innovation and entrepreneurship, and as a result staff are more likely to take risks within the safe boundaries of the organization.

Leadership in healthcare requires a leadership style that:

- Increases satisfaction/motivation among staff;
- Increases innovative thinking at all levels;
- Increases staff well-being and resilience;
- Increases and facilitates compassion toward oneself, each other and patients;
- Decreases overall stress among staff;
- Decreases burnout among staff.

Entrepreneurial leaders demonstrate characteristics of authentic leadership and compassion in the way they create trust, inspire followers, support, understand and empathize with them to build on their strengths. Authentic and compassionate entrepreneurial leaders are core to healthcare in their approach to meet the challenges they face and continue to have a positive impact on their followers even during turbulent times. In a similar context, transformational leadership characterizes leaders as charismatic and visionary with an ability to inspire, motivate and energize followers. They are por-trayed as being confident and motivated with a clear vision. As previously discussed, transformational leadership is recognized to include four elements: Idealized Influence; Inspirational Motivation; Intellectual Stimulation; and Individualized Consideration (Bass, 1985). Transformational leadership has been recognized as fundamental for innovative behavior within organizations. Thus, transformational leadership can act as a role model and motivate follow-ers to be more innovative in healthcare.

The effective integration of entrepreneurship and leadership in healthcare requires entrepreneurial leaders that create a vision, and facilitate and drive the exploration and exploitation of innovative opportunities among followers in order to generate better patient care. This can be best achieved through transfor-mational/charismatic and authentic/compassionate leadership. In healthcare, transformational leaders that are charismatic, authentic and compassionate have the ability to build trust and motivate followers to ignore self-interests and work for the greater good of the healthcare organization, which will result in significant accomplishments for the benefit of patients. The core focus is to articulate a vision that will convince followers to make changes that will lead to better health outcomes for patients. It is a coaching style of leadership that aspires to achieve organizational goals but is also focused on transforming followers which in turn will make leaders out of followers. Transformational leaders engage with followers to contribute to a vision of a high-quality healthcare system ensuring that it is safe, efficient, effective, timely, equitable and patient-centered, and take responsibility to ensure the delivery of excellent patient care. Building on the work of Kearney (2020: 16), entrepreneurial leaders in healthcare have the core focus on patients and the generation of patient value. Entrepreneurial leaders in healthcare need to demonstrate the following characteristics:

1. *Vision*: develop an inspiring, challenging but realistic vision that fully captures the core values and ideology of healthcare.
2. *Environment*: have a comprehensive knowledge of the internal and external environment; recognize the national and international challenges facing healthcare at a point in time, for example aging populations, Covid-19.
3. *Flexible*: be adaptable in embracing opportunities and change for the benefit of healthcare, and view change as a challenge for new opportunities to develop the field of healthcare.
4. *Teamwork*: encourage and support teamwork and demonstrate a multidisciplined approach that recognizes the potential capabilities of individuals and teams across the healthcare sector.
5. *Communication*: develop open, transparent communication and discussion with strong trust to develop an effective team that explores and exploits new opportunities that generate patient value.
6. *Motivation*: encourage and motivate each team member to be creative and generate innovative ideas, solve problems and improve patient care.
7. *Persistence*: create an encouraging and supportive environment and culture wherein all followers consider innovation as one of their tasks and demonstrate persistence in light of challenges and obstacles in their entrepreneurial endeavors.

IMPORTANCE OF LEADERSHIP FOR INNOVATION AND ENTREPRENEURSHIP IN HEALTHCARE

As we aim to address the unprecedented challenges of Covid-19 and continue to manage existing and growing healthcare needs, there is a necessity to be more flexible, adaptable, innovative and entrepreneurial to cope with those demands. Therefore, appropriate leadership is paramount in today's challenging healthcare sector. The rapid pace of change and complexities of healthcare requires leaders with core competencies in creativity, innovation and entrepreneurship and who have the ability to instill it throughout their organization. Healthcare leaders should behave entrepreneurially and undertake the mission, goals and objectives to lead their healthcare organization in a way that will generate greater patient value. Their strategies need to be flexible, and engender creativity, innovation and entrepreneurship, ensuring greater efficiency and effectiveness, utilization of resources, and delivering the highest standards of patient care.

Strong leadership is fundamental for successful entrepreneurship, particularly in healthcare where entrepreneurial behavior is not always supported. Such leadership support needs to demonstrate the facilitation and promotion of entrepreneurial activity throughout the healthcare organization. This support can take many forms, such as championing innovative ideas, providing appropriate time and resources, or embedding entrepreneurship as part of the healthcare culture. Innovation in healthcare is a key requirement to meet the major and potentially unprecedented challenges facing today's healthcare organizations. For this to be achieved, staff must be supported in their creative endeavors to identify innovations that address the challenges within healthcare and generate patient value. Leaders must therefore:

- *Create* an environment and culture that empowers the creative and innovative mindset of staff and give them the resources, motivation and support to thrive;
- *Enable* the generation and refinement of ideas, products, processes, services and technologies;
- *Transform* healthcare by ensuring leadership that protects those creative and innovative individuals from a bureaucratic environment and breaks the obstacles restricting their innovations.

Leaders must engage the right people, at the right time, in creative and innovative work. While some innovative breakthroughs are the result of one individual, more frequently innovations emerge from many contributions. Leaders can further enhance diversity by also going beyond the internal organization to external sources for creativity. Collaboration does not have to be restricted to the internal organization. Thus, utilizing core competencies among individuals at different stages of the creative and innovative process is crucial.

The challenges and complexity of the healthcare environment requires exceptional leaders that "can do more with less." Leaders must recognize the value of their team in the innovation process and understand that the most innovative members of staff are generally not at the top level of the organization. Innovations from frontline staff are invaluable as they have the day-to-day experience of the system, and need to be given the opportunity and support to delve into their creative expertise. Therefore, creativity, innovation and entrepreneurship can be developed through the right leadership, teamwork and collaboration, combined with time and resources in order to achieve and sustain optimal performance that will generate patient value.

Entrepreneurial Leadership that Drives Innovation in Healthcare

It is great for an organization to have an innovation process in place where creativity generates novel ideas while innovation incorporates the implementation of these ideas into new products, processes, services and/or technologies (as discussed in Chapter 2). It appears logical and relatively evident, however, that it is highly challenging and resource intensive. Organizations encounter many challenges and barriers in the innovation process. For this to be successful depends on internal and external forces that influence what is viable and what actually emerges. Entrepreneurial leaders need to drive innovation in healthcare through innovative collaboration throughout the innovation process (Figure 5.3).

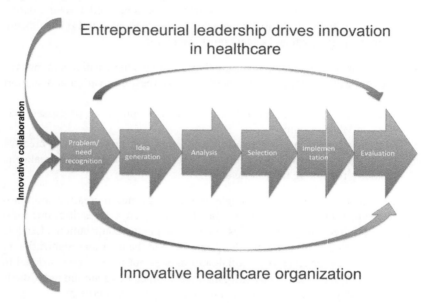

Figure 5.3   *Entrepreneurial leadership driving innovation in healthcare*

- Entrepreneurial Leadership – combined with transformational/charismatic and authentic/compassionate leadership provides an effective leadership for the development of innovation among healthcare professionals. Such leadership supports and facilitates the development through the innovation process from need, idea, analysis, selection, implementation and evaluation (further discussed above).

- Innovative Healthcare Organization – where the strategy, structure, culture, climate enables staff to be creative and innovative. While bureaucracy, red tape, rigidity, top-down communication and other factors are recognized as inhibiting the idea generation and implementation of innovation it is important that healthcare organizations find the right balance because too little structure and formality can be as inhibiting as too much.
- Innovative Collaboration – internal and external collaboration with all who engage in the innovation process, for example stakeholders. Innovation does not take place in isolation, particularly in healthcare; therefore, engaging with a diverse group of stakeholders is essential.

Entrepreneurial leaders have the passion to drive innovation and change, by developing and communicating a vision that motivates followers, and utilizes core competencies to explore and exploit opportunities that will lead to better healthcare outcomes. The success of a healthcare organization is strongly influenced by leadership. The entrepreneurial leader is the driving force for the development of innovation in healthcare.

SUMMARY

The field of healthcare has experienced an unprecedented challenge to healthcare professionals, frontline staff, patients and their families. Given the proliferation of Covid-19 globally, now more than ever before healthcare needs creative, innovative and entrepreneurial staff driven by appropriate leadership that will encourage, motivate and support creativity, innovation and entrepreneurial thinking and behavior as a major drive to bring about excellence in healthcare delivery and systems. Entrepreneurial leadership provides adaptability and flexibility with a willingness to take risks, and challenges assumptions in the best interest of patients. There are many opportunities to make meaningful innovations that can substantially enhance patients' lives. Healthcare professionals and leaders need to be transformational, charismatic, authentic, compassionate, creative, innovative and entrepreneurial to generate patient value. Such an entrepreneurial approach to leadership can develop innovations that go beyond the current pandemic and maximize the benefit to patients and staff indefinitely.

REFERENCES

Avolio, B.J. (2007). Promoting more integrative strategies for leadership theory-building. *American Psychologist* 62(1), 25–33.

Avolio, B.J. and Gardner, W.L. (2005). Authentic leadership development: getting to the root of positive forms of leadership. *Leadership Quarterly* 16, 315–38.

Avolio, B.J., Reichard, R.J., Hannah, S.T., Walumbwa, F.O. and Chan, A. (2009). A meta-analytic review of leadership impact research: experimental and quasi-experimental studies. *Leadership Quarterly* 20(5), 764–84.

Bass, B.M. (1985). *Leadership and Performance Beyond Expectations*. New York: Free Press.

Burns, J.M. (1978). *Leadership*. New York: Harper and Row.

Gilbert, P. (2014). The origins and nature of compassion focused therapy. *British Journal of Clinical Psychology* 53, 6–41. https://doi.org/10.1111/bjc.1204.

Kearney, C. (2020). Entrepreneurial leadership and its impact on the emergence of entrepreneurial ventures. In Ramadani, V., Palalic, R. and Dana, L.P. (eds.), Organizational Mindset of Entrepreneurship: Exploring the Co-creation Pathways of Structural Change and Innovation. Cham: Springer, 9–24.

Kernis, M.H. (2003). Toward a conceptualization of optimal self-esteem. *Psychological Inquiry* 14, 1–26.

Trzeciak S. and Mazzarelli A. (2019). *Compassionomics: The Revolutionary Scientific Evidence that Caring Makes a Difference*. Pensacola, FL: Studer Group.

Walumbwa, F., Avolio, B., Gardner, W., Wernsing, T. and Peterson, S. (2008). Authentic leadership: development and validation of a theory-based measure. *Journal of Management* 34(1), 89–126.

Suggested Reading

Avolio, B.J., Walumbwa, F.O. and Weber, T.J. (2009). Leadership: current theories, research, and future directions. *Annual Review of Psychology* 60(1), 421–49.

In this article, the authors begin by examining authentic leadership and its development, followed by work that takes a cognitive science approach. They examine new-genre leadership theories, complexity leadership, and leadership that is shared, collective or distributed. Each section ends with an identification of issues to be addressed in the future, in addition to the overall integration of the literature they provide at the end of the article.

Bagheri, A. and Akbari, M. (2017). The impact of entrepreneurial leadership on nurses' innovation behavior. *Journal of Nursing Scholarship* 50(1), 28–35. https://doi.org/10.1111/jnu.12354.

In this article, the authors examine the influence of entrepreneurial leadership on nurses' innovation work behavior and its dimensions. This cross-sectional study explores the impact of entrepreneurial leadership on the innovation work behavior of 273 nurses from public and private hospitals in Iran. The study found that entrepreneurial leadership had a significant positive impact on nurses' innovation work behavior and most strongly improved idea exploration, followed by idea generation, idea implementation and idea championing.

de Zulueta P.C. (2016). Developing compassionate leadership in health care: an integrative review. *Journal of Healthcare Leadership* 8, 1–10. https://doi.org/10.2147/JHL.S93724.

In this article, the author provides an integrative review of compassionate leadership in healthcare. The author asserts that developing leadership for compassionate care requires acknowledging and making provision for the difficulties and challenges of working in an anxiety-laden context. Tasks and relational care need to be integrated into a coherent unity, creating space for real dialog between patients, clinicians, and managers, so that together they can co-create ways to flourish.

Gillin, L.M. and Hazelton, L.M. (2020). Bringing an entrepreneurial mindset to health-care: a new tool for better outcomes. *Journal of Business Strategy* 42(4), 278–87. https://doi.org/10.1108/JBS-03-2020-0049.

In this article, the authors use a case study to examine the distinctive dimensions of entrepreneurial mindset – leadership, decision-making, behavior and awareness – within a practice-based healthcare (nursing) ecosystem and how these dimensions impact organization performance throughout the healthcare industry. This study validates research findings that entrepreneurial leadership encourages entrepreneurial behavior and an entrepreneurial culture supports the development of innovations. Opportunities for such cultural behavior are best understood by measuring the staff's and leaders' "entrepreneurial mindset."

Lai, F.-Y., Tang, H.-C., Lu, S.-C., Lee, Y.-C. and Lin, C.-C. (2020). Transformational leadership and job performance: the mediating role of work engagement. *SAGE Open*. https://doi.org/10.1177/2158244019899085.

In this article, the authors propose that transformational leaders use various behaviors to provoke followers' organizationally beneficial behaviors (e.g., better task performance and helping behaviors) through ignition of followers' work engagement. That is, employees inspired by transformational leadership are more likely to immerse themselves in the work, and, in turn, this is likely to result in better task performance and helping behaviors. In this study, the authors tested their hypotheses on a sample of 507 nurses working in 44 teams.

Larisch, L.M., Amer-Wåhlin, I. and Hidefjåll, P. (2016). Understanding healthcare innovation systems: the Stockholm region case. *Journal of Health Organization and Management* 30(8), 1221–41. https://doi.org/10.1108/JHOM-04-2016-0061.

In this article, the authors analyze the wider socio-economic context and conditions for such innovation processes in the Stockholm region, using the functional dynamics approach to innovation systems (ISs). Their analysis is based on triangulation using data from 16 in-depth interviews, two workshops, and additional documents. Their analysis reveals several mechanisms blocking innovation processes such as fragmentation and lack of clear leadership, as well as insufficient involvement of patients and healthcare professionals.

6. Innovation and entrepreneurship among individuals and teams in healthcare

QUESTIONS

How can effective teamwork in healthcare organizations develop innovations to address the growing needs of patients? What teamwork characteristics are essential for teams to identify and exploit healthcare opportunities? Why is communication so imperative to healthcare and how can this be enhanced to ensure the highest standard of care? How can leaders effectively drive individuals and teams to embrace innovation and entrepreneurship within healthcare organizations?

INTRODUCTION

Healthcare delivery is complex and challenging, particularly with growing needs of patients to address specific conditions, diseases, accidents and emergencies, or rare pandemics like Covid-19. Healthcare interventions of this nature require a team of multidisciplinary professionals to combine their competencies to deliver the most appropriate patient care. The need for multidisciplinary teams working together helps optimize the care provided to patients with complicated medical problems. This teamwork supports the need for further healthcare innovations to substantially evolve, to address the growing needs of patients. New innovations in healthcare, particularly medications and vaccines, take a significant amount of time to develop, receive full approval and implement as people's lives are at stake. The cost of healthcare globally is too high and in the United States it is excessive. There is a global need to develop innovations in healthcare that will generate greater patient value. Such innovations need to provide new and enhanced approaches to diagnosis, assessment, advice, and treatment that ensure the delivery of high-quality and safe care for all patients.

Over the years, the evolution of medicine has focused on the role and importance of teamwork. When leaders fully recognize and acknowledge current and future challenges in healthcare and embrace the competencies among staff by bringing them together to address complex problems and concerns, they are creating opportunities for greater innovation through effective teamwork. Leaders need to encourage behaviors and teamwork that are critical for innovation. No single individual is an expert in every area and therefore to deliver the highest standard of healthcare there is a dependence on multiple sources of expertise. Multiple perspectives in healthcare is paramount to provide the benefit of diverse knowledge and expertise. The delivery of healthcare requires many types of teams, across a multitude of professional specialist roles, in different structure, undertaking specific tasks. Healthcare leaders need to bring this expertise together and develop effective teamwork with clear coordination and collaboration within and across boundaries. Teams that work well together are more productive, contribute to higher levels of innovation and standard of care, and experience lower levels of stress. Effective teamwork can achieve greater innovation and enhance the quality and safety of healthcare delivery.

This chapter examines the importance of individuals and teams for the development of innovation and entrepreneurship among healthcare professionals to ensure they are continuously responding to the current and future needs of healthcare patients. Teamwork in healthcare is discussed to provide an understanding of the characteristics of effective teams and the importance of teamwork for innovation, quality and safety in healthcare delivery. Communication in healthcare is examined with strong emphasis on the channels of communication, barriers and skills required as a sender and receiver, and the importance of effective communication for the delivery of effective and safe patient care. Leading innovation and entrepreneurship is discussed to provide an understanding of the importance of individuals and teams within a healthcare organization that have the appropriate knowledge, skills and expertise, and equally are supported by leaders to champion opportunities for more innovations in healthcare delivery. Furthermore, a conceptual model of leadership for team effectiveness in innovation and entrepreneurship is presented. In addition, leading opportunities for innovation to address the changes in healthcare are examined, together with the importance of leading teams for innovation, quality and safety to address medical errors. Following that there is a discussion on leading an "After Action Review" as a way to learn from success and failure and develop further opportunities for innovation through this learning. The importance of entrepreneurial orientation in healthcare is examined. The final section of this chapter examines the importance of entrepreneurial orientation in healthcare.

TEAMWORK IN HEALTHCARE

Teamwork in healthcare is the ability of a group of individuals to work toward a shared purpose, to achieve greater efficiency and effectiveness, quality and safety, and improve patient outcomes in the delivery of care. Teamwork in healthcare has been defined by Xyrichis and Ream (2008: 232) as:

> A dynamic process involving two or more healthcare professionals with complementary backgrounds and skills, sharing common health goals and exercising concerted physical and mental effort in assessing, planning, or evaluating patient care. This is accomplished through interdependent collaboration, open communication and shared decision-making, and generates value-added patient, organizational and staff outcomes.

For teamwork to be effective the team must have common goals and a shared sense of purpose; there must be open and transparent communication and information sharing; and all members must be working in the best interests of patients and healthcare delivery. Effective teamwork is essential for both innovation and delivering the highest standard of patient care. Effective teamwork offers greater opportunities to synergize and be more creative and innovative. The timely diagnosis, assessment, advice and treatment can be complex, requiring specialized and diverse skills and effective teamwork. To manage this complexity, teams need to synthesize their competencies to deliver the highest quality of care to patients.

Globally there are aging populations, and increases in chronic diseases such as cancer, lung disease, diabetes and cardiovascular disease, which require healthcare professionals to take a multidisciplinary approach to healthcare. Additionally, healthcare professionals must work together to effectively and safely manage patients with multiple health problems. Effective multidisciplinary teamwork is essential to reduce medical errors and unnecessary patient harm and increase efficiency, quality, and safety of care. Therefore the growing demands of healthcare and the global requirements for innovation drive the need for effective teamwork. Hence, effective teamwork is paramount for developing a more successful and patient-centered healthcare delivery system. The success of the team is determined by the leader and team members' competencies, vision and perseverance to transform ideas into reality. Healthcare leaders need to nurture and develop the team to ensure the necessary levels of professionalism, ethics and values. Leaders need to support the team to function safely, achieve goals and overcome challenges while maintaining the highest standards and working in the best interests of patients as the priority.

Important characteristics of effective teams in healthcare:

- *Leadership*: Appropriate leadership with a shared sense of responsibility and accountability is fundamental for effective teamwork. The leader must support, facilitate and coordinate the activities of team members and ensure they are patient-centered and aligned to the organizational goals and objectives. Clear leadership creates higher levels of participation, commitment, motivation and support for innovation among team members.
- *Effective Communication*: This is imperative for successful teamwork to ensure open, honest, transparent, accurate, relevant, timely and complete information is recorded and communicated to all relevant healthcare professionals in the delivery of patient care. Ideas and approaches should be challenged in an open and constructive way to ensure best practice. Appropriate and accessible channels of communication must be used, which are available to all members.
- *Shared Goals and Objectives*: The team shares a common goal that is patient-centered and focused on the delivery of innovative, high-quality and safe patient care.
- *Professionalism*: Team members must undertake their roles and responsibilities with professionalism and integrity, and in an ethical manner. They must value each other's role and maintain the highest standards of healthcare delivery.
- *Respect*: Team members must respect and support each other and utilize the diversity of expertise to work effectively in the delivery of patient care.
- *Creativity and Innovation*: Team members are motivated to address problems and work together to seek opportunities for creativity and innovation, and find new and improved ways to deliver healthcare for the benefit of patients. They see mistakes as an opportunity to learn.
- *Performance/Outcomes*: Team members seek feedback that is accurate, reliable, transparent and timely. The team must agree and implement an appropriate course of action on all unsuccessful outcomes. There needs to be continuous focus on improving performance, quality and safety in the delivery of patient care.
- *Reflection*: Team members are committed to reflect on the lessons they learn in their day-to-day work and utilize those insights for continuous improvement and opportunities for innovation.

The above characteristics clearly distinguish an effective team from a pseudo team. Within healthcare, people need to work effectively as a team and this requires a clear understanding of the objectives and the shared objectives they are trying to achieve together as a team. There is no 'I' in teamwork but interdependent effective combination of efforts to achieve their objectives. It is through effective teamwork that competencies can be utilized and synergy can be achieved, leading to the delivery of more innovative and compassionate care. Regular meetings are necessary between team members to discuss and evaluate performance and identify ways to improve performance. They must identify any gaps or deviations that need to be addressed and ensure they are delivering the standard of care they are striving to achieve. Effective teamwork delivers higher standard and safer care that is more innovative, and team members work together in a way that motivates them, allows them to flourish, and enhances their well-being which is so important given the high risk of burnout among healthcare professionals (as discussed in Chapter 4). Hence, it is so important for leaders to develop effective teamwork in healthcare.

COMMUNICATION IN HEALTHCARE

Communication is the exchange of information between two or more people that must be accurate, relevant, concise, timely, and complete, and understood as intended by the sender, using the correct channels to communicate the message. The model presented in Figure 6.1 identifies the "communication process in healthcare." Communication in healthcare must rigorously ensure the accurate sharing of information with appropriate doctors, nurses, specialists, pharmacists and other hospital staff to ensure best diagnoses and treatment of patients. Equally, communication between the healthcare professional and patients must be respectful, accurate, clear, timely, compassionate and patient-centered.

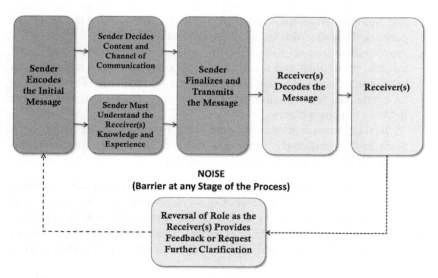

Figure 6.1   *Communication process in healthcare*

Channels of Communication

A channel of communication is the medium through which a message is sent to the receiver(s). The channels of communication can be verbal, written, and electronic (which can include verbal and/or written). The most appropriate channel must be adopted for the message that is being communicated to ensure it is received and understood as intended. This is particularly important when communicating with patients. With the increase in the availability and use of electronic devices the opportunity to communicate internally and externally (with patients) in new and novel ways has grown significantly in recent years.

Channels of communication in healthcare include the following:

- Verbal Communication
    - *Face-to-Face*: Includes both verbal and nonverbal signals, which must be consistent for message credibility and clarity. It generates the highest level of information richness. Nonverbal communication (e.g., body language, facial expression, eye contact, tone of voice) should be consistent with the verbal communication thus providing greater clarity and meaning. It provides opportunity for immediate feedback.
    - *Video Conferences/Online Platforms*: Online mobile conferences and meetings using, for example, Zoom, Blackboard Collaborate, or MS Teams are becoming more frequent particularly during Covid-19. When participants fully engage with cameras and microphones activated, the inclusion of verbal and nonverbal cues provides high information richness. It is also very cost effective, time efficient and safe during Covid-19. Online platforms facilitate meetings across many different regions. The use of online platforms in healthcare has increased substantially during Covid-19 not only among healthcare staff but also interaction and virtual appointments with patients.
    - *Verbal Communication Electronically Transmitted*: Includes telephone conversations and other electronic channels such as Skype or Zoom, with no camera connected. With the exception of tone of voice and silence, this form of communication does not facilitate nonverbal cues. However, there is information richness once the verbal communication is clear and concise.
- *Written/Electronic Communication*: Letters, emails, reports, text messages that are communicated to individuals and/or groups. Ensure appropriate professional grammar, punctuation and language, being mindful and respectful of your audience. Individuals generally think more concisely about what they document in writing than what they say when speaking. Written communication is particularly important for more complex messages. It provides a formal documented record of the communication.

While feedback is not usually immediate, it can be requested to ensure understanding.

Barriers to Communication in Healthcare

A barrier of communication is any obstacle in the communication process from the sender, receiver or external factors that inhibits the process of effective communication. Communication barriers are all too common among healthcare professionals and such barriers can be detrimental to patient outcomes. Barriers to effective communication in healthcare can include the following:

* Socio-cultural Barriers
    * Language: Lack of fluency in the language and inability to understand the nuances of the language.
    * Jargon: Unexplained medical terminology or jargon.
    * Culture Values and Beliefs: National culture has specific values and beliefs that are not always understood by other nationalities. Healthcare organizations have healthcare professionals and staff from many different cultures. Despite their specialism, communication across cultural boundaries has a higher risk of misinterpretation due to different views, values, beliefs and religions.
    * Stereotyping: Attempts to predict individual behavior based on their membership of a group or more specifically to make assumptions about others based on, for example, gender, race, religion or ethnicity. This can result in significant inaccuracies and lead to a major breakdown in communication.
* Psychological Barriers
    * Perception: Individuals have perceptions of reality. They behave according to those beliefs and that influences behavior. Therefore, information that is in conflict with those perceptions is filtered.
    * Poor Listening Skills: Failure to fully engage and listen with full attention. Few people listen with complete attention for more than a few seconds at a time.
    * Emotional Interference: Both positive and negative emotions can be a barrier to communication both in sending and receiving messages. A more balanced objective approach is more effective.
* Organizational Barriers
    * Information Overload: The challenges in healthcare organizations result in constant information overload. Information is coming to staff from all channels and directions relating to patients and other factors with the expectation of a timely response.

- Message Filtering: When information is passed on to others the message can be filtered which dilutes the clarity of the message.
- Conflicting Messages: Where there are conflicting messages in health-care, credibility is undermined and the risk of error is increased.
- Communication Climate: Healthcare needs open and accessible channels of communication among and between staff at all levels of the organization.

Communication Skills for Senders and Receivers

- Communication Skills for Senders with Team Members and Patients:
  - Send accurate, relevant, timely and complete messages.
  - Encode messages using appropriate language and terminology that the receiver(s) will understand.
  - Select the appropriate channel(s) of communication for the message.
  - Consider the context (information that surrounds the communication, e.g., relational, environmental and cultural) as well as the content of the communication. This is particularly important when communicating across cultures where some cultures are high-context (e.g., China, Japan, Korea) and others are low-context (e.g., German, Australia, America).
  - If more than one channel is being used, ensure consistency (i.e., face-to-face communication includes both verbal and nonverbal communication; ensure what is said is consistent with the tone of your voice, facial expressions, and all non-verbal cues). Consistent, reliable communication builds trust and credibility among the team.
  - Be honest, respectful, empathetic and compassionate in your communication.
  - For greater clarity and objectivity, consider yourself in the position of the receiver by reversing roles. Consider if you were the receiver of this message – would it be received and understood as you intend? This is an effective way to become more objective in your communication.
  - Ensure a feedback mechanism is included in the message – ask questions, ask for feedback to ensure that the message was received and understood as intended.
- Communication Skills for Receivers with Team Members and Patients:
  - Pay close attention to the message being communicated. Avoid and remove any distractions or disruptions.
  - Listen actively with interest and curiosity.
  - Do not interrupt until the opportunity arises to ask questions, and clarify your understanding.

- Be honest, respectful, empathetic and compassionate in your response.
- Ensure the use of appropriate language. When communicating with patients avoid jargon or medical terminology that may not be understood.
- Understand different linguistic styles and contexts, particularly across cultures.
- Do not make assumptions, engage in the feedback process and become the sender.
- Repeat in your own words what was communicated to ensure accurate interpretation.

Importance of Effective Communication in Healthcare

The importance of effective communication cannot be overemphasized when delivering value-based patient-centered healthcare. Medical errors due to communication failure are a major problem and concern in today's healthcare organizations. Therefore, effective communication can reduce and/or alleviate these errors with more concise information sharing, more efficient and effective interventions, enhanced quality and safety of care, improved staff morale, and improved patient outcomes and satisfaction. Healthcare professionals need to collaborate and work together as a team, clearly communicating and sharing information and synergizing the diverse knowledge and skills to make the best decisions for the delivery of patient care.

Healthcare professionals need to communicate in an understandable manner, and avoid jargon or terminology that will not be understood; they need to provide precise instructions and concisely answer questions honestly, respectfully, thoroughly and compassionately, and this will contribute to higher standard of care. Clarity in communication and information with compassionate and empathetic two-way communication with patients can result in patients being more engaged in their own care and feel more willing to disclose all relevant information and adhere to recommended medical treatment. Additionally, when communicating with patients and caregivers, they must provide clear discharge, medication instructions and follow-up care; this will reduce confusion, unnecessary readmissions and preventable errors and harm. Once this is achieved there will be a more positive patient experience resulting in a greater understanding and adherence to their treatment plan. Otherwise, errors will increase, efficiency and effectiveness will be reduced, and quality, safety and patient care will be compromised.

Communication is paramount for effective teamwork and must be evident vertically from the top down and the bottom up and horizontally across the delivery of healthcare. Effective teams need to be built on trust, respect and collaboration. Team members need to feel respected, heard and empowered to contribute to decision-making. This helps build trust and inclusivity, which in turn creates more information sharing. When important decisions need to be made all team members should be present and all information should be readily available and communicated. The participation of all relevant team members to share patient information, evaluate plan options and determine the best course of patient care, should in turn reduce the likelihood of error and harm. Effective communication among team members can increase satisfaction, staff morale and the quality of work relationships, all of which contribute to positive staff and patient outcomes.

Leaders must use appropriate channels of communication to interact with their teams, other healthcare professionals, staff, and patients, develop an open-door policy, and create a culture that strives to advance communication excellence. Communication can be formal and informal. Leaders need to be aware of the informal "rumors," "gossip," "water cooler" and "coffee machine" conversations and information, as what is communicated can be somewhat exaggerated or possibly distorted. This informal misinterpretation is reduced when the leaders have clear formal communication systems in place. Therefore, the stronger the formal communication channels, the weaker the informal channels. Clarity in communication is vital, particularly in this digital age when electronic messages such as texts and emails can be sent quickly and if they are not reviewed prior to sending can contain errors or lack clarity. The way information is communicated is very important because the delivery of care involves numerous patient handovers between healthcare professionals within and across departments, as well as interaction with healthcare professionals with diverse areas of specialism and nonmedical administration. This requires the ability to clearly explain, actively listen and demonstrate compassion. This has a significant effect on relationships with leaders, colleagues, patients and caregivers.

LEADING INNOVATION AND ENTREPRENEURSHIP AMONG INDIVIDUALS AND TEAMS

The knowledge, skills and abilities of healthcare professionals are imperative to healthcare organizations where patients' lives are at stake. Innovation does not exist without people who have the competencies to champion ideas. Having the right people, with the right skills, who are supported to deploy their creativity and share their competencies and expertise with other team members is paramount to bring about innovations that deliver the highest standard of patient care. Innovative and entrepreneurial healthcare organizations have a supportive senior management team, with a transformational and entrepreneurial approach to leadership (as discussed in Chapter 5), which is flexible and adaptable to change, and has open two-way channels of communication, an innovative future-oriented mindset, and a culture that embraces and encourages innovation and entrepreneurship among individuals and teams.

For healthcare organizations to effectively develop innovation and entrepreneurship among staff, they require the following:

- Leadership to support, facilitate and motivate individuals and teams in their innovative and entrepreneurial endeavors. Leaders need to give the team the freedom to disagree and to challenge ideas in order to synergize and reach the best solution. The degree of openness among team members is determined by the openness of the leader.
- A culture that embraces staff creativity and drives innovation and entrepreneurship.
- Individuals and teams who have the knowledge, skills and abilities to engage in the process of innovation, and explore and exploit viable innovative opportunities.
- The ability to develop effective teamwork within departments, cross-functional and across healthcare organizations including universities, medical device companies and pharmaceutical companies that can work together to develop innovations for the betterment of healthcare. This supports the utilization of the competencies of individuals with different specializations at different levels across the healthcare sector. Teamwork is so important to healthcare with the impact of a global pandemic and the proliferation of technological advancements and developments, and the pressurized necessity to do more.

Healthcare leaders need to be entrepreneurial (as discussed in Chapter 5) and support individuals and teams to achieve their full potential. The leader needs to understand the internal and external environment. They must be visionary and have a futuristic view to address the needs of healthcare. Leaders that drive innovation have the ability to determine a great vision and communicate that in a way that followers want to work together and be part of that vision for the benefit of healthcare. This may create challenges and bring about change for some healthcare organizations where healthcare professionals hold specific roles and identities.

Effective leadership that develops individuals and teams to be more innovative and entrepreneurial will significantly improve the outcomes and increase the efficiency and effectiveness in the delivery of patient care. As indicated in Figure 6.2, this in turn can deliver more innovative, higher quality and safer patient care; increase responsiveness to address both healthcare and patient needs; increase the number of successful healthcare innovations; and increase well-being and motivation among healthcare professionals which in turn will lead the world to more responsive and innovative healthcare.

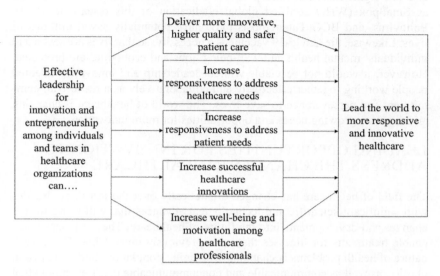

Figure 6.2   Leadership for individual and team effectiveness in innovation and entrepreneurship

We have seen strong leadership and teamwork in the innovative responsiveness in the search for a vaccine during the Covid-19 pandemic. Scientists and pharmaceutical companies like Pfizer, Moderna, Johnson & Johnson, Oxford/AstraZeneca were racing to develop a vaccine. In normal circumstances vaccines take on average 4–12 years of research and testing before they are approved. However, in this pandemic there is a global urgency for a vaccine – scientists are working relentlessly to produce a safe, effective, risk-free vaccine. This shows strong leadership, teamwork and collaboration among scientists, academics, healthcare professionals, universities, hospitals, pharmaceutical companies and governments. The world has united in working to develop a vaccine and therefore the responsiveness is significantly faster. Additionally, significant investments have been made; however, the vaccine testing process must still rigorously progress through the development process from (1) research and discovery; (2) pre-clinical testing; (3) phase 1 clinical trials; (4) phase 2 expanded clinical trials; (5) phase 3 efficacy trials; (6) seeking approval. The development process and, for example, the European Medicines Agency (EMA) and United States Food and Drug Administration (FDA) evaluation is rigorous before approval is permitted. Following approval there is ongoing surveillance to identify any longer term implications because the risk to human lives is too high. Vaccines provide a major medical benefit and are significant innovations to the field of healthcare. Vaccines such as Smallpox (WHO certified global eradication of this disease in 1980), Poliovirus, and BCG Tuberculosis (TB) have potentially saved millions of lives. Likewise, the Covid-19 vaccine is a necessity, so that lives are saved and individuals' mental health and well-being, jobs and economies are protected. However, it would not be viable without leadership and innovative talented people working together effectively and collaboratively as a team, with commitment and perseverance to save lives. The world of healthcare is changing and there are growing needs and opportunities for more innovation.

LEADING OPPORTUNITIES FOR INNOVATION TO ADDRESS THE CHANGES IN HEALTHCARE

The field of healthcare has changed dramatically over the last three decades with significant scientific and technological advances that will bring further changes and developments into the future of healthcare. These advancements enable treatments for illnesses that were previously untreatable. The overall nature of health problems is changing with aging populations and increases in obesity, as well as communicable and noncommunicable diseases. Innovation is not a matter of choice but of necessity, to work toward preventing as well as treating the many communicable and noncommunicable diseases.

It is through effective leadership and teamwork that game changing innovative solutions can be developed, for example solutions for prevention or earlier diagnoses of chronic diseases such as cancers, cardiovascular disease and diabetes, solutions to support lifestyle changes and greater public awareness to change behaviors and increase the health and well-being of people to reduce their chances of getting preventable diseases. Advanced solutions are required in diagnostics, remote assessment, advice and treatment, particularly during Covid-19 when there is so much pressure on healthcare yet there is a growing number of people in need of medical care for the continued growth in non-Covid-19 conditions and diseases. Solutions in, for example, AI, precision medicine and electronic health records, would help greatly.

While there have been many innovations in healthcare there is so much more to achieve. Leading effective teams provides the opportunity for healthcare professionals to contribute to addressing challenges as opportunities for innovation in healthcare delivery.

Leading Teams for Innovation, Quality and Safety to Address Medical Errors

Effective teamwork is an essential component of healthcare delivery in terms of high quality and safety in patient centered care and the development of innovations that will further advance the field of healthcare. Team-based delivery of care ensures all medical professionals work together for the benefit of patient care. This is paramount given the extremity of medical errors that annually result in death. It is estimated that in the United States, medical error is the third largest cause of death (Makary and Daniel, 2016). Harm is the unfolding result of a series of medical events, which have astounding consequences. Harm includes hospital-acquired infections, diagnostic errors, surgical errors, medication errors, misdiagnoses, delayed diagnoses and patient falls, all of which have a detrimental impact on patients, families, healthcare professionals and their organization, and society at large. Medical errors need to be recognized globally and addressed accordingly with appropriate leadership, teamwork and collaboration by sharing sound scientific methods and innovations for prevention. Hence, effective leadership and teamwork is essential for developing an efficacious approach to ensure innovation, quality and safety in the delivery of patient care.

Leading an After Action Review for Innovation

Given the complex and dynamic healthcare environment there is a necessity for continuous learning and development. Leaders have a responsibility to ensure that the team have clearly defined goals and objectives that are patient-centered and provide them with a continuous assessment and evaluation of performance/outcomes. Within healthcare, there are daily challenges; how leaders manage those challenges can determine how the team and delivery of care advances and develops. Leaders need to drive effective teamwork and open communication so all successes and failures are reviewed to fully understand what works well and what can be further developed. Appropriate learning and development needs to take place when there is success and failure. Most significantly, any failures that have occurred need to be identified and reported with effective action undertaken to ensure this does not happen again. The number of medical errors and harm globally is astounding and healthcare organizations need to address these errors as quickly and effectively as possible and take appropriate corrective action to ensure they are not repeated.

An After Action Review (AAR) is a way to support the evaluation of successes and failures in healthcare. According to the WHO, an AAR is a qualitative review of actions taken to identify and record best practices and challenges in response to a public health event or project. The review must be done in a timely manner. The review needs to identify (1) what works well; (2) what did not work; and (3) what would be different next time. An AAR can be used effectively in healthcare organizations to facilitate healthcare professionals and staff to assess and evaluate an event and determine how to sustain and build on successes and ensure failures will not happen again. This can be achieved by gaining a greater understanding of the following:

- the gap between "actual outcome" and "expected outcome";
- why there was a difference between the "actual outcome" and the "expected outcome";
- what worked well and what was unsuccessful;
- what learning can be gained and shared among team members and other staff to guarantee improvements.

The objective is to support all team members to learn and develop, and identify changes required and ways to further improve outcomes in the delivery of care. Likewise, even when an event is successful it is good to understand why it went well and what can be done to replicate this success in the future. There needs to be honest, open, transparent communication and information sharing among leaders and team members at all times.

While AARs are used as a tool to support continuous learning and improvement, their benefit can go beyond this. Leaders that promote the use of AARs can create a safe, equitable, respectful environment that supports constructive teamwork, communication and decision-making which in turn can enhance solutions for the generation of ideas to address problems in the delivery of care. This can potentially lead to more opportunities for innovation that can be effectively implemented within healthcare.

ENTREPRENEURIAL ORIENTATION IN HEALTHCARE

Entrepreneurial orientation (EO) is one of the most established concepts within the field of entrepreneurship. EO reflects the objectives of the organization in relation to exploring and exploiting opportunities. Miller (1983) originally delineated EO as a unidimensional construct. EO is a strategic orientation that is characterized by innovation, risk-taking and proactivity. EO organizations take more risks and are more proactive in their pursuit of innovative opportunities. EO represents an organizational-level proclivity toward entrepreneurial behavior within existing organizations and has more recently been recognized as important to the field of healthcare. It demonstrates the leader's vision and the organizational requirements to develop innovations that generate patient value.

Within healthcare, the innovation dimension refers to the organization's interest and commitment to conscientiously explore and exploit opportunities for the development of new products, services and processes that will benefit the field of healthcare. It reflects a willingness to diverge from the status quo of healthcare and embrace new opportunities. The risk-taking dimension refers to the level of risk the healthcare organization and its leaders are willing to take, and realistically should take, when the outcomes are uncertain and patients' lives may be at stake. Proactivity refers to the extent the organization supports and facilitates the development and implementation of innovations in advance of other competing healthcare organizations. Collectively, these three dimensions are recognized as representing the overall degree of EO within an organization (Covin and Lumpkin, 2011). When an organization undertakes higher levels of these dimensions they are recognized as being more entrepreneurial.

EO is recognized as an important component for organizational success and enhances organizational outcomes and performance across many sectors. EO is important to healthcare due to continuous global changes in healthcare systems, where and how healthcare is delivered, the demands for certain services such as diabetes which has a growing global prevalence, and cardio-vascular diseases which, according to the WHO, are globally the number one cause of death. In response to the growing pressures on healthcare systems, healthcare organizations have demonstrated innovation and entrepreneurship through, for example, technological advancements and developments, for example robotics, AI, less invasive surgical procedures, reduction in waiting times, and more day-care procedures, all of which can better utilize resources and enhance patient satisfaction and recovery.

For EO to emerge, the organizational environment must value and drive an entrepreneurial spirit and culture. Furthermore, EO must be facilitated and supported by organizational leaders, and they must create a culture where problems are seen as opportunities. For EO to develop, leaders can extend the utilization of resources and competencies through teamwork and implement new approaches to delegate autonomy to staff, decentralize decision-making, and to become more flexible and adaptable to embrace opportunities for the benefit of patients. EO can provide insights into the leadership, value and outcome of entrepreneurial behavior within healthcare organizations. Therefore, healthcare organizations that drive EO have the opportunity to provide superior patient value and better patient outcomes.

SUMMARY

The field of healthcare is complex, multifaceted and diverse. Healthcare must be innovative and entrepreneurial to address patients' needs and the health and well-being of society. With aging populations and growing numbers of complex diseases, healthcare organizations can deliver higher standards, and better quality and safer care in a more timely, efficient and effective way if they are more innovative and entrepreneurial. To manage this, effective multidisciplinary teamwork is a necessity to ensure innovation that can adhere to delivering the highest standard of patient care. This cannot happen without effective leaders, focused individuals who have the ability to encourage and support innovation among individuals and team members, working toward the same shared goals and objectives, ensure clear open channels of communication and information sharing, and have a commitment to innovation to deliver the highest standard of patient care.

Through effective leadership and teamwork there is no reason why a strong momentum for innovation and entrepreneurship demonstrated globally cannot continue beyond Covid-19 to more readily develop and effectively respond to current and future needs of healthcare.

REFERENCES

Covin, J.G. and Lumpkin G.T. (2011). Entrepreneurial orientation theory and research: reflections on a needed construct. *Entrepreneurship Theory and Practice* 35(5), 855–72.

Makary M.A. and Daniel, M. (2016). Medical error: the third leading cause of death in the U.S. *British Medical Journal* 353, i2139. https://www.oliveviewim.org/wp-content/uploads/2018/10/Makary-2016-3rd-leading-cause-of-death.pdf.

Miller, D. (1983). The correlates of entrepreneurship in three types of firms. *Management Science* 29(7), 770–91.

Xyrichis, A. and Ream, E. (2008). Teamwork: a concept analysis. *Journal of Advanced Nursing* 61(2), 232–41.

Suggested Reading

Keiser, N.L. and Arthur, W., Jr. (2020). A meta-analysis of the effectiveness of the after-action review (or debrief) and factors that influence its effectiveness. *Journal of Applied Psychology* 106(7), 1007–32. https://doi.org/10.1037/apl0000821.

In this article, the authors examine the effectiveness of the after-action review (AAR) – also commonly termed debrief – and four training characteristics within the context of Villado and Arthur's (2013) conceptual framework [see https://www.researchgate.net/publication/235377757_The_Comparative _Effect_of_Subjective_and_Objective_After-Action_Reviews_on_Team _Performance_on_a_Complex_Task]. Based on a bare-bones meta-analysis of the results from 61 studies (107 ds [915 teams and 3,499 individuals]), the AAR leads to an overall d of 0.79 improvement in multiple training evaluation criteria. Overall, this study suggests that the effectiveness of the AAR should be understood as a function of the combined influence among multiple inter-acting characteristics.

Moser, K., Dawson, J.F. and West, M.A. (2018). Antecedents of team innovation in health care teams. *Creativity and Innovation Management* 28, 72–81.

In this article, the authors extend previous research on team innovation by looking at team-level motivations and how a prosocial team environment, indicated by the level of helping behaviour and information-sharing, may foster innovation. Hypotheses were tested in two independent samples of health care teams (N_1 = 72 teams, N_2 = 113 teams), using self-report measures. Results supported the hypotheses of main effects of both information-sharing and helping behaviour on team innovation and interaction effects with team size and occupational diversity.

Ratna, H. (2019). The importance of effective communication in healthcare practice. *Harvard Public Health Review*, 23, 1–6.

In this article, the author discusses multiple components to effective communication in a healthcare setting: healthcare literacy, cultural competency and language barriers. The purpose of this review is to analyze the components of effective communication in a healthcare setting, cite current professional standards for each and propose solutions for improvement.

Rosen, M.A., DiazGranados, D., Dietz, A.S., Benishek, L.E., Thompson, D., Pronovost, P.J. and Weaver, S.J. (2018). Teamwork in healthcare: key discoveries enabling safer, high-quality care. *American Psychologist* 73(4), 433–50. https://doi.org/10.1037/amp0000298.

In this article, the authors synthesize the evidence examining teams and team-work in healthcare delivery settings in order to characterize the current state of the science and to highlight gaps in which studies can further illuminate our evidence-based understanding of teamwork and collaboration. The authors highlight evidence concerning (a) the relationship between teamwork and multilevel outcomes, (b) effective teamwork behaviors, (c) competencies (i.e., knowledge, skills, and attitudes) underlying effective teamwork in the health professions, (d) teamwork interventions, (e) team performance measurement strategies, and (f) the critical role context plays in shaping teamwork and col-laboration in practice.

Schippers, M.C., West, M., and Dawson, J. (2015). Team reflexivity and innovation: the moderating role of team context. *Journal of Management* 41(3), 769–88. https://doi.org/10.1177/0149206312441210.

In this article, the authors developed and tested a team-level contingency model of team reflexivity, work demands and innovation. They argue that highly reflexive teams will be more innovative than teams low in reflexivity when facing a demanding work environment. A field study of 98 primary health care teams in the United Kingdom corroborated their predictions: team reflexivity was positively related to team innovation, and team reflexivity and work demands interacted such that high levels of both predicted higher levels of team innovation. These results are discussed in the context of the need for team reflexivity and team innovation among teams at work facing high levels of work demands.

Smith, B. and Jambulingam, T. (2018). Entrepreneurial orientation: its importance and performance as a driver of customer orientation and company effectiveness among retail pharmacies. *International Journal of Pharmaceutical and Healthcare Marketing* 12(2), 158–80. https://doi.org/10.1108/IJPHM-07-2017-0038.

In this article, the authors examine how entrepreneurial orientation and customer orientation influence healthcare (retail pharmacy) industry performance. Using a sample of US retail pharmacies, the study applies partial least squares structural equation modeling to identify the direct and indirect effects of the entrepreneurial orientation constructs on company performance. The study finds that the entrepreneurial orientation has a significant impact on customer orientation and company effectiveness.

7. Understanding and leading design thinking in healthcare

QUESTIONS

What is design thinking? How can design thinking be used to create significant innovation in healthcare? Are there steps that can be followed to implement design thinking on an individual or organizational basis? Are there good examples of the successful use of design thinking in healthcare? How can leaders drive design thinking in healthcare?

INTRODUCTION

Increasing creativity and innovation is becoming an important strategic goal for healthcare. However, healthcare organizations are challenged in achieving this in addition to their specific day-to-day tasks. Leaders need to increase staff engagement, motivate, and facilitate creative thinking and problem solving. While leaders can have meetings that facilitate and motivate intelligent and enthusiastic team members to generate interesting ideas and assess and evaluate their viability, there needs to be continuity and support to ensure this moves beyond the meeting and is part of the strategy.

There is no doubt that there is a continuous need for creativity and innovation in healthcare. These needs have been further escalated due to the Covid-19 pandemic, which requires even more innovative approaches to increase efficiency and effectiveness and enhance patient outcomes. The scale and exponential growth of Covid-19 cases globally into 2021 and beyond has resulted in implementing public health measures on a scale that has previously not been experienced. These necessary public health measures (e.g., restricted movement, staying at home as much as possible, reducing the number of contacts to your household, physical distancing, hand hygiene, face coverings, cough etiquette, necessary travel only, curfews, closures of schools and universities, closure of nonessential business) attempt to reduce the number of Covid-19 cases, hospitalizations and mortality. This further highlights the complexity, unpredictability, ambiguity and volatility of healthcare, with the urgency for timely innovative responses to address immediate and unprecedented challenges.

Innovation does not happen without people and the utilization of core competencies among healthcare professionals can generate innovations that address current healthcare inefficiencies and lead to improved patient outcomes. These innovations need to address patient needs and be supported by leaders and key stakeholders. Within healthcare, it is every leader's and healthcare professional's goal to improve the patient experience and outcome. Design thinking is a creative and innovative approach to address problems by obtaining a greater understanding from the perspective of end users in order to more succinctly address those problems and develop better solutions. It is a patient centered, collaborative approach to innovation. Design thinking requires that healthcare providers have a greater understanding of and empathy toward patients, recognize patients' needs and challenges, and work to develop innovations to address those problems. Empathy is central to design thinking. Design is focused on developing a greater understanding of patient needs rather than making assumptions based on their own professional experience. Design thinking has been recognized as a driver of innovation. An effective design has an in-depth understanding of patient needs within their specific environment by testing viable solutions. Design thinking can therefore result in more defined solutions with more successful outcomes. The healthcare system can substantially benefit from design thinking as an effective approach to innovation in understanding and addressing the most pertinent patient needs. Hence, better design can save lives and therefore healthcare can substantially benefit from design thinking.

The objective of this chapter is to examine design thinking in healthcare. Design thinking is discussed to provide an understanding of the meaning and nature of design thinking in healthcare. The five core elements of design thinking are presented. Design thinking for creative solutions to healthcare challenges as well as embracing design thinking and the benefits of design thinking in healthcare is discussed. Following a discussion on leadership and organizational support, this chapter emphasizes the importance of leadership commitment, leading and managing change, resistance to change, and leadership and organizational culture. The chapter concludes with a discussion on effective leadership and design thinking in healthcare.

WHAT IS DESIGN THINKING IN HEALTHCARE?

Design thinking in healthcare can be defined as taking a creative and patient-centric perspective to address needs and identify and solve problems. This is achieved through defining the problem and emphasizing ideation and prototype models, testing them, and selecting improvements to generate feedback for redesign and implementation. It is an effective way to gain insights from the patient on the new product, service and/or experience in order to develop better solutions to address patients' needs. Design thinking in healthcare is about putting the patient first, and gaining an in-depth understanding of their experiences and challenges in order to determine the best solutions to address those needs. Design thinking requires hard work, ability, perseverance and commitment to turn challenges into opportunities. Design thinking must be viable, feasible and desirable to generate and enhance patient experience and outcomes. It is a relatively new approach for healthcare that can drive innovation and effective collaboration. It is through the collaboration of cross-functional teams that different levels of expertise are brought forward, with different perspectives, to delve deeper into the development of a viable innovation and design. It is action oriented to discover new innovations that provide solutions to problems. The start of the design process is escalated by the recognition of the gaps and limitations of the current state and the drive and commitment to take action to address those problems. Design is not just about designers but empathizing and engaging with end users to fully understand their experience and needs. Therefore, design thinking in healthcare prioritizes empathy to address the needs, wants and expectations of the end user. It embraces the opportunity to fully understand a problem with the core objective of developing an effective and innovative solution that patients need and want.

CORE ELEMENTS OF DESIGN THINKING

Within the field of healthcare, design thinking is an innovative approach to bring different stakeholders together to work through core elements. There are usually five key elements in design thinking: (1) problem empathy and definition; (2) ideation; (3) prototype; (4) test and select; and (5) implementation.

Problem Empathy and Definition

This first element in this process is empathizing and defining. Empathizing is central to design thinking and requires the ability to objectively observe, engage and closely monitor and listen intensely to patients. This requires in-depth research to gain a comprehensive understanding of the needs of the specific population group and the challenges they experience. Accurately and concisely defining the problem is frequently the most challenging aspect of design thinking; if the specific problem is not clearly defined, then the solution, if found, will not address the right need. Defining the problem should be a team effort with leaders encouraging active participation from each team member. Defining the problem requires observation so there is a clear understanding of what the patients actually experience versus what they say they experience. This also requires a cross-functional approach to problem solving to facilitate a deeper understanding of the issues involved. There needs to be total objectivity and any preconceived assumptions must be dismissed so that an accurate definition of the problem can be developed to support and facilitate creative and innovative solutions.

Ideation

Once the problem is defined, the second element focuses on brainstorming to generate as many options as possible. The focus is on moving beyond the obvious and coming up with new and better innovative solutions. The objective of design thinking is to create many solutions to address the problem even if one solution appears obvious. For this to be effective, leaders need to engage team members and other relevant individuals such as patients and stakeholders so there are multiple and diverse perspectives. Multiple perspectives achieve greater synergy and therefore should provide a richer breadth of solutions.

Prototype

The third element requires the building of real models to provide a sample of the proposed idea. Visual cues and demonstrations are important to us as individuals, so seeing a prototype helps the proposed solution become more vivid. The faster a prototype is presented, providing clarity and understanding, the easier it is to gain acceptance from key patients and stakeholders. It is important that the most viable solutions are carefully developed and evaluated, so they can be further reviewed and refined. Ideally, a prototype provides the opportunity to learn fast and effectively, make mistakes early on and address them quickly, saving time and resources. Leaders need to create a culture that allows each solution to develop so the best one can emerge, or a combination of ideas to develop a more effective solution.

Test and Select

The fourth element is focused on selecting the best solution from the many solutions proposed in the previous element. Prototypes of the proposed solution are brought to the stakeholders to obtain feedback and further review, and refinement of prototypes takes place as necessary. Vigorous testing takes place to ensure the selected solution is the best option.

Implementation

The final element is implementation. Once the best option is tested and selected, the solution is then implemented. The more significant the change, the more challenging it is to implement. Design thinking requires change and the risk associated with that change which is difficult for healthcare professionals and organizations to accept. It is not a one-time implementation but one that requires feedback so there is opportunity for continuous improvement and innovation.

DESIGN THINKING FOR CREATIVE SOLUTIONS TO HEALTHCARE CHALLENGES

Design thinking generates creative solutions to healthcare challenges by putting personal perspectives aside, being objective and delving into the patient's experience and defining the problem. This provides a deeper understanding of patient challenges as well as questioning potential perceptions and biases about patients with certain conditions, illnesses and diseases. This can open up a new array of questions not only for design thinking to address problems but also to support patients and provide higher standards and quality of service provision to them in their current situation. Greater insights are achieved by engaging in the users' experience. This also helps in understanding patients' needs, not just what is perceived as best practice as "one size does not fit all," but providing innovators with new insights and possibilities. This facilitates understanding and developing what is most important to patients, supporting a more focused approach to enable team members to identify a number of potential solutions. This helps weigh out the pros and cons of the success of each viable idea, understanding the value of the potential solution. Team members need to be committed and confident that the final solution provided has gone through a rigorous selection process.

For successful outcomes in healthcare, innovation needs to ensure the following:

- *Better solutions to address healthcare needs and problems*: To find the best solutions to address existing and likely future needs and problems requires deep engagement in the design thinking process. The right questions must be asked to find the appropriate solutions. For a truly valuable solution to be developed, patients and other relevant stakeholders must be included in the process. While this can be challenging to manage, if properly led it can provide invaluable insights.
- *Minimal risk*: Risk and uncertainty is inevitable, particularly in more advanced innovations that are breakthrough rather than incremental.

However, with healthcare there is a need to be mindful of the risk that can be taken to ensure that the well-being of patients is never jeopardized. Leaders must be willing to let go of ideas that have questionable risk and consequences and focus on the creative ones that are most viable.

- *Staff embracing the opportunity*: For design thinking to work well in the organization it must be supported and embedded in leadership and embraced by staff. This can be achieved when it is driven by leaders that encourage and support staff to engage in the design thinking process.

By demonstrating a strong empathetic approach and involving patients and other relevant stakeholders in defining the problem and working toward the development of a solution, there is a greater acceptance of the proposed innovation. This was emphasized at GE Healthcare in their need to fully understand the experience of children when undergoing CT scans, X-ray procedures and MRI scanning. While technological advancements and developments have changed the field of healthcare, some procedures are not the most pleasant experiences for patients, and can be particularly difficult for children. Therefore it is not just about the cutting-edge technological advancement in diagnostics procedures but also the impact these procedures have on patients. Diagnosis, assessment, advice and treatment needs to provide patients with a positive experience, where patients feel safe and secure. This is paramount in healthcare where patients are at their most vulnerable. GE Healthcare has contributed to this patient-centered approach in making procedures more pleasant by redefining the experience of an MR exam for children with an "Adventure Series" of scanner environments led by Doug Dietz, principal designer at the company (see https://thisisdesignthinking.net/2014/12/changing-experiences-through-em pathy-ge-healthcares-adventure-series/). Design needs to look, feel and work in a way that is best for the patient and enhances their experience. By focusing on the patient's needs with empathy, they are making the innovation richer and more rewarding. When patients have a positive experience this increases their level of satisfaction, reduces their levels of stress and anxiety, reduces the amount of re-admissions, and provides greater utilization of resources which helps reduce unnecessary costs. This emphasizes the need for empathy and taking a patient-centered approach to innovation and design in healthcare. Design thinking in healthcare transforms innovative ideas into real-life solutions that change the delivery of patient care.

Embracing Design Thinking in Healthcare

Healthcare is a challenging and complicated industry, with this complexity further escalated due to the Covid-19 pandemic. When such complexity exists there is too often a focus on maintaining the status quo rather than a drive for innovation and change for the benefit of patients and society at large. The reality is that "nothing changes, if nothing changes" and therefore innovation is paramount to bring about positive changes at all levels of healthcare. Design thinking has been embraced by the Mayo Clinic in their Center for Innovation, and it drives their innovation. They focus on addressing patients' needs through incubator designs that shape the delivery of future patient care. Mayo take a patient-centered approach and use design methods such as ethnography and observations techniques, visualization, prototyping, sketching, storytelling, and brainstorming. Design thinking is congruent with the values of the Mayo Clinic that focus on the patient, research and teamwork (see http://centerforinnovation.mayo.edu/design-in-health-care/).

While design thinking takes significant time, expertise, effort, perseverance, resilience and confidence on the part of leaders and their teams however, the results can be life changing. It is the leaders and team competencies that understand the industry and recognize existing gaps and limitations, and can engage in the process of design thinking more efficiently and effectively. This requires significant competencies with minimal room for mistakes and errors and, most significantly, no such mistakes or errors when dealing with patients' lives. To continue to grow and develop the field of healthcare it is imperative that healthcare leaders, healthcare professionals and staff work together and challenge themselves to embrace a more objective approach to work; this can be effectively facilitated through design thinking.

Despite the rightful regulation of the healthcare industry there is no reason why healthcare leaders cannot drive greater innovation to contribute to their organization and potentially the industry. Patients rely on healthcare at their most vulnerable and fearful moments. When patients receive a diagnosis which at times can be life-changing or, more seriously, close to end of life situations, the impact of this is deeply profound for the individual and their loved ones. Therefore, it is the responsibility of healthcare professionals to work to the highest standards to "heal patients" as much as medically possible, to "treat patients" in need of necessary treatment, and to ensure that they always demonstrate "care, compassion, comfort, and respect" for patients.

Design thinking is an important aspect of healthcare and can be utilized through effective interaction among the diverse specialisms and expertise throughout healthcare and beyond. Design thinking provides the opportunity to address confusion and offer clear and purposeful action and more positive patient experiences and outcomes. The field of healthcare has the opportunity to engage more in design thinking and see healthcare through the design lens.

Benefits of Design Thinking for Healthcare

- Design drives innovation – achieving innovation requires exceptional commitment in understanding patient needs, identifying gaps and limitations, and developing innovations to address those needs.
- Design provides a sense of awareness – by being present, engaging with others and communicating effectively, asking questions and seeking clarification, a greater understanding of the needs of others can be gained.
- Design generates opportunities – empathy and compassion for patients drives the design process to help recognize and seek opportunities that can support change for the benefit of patients.
- Design builds connections – there are opportunities to connect and learn from other industries to build truly valuable designs in healthcare.
- Design develops teamwork – engaging openly and honestly with others builds trust, collaboration and authentic relationships among leaders and team members.
- Design helps motivate people – having the opportunity to be part of something bigger inspires and motivates people in their roles, giving them the chance to contribute to designing solutions.
- Design provides clarity – prototypes help assess and evaluate what is most viable, thus increasing efficiency and effectiveness and reducing costs.
- Design for tomorrow's innovation today – having a future-oriented mindset helps in envisioning and aspiring to achieve the ideal outcome and working toward achieving this through design.

LEADERSHIP AND ORGANIZATIONAL SUPPORT

Even if the elements of design thinking are adhered to, for it to be successful there is a need for leadership and organizational support and commitment. Effective leadership is required, which instills motivation among team members, and provides direction and momentum on the journey to innovation. An in-depth study on leading design thinking undertaken by Bason and Austin (2019) included twenty-four projects across five countries that recognized that effective leadership is paramount to success. In engaging in design thinking, a healthcare organization must recognize that it could fail. This failure is not always negative as it is learning that can lead to future success. Such failure needs to be considered part of the cost of successful innovation. As part of the process, design thinking develops alternatives before a viable solution is selected for implementation. Design thinking is an essential tool for providing greater simplicity and taking into account empathetic, thoughtful and human perspectives. Leaders need to demonstrate their commitment and support for design thinking by challenging the status quo, thinking "outside the box" in how they connect unrelated ideas in new ways, and engage and collaborate with their team in the design thinking process. Leadership commitment and organizational support is necessary to develop the chances of successful implementation in design thinking.

Leadership Commitment

Leaders must link design thinking initiatives to the strategic organizational goals and objectives. Leaders and top management teams must openly endorse and demonstrate their commitment and support for design thinking throughout the organization. For design thinking methods to be successful, leaders need to work with their teams and communicate and collaborate to address any challenges that are encountered. Leaders need to show their commitment and demonstrate an appropriate balance between leading and doing. Without this clear commitment, staff will not embrace and engage in the practice of design thinking. This is important so that staff at all levels recognize the value of design thinking in the organization and as part of their own role. Leaders need to manage resistance to using design thinking through appropriate communication, training and development. While design thinking does not address all problems, ideally design should result in innovation. Given the nature of healthcare and the patient-centered approach, design thinking can begin by focusing on addressing a small problem with significant potential for further development.

Leading and Managing Change

Change is always a challenge, especially in the complexity of healthcare environments where there are so many rules and regulations that rightly need to be followed. Additionally, there are many individuals within healthcare with diverse and at times conflicting goals and objectives. Forces for change can be as a result of external environmental factors such as patients, stakeholders, governments, regulations, legislation, and technological and medical advancements. Internal environmental factors include activities and decisions for change due to certain outcomes and/or feedback. However, change is also important particularly when gaps and limitations are identified, and there is a clear gap between existing performance/outcomes and desired performance/ outcomes. Continuing with something that is not working reduces efficiency and effectiveness, increases costs, and compromises the delivery of the highest standard of patient care. Leaders need to have a comprehensive understanding of healthcare trends, patterns and needs to address problems and explore and exploit viable opportunities. This requires effective leadership and management of change among individuals and teams to address the performance gaps identified.

There are many change management frameworks that can be used by leaders to facilitate the change process. However, it is not just the *process* of change that is important, as leaders need to ensure that they are supporting a *successful* change through effective leadership, knowledge sharing, communication, engagement, collaboration with relevant stakeholders, training, and assess-

UNFREEZE   CHANGE   REFREEZE

- Recognition of what   - Transition to a new   - Embed the changes
  needs to change   state   into the culture
- Create the need for   - Ensure open   - Ensure leadership,
  change   transparent   training and
- Ensure effective   communication   education
  leadership support   - Effective teamwork   - Applaud success
                              with engagement,
                              collaboration and
                              participation
                              throughout the
                              process of change

Source: Kurt Lewin (1951).

Figure 7.1   Lewin's change model

ment and evaluation.

Lewin's (1951) change model

Kurt Lewin is recognized as the father of change management with his three-stage change model: Unfreezing, Change, and Refreezing (Figure 7.1) or "Changing as Three Steps" (CATS).

Lewin's model starts with *unfreezing* focuses on recognition of the need to change, clearly defining the problem, and altering the factors that maintain the current state; *change* focuses on introducing new desired ways of doing things and the implementation of change; *refreezing* focuses on stabilizing the change within the organization and ensuring the new norm becomes part of the organizational culture. While Lewin's model focuses on the three steps it is important that leadership support and team engagement are demonstrated at each stage in order for the change to be accepted and become part of the new state. While Lewin's three-step model can be applied to most change situations, however,

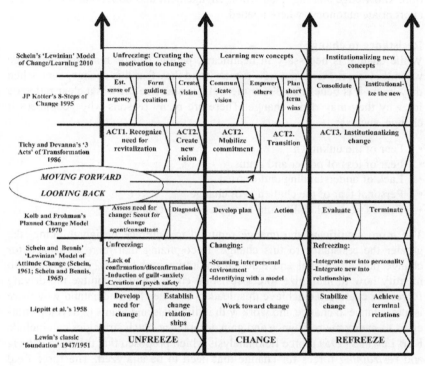

Source: Cummings et al. (2016: 42).

Figure 7.2   *CATS model*

change in healthcare is not an easy process.

There are many change models (some are outlined in Figure 7.2) and Lewin's three-step model has been the basis for the development of many other change models over the last seven decades. Cummings et al. (2016) clearly demonstrate in Figure 7.2 how a number of change models use the CATS model as their foundation.

The world of healthcare is now more complex and challenging than ever, requiring healthcare organizations to undertake immediate change if they are to continue to deliver high standards of healthcare and manage Covid-19. Leaders need to drive this change and work with their teams to overcome resistance to change. The transformational style of leadership can positively impact organizational change and work to manage resistance to change. Transformational leadership supports staff with open, transparent communication, knowledge sharing, teamwork, engagement and collaboration, allowing appropriate autonomy where needed.

Resistance to change

While change is necessary in healthcare, people can be resistant to change when they are moving into new territory and they fear this change, even when they know it is beneficial. From the staff perspective there is a clear rationale for why they may resist change. There are many reasons why people resist change, such as:

* Fear of the unknown
* Fear of loss of power and status
* Lack of understanding and/or trust
* Personal fear of the challenge of change
* Fear of personal ability and competencies to change.

The more significant the change required to embrace design thinking, the greater the resistance to this change. Recognizing that there is a need for change due to internal and external environmental factors, leaders need to identify how to minimize forces resisting change and maximize the driving forces for change. To achieve this, leaders first need to understand why there is a resistance to change and work with individuals and teams to develop strategies to overcome resistance and gain acceptance. Such strategies can include Kurt Lewin's (1951) force field analysis which proposed that there are *driving* and *restraining* forces for change that need to be analyzed. The force field analysis can be undertaken to identify how significant the proposed change is, and predict the success of the change. Driving forces positively influence the situation toward change; restraining forces negatively influence the situation, making it difficult to progress change (Figure 7.3). Equilibrium is achieved when the driving and restraining forces are equal. To implement a change, leaders need to analyze the driving and restraining forces. The strength of the arrows will demonstrate which forces on the driving and restraining side are stronger than others. This provides clarity of the forces that influence the change, and by addressing the restraining forces, the driving forces should be strong enough to support the desired change. Successful change can be achieved by developing the driving forces, or reducing or removing the restraining forces. The process of change should be monitored and evaluated to ensure that the desired change is being achieved.

Change models and strategies play a significant role in supporting the change. However, the leader's approach is fundamental in facilitating successful change through transparent communication, engagement, collaboration, participation, negotiation, education, and, when necessary, ensuring appropriate training is provided. This will provide individuals with clarity on:

(i)   Why change is required
(ii)   What change is required

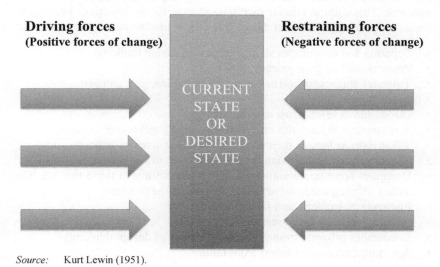

Driving forces
(Positive forces of change)

CURRENT STATE OR DESIRED STATE

Restraining forces
(Negative forces of change)

Source: Kurt Lewin (1951).

Figure 7.3   Force field analysis

(iii)   How change can be achieved
(iv)   What role each team member plays in the change process.

Effective leaders understand the feelings and emotions that change incurs. Therefore leaders need to ensure psychological safety to drive action towards innovation. When people feel part of this process, have clarity on what is required, and are familiar with design thinking, it can then be effectively adopted to find viable solutions to problems.

Leadership and Organizational Culture

The overall culture needs to embrace design thinking at all levels. When the organizational culture has a clear vision, encourages innovation and supports staff in their endeavors, demonstrating characteristics such as trust, respect and compassion in their people, as well as facilitating creativity, they are better able to engage in the development of design thinking. An organizational culture of this nature in healthcare provides a conducive environment for healthcare professionals and staff to take ownership of their positions and do everything to deliver the highest standard of care and seek ways to continue to develop this standard of care. Leaders need to support this culture and allow their team members to take chances and move forward without a guarantee of the outcome. This cultural climate facilitates change for the benefit of healthcare. Leadership characteristics for design thinking in healthcare organizations are:

- Supports and encourages staff to engage in design thinking;
- Protects staff on their journey;
- Tolerates and accepts mistakes as part of the learning process;
- Leads by example;
- Builds and develops trust among staff;
- Advises staff in line with core organizational goals and objectives;
- Takes risks as long as they do not put people's lives in jeopardy;
- Shares a vision and passion for the betterment of healthcare;
- Delegates appropriate autonomy and responsibility to those that are best suited with required competencies to address the problem;
- Encourages, supports and facilitates creativity;
- Actively engages in the search for new ideas;
- Encourages progress through all the elements of design thinking;
- Applauds success and learns from failure.

EFFECTIVE LEADERSHIP AND DESIGN THINKING IN HEALTHCARE

Design thinking is focused on finding the best patient-centered solutions, and designers aim to go to a deeper level of empathy to achieve an in-depth understanding of end users' needs by being objective and endeavoring to see the situation from their perspective. Through the design process they need to focus on patients' needs first and foremost. They need to be clear on what they are aiming to achieve and for what patient cohort they are aiming to achieve it. Within healthcare, effective leaders have the drive and motivation to make a difference that will change the world of healthcare for the better. Leaders need to be supportive of the elements of design thinking and how iterative, prototyping and testing processes bring about numerous ideas, many of which are not viable as they proceed to find the best solution. Leaders need to work with healthcare professionals so they engage in the process with clarity on how their design can impact patients. Leaders need to actively support and facilitate the process and support staff through the challenges of design thinking when things do not go to plan. Failure is part of the journey and provides the greatest learning for progress to be made. It is those challenges that can provide opportunities to delve deeper into the discovery of new opportunities for innovation.

Patients can, for example, experience fear, confusion, concern, anxiety, discomfort and embarrassment as they go through diagnosis, assessment, and treatment. What the medical professional believes is helping to treat or cure the patient can be different from the patient's experience and feelings. It is not just about the destination but the journey patients are brought through to reach that destination, and providing them with the best possible experience as they go on that journey. Therefore, design thinking provides a deep understanding from the patient's perspective and helps develop better solutions. Leaders need to create an openness to recognize existing problems as opportunities for innovation and support design thinking as part of this process. Leaders need to have an overarching view of the design thinking project and engage with their team, particularly at times when things are not going to plan and anxiety levels can elevate due to risk of failure. They must continue to support, motivate and encourage the team at times of distress while also working with them on alternative options to move the project forward. Effective leaders need to find the right balance so they are proactively working with the team during challenging times but can also stand back and let the team flourish when they are achieving their goals. Leading design thinking projects in healthcare is particularly challenging, but the value it can in time generate for patients makes it all worth the journey.

SUMMARY

Design thinking is an innovative approach to problem solving that is solution-focused. The focus is on empathy which drives a more patient-centered approach to healthcare. Through design thinking, new approaches to diagnosis, assessment, treatment and monitoring can be achieved that can benefit patients and help improve healthcare. Design thinking can benefit the field of healthcare by transforming the experience and delivery of care with a patient-centered focus that provides viable and effective interventions to address current and future problems and challenges. By involving patients and relevant stakeholders in defining the problem and developing solutions, there will be greater willingness and acceptance to embrace design thinking and the change it brings to the organization. For many healthcare organizations, design thinking brings about change and effective leadership is imperative in bringing design thinking to fruition. It is through leadership, staff engagement and empowerment, and openness to knowledge sharing and communication that will support each stage of the process of change. Leaders must empower their team to be creative and innovative in how they address problems so they can improve patient outcomes, the overall healthcare system and contribute to society at large. The leadership of design thinking and how this process is managed will strongly influence its success or failure.

REFERENCES

Bason C. and Austin, R.D. (2019). The right way to lead design thinking. *Harvard Business Review* (March–April). https://hbr.org/2019/03/the-right-way-to-lead-design-thinking.
Cummings, S., Bridgman, T. and Brown, K.G. (2016). Unfreezing change as three steps: rethinking Kurt Lewin's legacy for change management. *Human Relations* 69(1), 33–60.
Lewin, K. (1951). *Field Theory in Social Sciences*. New York: Harper & Row.

Suggested Reading

Altman, M., Huang, T.T. and Breland, J.Y. (2018). Design thinking in healthcare: systematic review. *Preventing Chronic Disease: Public Health Research, Practice, and Policy* 15, 180128. http://dx.doi.org/10.5888/pcd15.180128external icon.

In this article, the authors' objective is to determine how design thinking has been used in health care and whether it is effective. The authors collected data on target users, health conditions, intervention, design thinking approach, study design or sample, and health outcomes. Twenty-four studies using design thinking were included across 19 physical health conditions, two mental health conditions, and three systems processes. Twelve were successful, 11 reported mixed success, and one was not successful. All four studies comparing design thinking interventions to traditional interventions showed greater satisfaction, usability and effectiveness.

Bason C., and Austin, R.D. (2019). The right way to lead design thinking. *Harvard Business Review* (March–April). https://hbr.org/2019/03/the-right-way-to-lead-design-thinking

In this article, the authors studied almost two dozen major design-thinking projects within large private- and public-sector organizations in five countries and found that effective leadership is critical to their success. They focused not on how individual design teams did their work, but on how the senior executives who commissioned the work interacted with and enabled it. The authors assert that those who are unfamiliar with design thinking need guidance and support from leaders to navigate the landscape and channel their reactions to the approach. The authors have identified practices that executives can use to stay on top of such innovation projects and lead them to success.

Kim, S.H., Myers, C.G. and Allen, L. (2017). Healthcare providers can use design thinking to improve patient experiences. *Harvard Business Review*, August 31. https://hbr.org/2017/08/health-care-providers-can-use-design-thinking-to-improve -patient-experiences.

In this article, the authors discuss how design thinking has taken hold in healthcare, leading to the development of new products and improved design of spaces. Yet according to the authors it remains underused in addressing other important challenges, such as patient transportation, communication issues between clinicians and patients, and differential treatment of patients due to implicit bias, to name just a few. If more leaders embrace design thinking, they can leverage a deeper understanding of patients to solve such problems, achieving better clinical outcomes, improved patient experience, and lower costs along the way.

Roberts, J.P., Fisher, T.R., Trowbridge, M.J. and Bent, C. (2015). A design thinking framework for healthcare management and innovation. *Healthcare* 4(1), 11–14.

In this article, the authors lay out how design thinking applies to healthcare challenges and how systems might utilize this proven and accessible problem-solving process. The authors show how design thinking can foster new approaches to complex and persistent healthcare problems through human-centered research, collective and diverse teamwork and rapid prototyping. They introduce the core elements of design thinking for a healthcare audience and show how it can supplement current healthcare management, innovation and practice.

Thakur, A., Soklaridis, S., Crawford, A., Mulsant, B. and Sockalingam, S. (2020). Using rapid design thinking to overcome COVID-19 challenges in medical education. *Academic Medicine: Journal of the Association of American Medical Colleges* 96(1), 56–61. https://doi.org/10.1097/ACM.0000000000003718.

In this article, the authors discuss how design thinking offers creative and innovative solutions to emergent complex problems, including those related to training and patient care that have arisen as a result of the Covid-19 pandemic. They discuss how design thinking can accelerate the development and implementation of solution prototypes through a process of inspiration, ideation and implementation.

Valentine, L., Kroll, T., Bruce, F., Lim, C. and Mountain, R. (2017). Design thinking for social innovation in healthcare. *The Design Journal* 20(6), 755–74. https://doi .org/10.1080/14606925.2017.1372926.

In this article, the authors propose a strategic framework for fostering a culture of design thinking for social innovation in healthcare. Drawing upon the theory of design (and its thinking), in conjunction with global and national healthcare strategies and policies, the authors critically reflect on pedagogical approaches for enhancing the curriculum in design as a means of discussing the need for new thinking in health.

PART IV

Making it all happen: a future-oriented mindset

8.   Women in leadership, innovation and entrepreneurship in healthcare

QUESTIONS

Why are women still underrepresented in senior and executive leadership roles in healthcare organizations? What are the key barriers for women to obtain senior leadership roles and how can they be more effectively addressed? What is the "impostor phenomenon" and how can women overcome such a phenomenon? How can leaders effectively support women to progress and advance to more senior leadership roles and embrace innovation and entrepreneurship within the field of healthcare? What is the meaning and value of "inclusivity" in healthcare organizations?

INTRODUCTION

Healthcare is one of the largest sectors in the world. There is a need for senior leadership, innovation and entrepreneurship to have a greater level of gender diversity in today's healthcare workforce. Although women hold leadership roles in healthcare, their number and the accessibility they have to more senior leadership roles is not equitable. Greater attention is being given to the disparity of women in leadership roles in the global healthcare system. The global healthcare workforce is over 43 million (WHO, 2017), which is represented by 70 percent of women (Boniol et al., 2019). While women represent a strong majority of healthcare professionals and are successful at supervisory and middle management level, there is minimal female representation in senior and board level leadership roles. This underrepresentation of women in senior leadership roles within healthcare is global. Hence the issue is not about the education, training and recruitment of "women in healthcare" but the limited number of "women in leadership" in healthcare. While data show there has been an increase in women in leadership roles, they consistently indicate inadequate gender parity in leadership roles, particularly among the more senior leadership roles in healthcare. This disparity at senior level is questionable given all the changes, advancements and developments that are taking place in the field of healthcare. There is a need to address those gender inequalities and discrimination, and support women with equal opportunities in professional development and leadership roles (Boniol et al., 2019).

Women need to be empowered to engage in healthcare innovations and entrepreneurial activities in their role as healthcare professionals. Healthcare organizations need to motivate, support and facilitate women to advance and develop in their careers through equal opportunities for leadership roles and engagement in innovations that advance and develop the field of healthcare and lead the world to a more equitable and innovative healthcare system.

The purpose of this chapter is to examine women in leadership, innovation and entrepreneurship in healthcare. Women in leadership in healthcare, the barriers they may experience, and how they can work to overcome those barriers is discussed. This is followed by a focus on successful behaviors for women in leadership roles. The "impostor phenomenon" and how to address and overcome its challenges is examined. Following a discussion on women in innovation and entrepreneurship in healthcare, the importance of appropriate leadership to support women in innovation and entrepreneurship in healthcare is presented. The final section examines the importance of inclusivity in healthcare organizations with specific focus on gender diversity. The final section of the chapter presents a summary.

WOMEN IN LEADERSHIP IN HEALTHCARE

There is growing focus and discussion around equity for women in leadership roles. While a certain level of progress has been made in the advancement of women in leadership roles, more is required to achieve greater equity for women to advance and progress the corporate ladder. This inequity is highlighted particularly in the field of healthcare where women represent 70 percent of the global healthcare workforce yet are significantly underrepresented when it comes to holding senior leadership roles. It is recognized that the majority of senior leadership roles are held by men; however, research shows that it is women who have what is required to effectively lead (Chamorro-Premuzic and Gallop, 2020). As of 2015, almost half of all doctors across OECD countries are women, with the exception of Japan and Korea (20% female doctors), and Latvia and Estonia (over 70% female doctors) (OECD, 2017). Between 2000 and 2015 there has been an increase in the number of female doctors in all OECD countries, which grew to 38 percent in 2000 and 46 percent by 2015, and is continuing to grow (OECD, 2017). Yet, globally, women continue to be significantly underrepresented in leadership roles, experiencing many challenges that inhibit their career potential for advancement and development.

For healthcare to effectively transform and embrace innovation there is a need for a more equitable approach globally across healthcare systems for the inclusion of more women in board rooms and in senior leadership roles.

Having a greater gender balance in senior leadership roles can provide greater diversity in mindsets and perspectives, and greater opportunity to synergize and contribute more innovative ideas. The inclusion of women in more senior leadership roles is of benefit to the individual women, their colleagues, healthcare organizations, patients, the profession as a whole, and society at large.

There is a need to support women equally in the advancement and development of their careers and provide them with equal opportunities as their male counterparts, ensuring the best person is selected for each specific leadership role. Equally, women need to be prepared to take on more senior leadership roles and proactively bring themselves forward in order to further advance the positive impact they can have on the healthcare sector. Women usually wait for an invitation from a more senior leader to validate their "readiness" to apply for a leadership role; however, in contrast, men are more likely to be self-confident that they are "sufficiently ready" to apply for a leadership role (Chyu et al., 2021). This is not advocating a divide between men and women but rather a recognition of the value both genders bring to healthcare and ensuring that there is a fair and transparent representation of both at board level and in senior leadership roles. The core objective is to ensure that gender does not predict accessibility to senior leadership roles, career advancement and development within the global field of healthcare.

Barriers for Women in Leadership in Healthcare

Women working globally in the complexity of healthcare systems experience many challenges and barriers as they strive for career advancement and development, most significantly when they are working toward more senior leadership roles. These challenges can be cultural, institutional and also on a wider global scale. The "glass ceiling," a phrase first introduced in the 1980s, refers to the invisible barriers that many women experience in their goal to progress up the corporate ladder to senior leadership and executive roles which the majority can only progress to a certain level before they experience numerous obstacles. The glass ceiling inhibits women as well as the healthcare organization and the wider healthcare system from achieving its full potential – for many women the glass ceiling can feel indestructible. The glass ceiling reduces the value that can be achieved through gender diversity in leadership roles. The traits that are so commonly encouraged in men are the same traits that can meet resistance when demonstrated by women.

There have been many studies focusing on the barriers women experience in pursuit of executive and senior leadership roles. Chisholm-Burns et al. (2017: 321) asserted that "such barriers include cultural biases and stereotypes, challenges involving work–life balance, and a lack of mentors and sponsors." The lack of mentors and sponsors for women at senior level can inhibit women from being supported to gain opportunities for growth and progression to more senior leadership roles. Mentoring is an important relationship between two people, where one is more experienced and can provide specific support to the other who has the potential to advance. It is appropriate that women leaders can mentor other women who are striving for more senior leadership roles. However, given the underrepresentation of women in more senior leadership roles, there is a clear absence of female role models which further challenges women that are seeking leadership roles.

A study undertaken by Kalaitzi et al. (2019) on women in leadership in healthcare in Greece and Malta found the following barriers in each country:

> Work/life balance (17%), lack of family (spousal, namely, husband, wife, partner, mate, significant other) support (12%), gender gap (10%), gender bias (8%) and lack of social support (6%) featured in Greek interviewees' experiences and perceptions across healthcare settings. The top-ranking barriers presented in Malta included work/life balance (13%), culture (12%), lack of family (spousal) support (11%), stereotypes (9%), gender bias and lack of social support both ranked at 6%. (Kalaitzi et al., 2019: 48)

Like most industries, more senior leadership roles within the field of healthcare require full commitment above and beyond the working day which can be a major challenge for many women who are trying to balance a working life and family responsibilities. Therefore, for many women, disparities may also exist in terms of the proportion of family responsibilities they have to provide in comparison to their male counterparts.

Overcoming the Barriers for Women in Leadership

Recognizing the barriers for women in leadership helps understand what actions are necessary in order to work toward overcoming those barriers and achieving greater parity. While breaking the glass ceiling is complex and challenging, it does need to be destroyed by women and for women. This can be achieved with the support of governments, employers, universities and women working together to overcome the barriers that are suppressing the progression of women in leadership. Governments have the power to promote gender equality and, when necessary, enforce policy and legislation to protect women from discrimination. Employers need to be actively committed to gender diversity and equity, and make this part of the organizational culture before any glass ceiling can be broken. Universities can promote gender diversity in their leadership programs that can create the women leaders of tomorrow today.

While it is challenging to face such barriers Chisholm-Burns et al. (2017) asserted the following strategies to overcome these barriers:

> interventions to reduce gender bias, leadership development programs, access to mentors and sponsors, and changes to family-related policies should be addressed on the individual, institution/employer, professional leadership/organization, and societal levels. (Chisholm-Burns et al., 2017: 321)

Greater objectivity, equity and fairness is required to remove the barriers that are so inhibiting to women as they strive for more senior leadership roles. Leadership development provides the necessary tools to advance and ensure that individuals have the ability to achieve a high standard of performance. Leadership development is important for the individual, the team and the organization, because developing and demonstrating personal leadership qualities and effective skills in working with and leading others benefits the entire organization. This should be equally provided to men and women that have the potential to advance to more senior leadership roles. Leadership development is important for organizational success and this success has the potential to be at a higher level when there is greater gender parity.

Women need to empower themselves and each other as they work toward achieving gender parity. Women can support each other by promoting each other's ideas. They can sponsor each other by sharing opportunities to maximize the overall benefit for the group by recognizing the core competencies of each other and synergize as a group to embrace opportunities and achieve equity as future leaders in healthcare.

While overcoming the barriers to achieve gender parity is challenging, it is realistically achievable given the caliber and expertise of women in healthcare. Both men and women need to support gender diversity and an equitable representation in senior leadership roles. Most significantly, healthcare systems and organizations need to be proactive by ensuring equitable representation of women in more senior leadership roles. They need to create a culture of inclusivity and incentivize mentorship so women are equally supported in their career advancement and development, and there is equal opportunity for senior leadership roles so the best candidate is selected for each role.

Women in Leadership: Behaviors for Success

Successful women that are working to advance their way up the corporate ladder have to be strategic and at times take themselves out of their comfort zone. Women need to push forward, taking every opportunity that gets their work and contribution recognized by senior stakeholders and the wider healthcare community. It is the combined value of embracing those opportunities with perseverance and commitment that works toward longer-term success and development.

Women need to be focused on where they are and where they want to go in their career. Women are recognized to leverage traits such as compassion and empathy, which are key to the field of healthcare. Yet women have limited success in obtaining more senior leadership roles in healthcare. When given the opportunity there is no reason why women cannot compete equally for more senior leadership roles. Reports show that early in the pandemic the mortality rates from Covid-19 were lower in countries with female political leaders, who developed an effective national response. While there are some variations, in general women were faster to lockdown the country and got people on board in how they expressed compassion and empathy toward the challenges people were experiencing. While there are highly successful women in leadership there are more women that have high potential but are not getting the opportunity to excel. Women need to become their own best advocate, confidently promote themselves and their competencies, and clearly state what they want to achieve. The following behaviors are important for women to advance in their careers:

- Strengths: Know your strengths and utilize them to seek further opportunities that demonstrate the value you continue to bring to the organization. Women need to have self-belief to fully realize their strengths and reach their potential.
- Competence and Confidence: Demonstrate competence, a positive attitude, self-assurance and confidence in what you do and can do. Promote yourself and your knowledge, skills and abilities with confidence, demonstrating expertise, leadership, intelligence, empathy, compassion and integrity.
- Network: Instrumental to leadership and leadership development is being a member of key networks because cultivating strong internal and external networks can support career advancement. Networks can generate many important opportunities in terms of relationship development, gaining recognition and creditability within your specialism and potential promotional opportunities. Both men and women need to have equal access to the key networks that can support them as they strive for senior leadership roles.
- Strategic Mindset: Demonstrate the ability to think strategically with an open and objective mindset, which is focused on moderate risk taking and innovation, with emphasis on the short, medium and long term.
- Career Progression: Have a realistic plan for career progression, and engage with management to get the support needed to progress and advance to the next level.
  - Coaching: Engaging with a coach can really support progression. With a coach a development plan can be designed recognizing core strengths

and identifying ways to best leverage those strengths while also identifying weaknesses and ways to address them.

Women globally across all sectors including healthcare struggle to obtain a senior leadership role and be part of the senior management team due to glass ceilings, competing goals and aspirations, and lack of support and guidance within the internal and external organization. Organizations need to be equitable and transparent in how the promotion process works. Leaders act as role models whose behavior is frequently imitated by their team members. Therefore, it is paramount for the organization to have a role model that will inspire and motivate staff to aspire to the highest standards of care, allowing their staff to advance and develop in their careers. Once the organization embraces equity, diversity and fairness they will select the best leader in terms of qualifications, competencies, experience and leadership style that will support the organizational culture, thus creating more opportunities for women in leadership, which in turn will lead the world to further enhance the delivery of healthcare.

THE IMPOSTOR PHENOMENON

The impostor phenomenon (also referred to as impostor syndrome) is a concept defined by Aubeeluck et al. (2016: 104) as "an 'internal experience of intellectual phoniness' exhibited by individuals who appear successful to others, but internally feel incompetent." This is associated with intelligent high-achievers, predominately women and those that strive for perfectionism. Men are more likely to take ownership of their success whereas women are more likely to associate their success with external factors such as luck. A study undertaken by Exley and Kessler (2019) on 1,500 workers found a substantial gender gap in self-promotion, with men rating their performance 33 percent higher than women that performed equally. These findings are concerning, in that women offer a weaker evaluation of their past performance and future ability, minimizing their achievements in comparison to men. Women need to overcome their fear and apprehension of self-promotion, recognize their competencies and values, and emphasize their contribution to innovation.

The challenges for those that experience impostor phenomenon is that, notwithstanding their high academic and professional achievements, they do not believe they are intelligent and feel they are fooling those that think otherwise. No matter what they achieve it does not change their impostorism. Hence, it is evident among healthcare professionals when they have an inability to recognize their own achievements and feel they are a fraud within their profession. Impostor phenomenon is more common than many would think and it is not limited to any specific medical profession or speciality.

The impact of impostor phenomenon on individuals can be significant, resulting in overworking and studying to address their perceived competency gaps or limitations. This can result in increased anxiety, depression, fatigue, burnout, lower job satisfaction and reduced job performance, withdrawal from colleagues, and lack of motivation for career advancement and development. Furthermore, impostor phenomenon can result in individuals holding back from career advancement opportunities which, in turn, is also being recognized as a factor for the limited number of women holding senior leadership roles in healthcare.

Overcoming Impostor Phenomenon

Impostor phenomenon is virtually ubiquitous, impacting many professions. Individuals must recognize the impact of impostor phenomenon and take action to manage this by building their confidence, enhancing emotional health and well-being, and working to mitigate potential negative consequences. High-achievers usually underestimate their ability and performance whereas low-achievers usually overestimate their ability and performance. When women underestimate their skills and abilities they are impeding themselves from pursuing leadership roles. While everyone doubts their ability at times, women are more likely to allow their doubts to prevent them from moving forward in comparison to men.

It is important for high-achieving women not to allow their thoughts to control them and to take a more objective view of their core competencies and work to develop their confidence and personal and professional growth. They must make a strong commitment to change, and change the internal dialogue communicating positively to themselves where they recognize, acknowledge and accept what they have achieved, and that they are both "intelligent" and the best person for the job they hold. In doing this continuously over time they will transition and start to believe in their competencies and overcome the burden of feeling a fraud within their profession. This will allow them to be more engaged in their accomplishments and advance in their personal and professional development.

Leaders need to recognize and manage impostor phenomenon as it will not disappear by being ignored. Impostor phenomenon can lower self-esteem and result in poor performance. Impostor phenomenon must be recognized at senior management level and appropriate support must be in place for leaders at all levels to work to address and alleviate it. Leaders can develop a work environment that supports individuals in their endeavors and builds confidence in individuals' competencies. This can be done through peer support, mentoring and coaching that provides positive and constructive feedback that allows individuals to develop their strengths and grow. Likewise, it is also imperative that leaders model appropriate behavior, demonstrating competence and confidence with the ability to manage the challenges within healthcare, address errors and take appropriate corrective action in the best interest of patient care.

WOMEN IN INNOVATION AND ENTREPRENEURSHIP IN HEALTHCARE

The field of healthcare is surrounded by creative minds that need to be nurtured and developed to fully realize their potential to lead the world to better health. However, a gender imbalance of women in innovation and entrepreneurship in healthcare creates a gap in the development of more diverse innovations. This is a loss for women to professionally advance and progress the field of healthcare and a loss for society in terms of the value such innovations can generate. In the era of Covid-19, innovation is front and center to healthcare, and women need to be empowered and supported to develop and drive initiatives that generate new innovations in healthcare, which will also help them advance and develop in their careers. This requires equal opportunities and access to resources as well as flexibility and support to pursue viable opportunities. This helps inspire women, promotes greater diversity, and increases the number of women that explore and exploit innovations in healthcare. Women that engage in innovation and entrepreneurship add a new mindset and help promote innovations across many diverse areas of healthcare including a greater focus on female health issues and concerns. This helps push for innovations beyond what was considered possible.

Over recent decades there has been an explosion of innovations in many areas of healthcare, for example gastrointestinal endoscopy and robotic surgery, all of which have been developed to improve quality of life through more innovative approaches. Innovations in healthcare need to be bold, forthcoming and action oriented. They should be clearly focused through every stage of the innovation process from idea through to implementation of the product, service or process. Women need to engage in this process by utilizing their competencies and day-to-day experience of clinical practice to develop innovations that bring new products, services or processes to market or develop innovations specific to their current healthcare role. As the field of healthcare faces major challenges to improve quality and safety, increase accessibility, increase efficiency and effectiveness, and reduce costs, innovation and entrepreneurship is paramount for all healthcare providers. Entrepreneurial women in healthcare can seek opportunities for innovations that can contribute to the transformation of healthcare.

Entrepreneurship in healthcare is particularly challenging due to the barriers and rigidity of the structure and culture of healthcare organizations. Overcoming those barriers can be achieved through effective leadership that supports and facilitates innovation and entrepreneurship among staff at all levels. Innovation and entrepreneurship in many cases is not gender-neutral, particularly in certain areas of science and technology. There are many reasons for gender disparities for women in innovation and entrepreneurship (e.g., family responsibilities, diverse career aspirations, time due to current work challenges, lack of appropriate mentorship, cultural stereotypes, lack of funding, gender biases, professional isolation and poor leadership). Some are within the control of each individual; however, there are many institutional and societal factors outside the control of any women that need to be addressed nationally and globally. Hence, more women in innovation and entrepreneurship would substantially increase the degree to which innovation occurs in healthcare, and this in turn would increase the number of successful innovations. Supporting more women in entrepreneurship is paramount to explore and exploit more viable innovations in healthcare. Therefore leaders must equally motivate and support both men and women in their entrepreneurial endeavors.

Leading Women in Innovation and Entrepreneurship

Within healthcare, innovation and entrepreneurship is the result of individuals that develop new ideas and new ways of doing things, bringing about change and taking moderate risks to achieve greater organizational success and generate patient value. Healthcare innovators and entrepreneurs seek and pursue opportunities with perseverance and passion, demonstrating flexibility, confidence and commitment. For this to be achieved, there needs to be strong and committed leadership to build an environment that drives innovation and entrepreneurship, particularly among all staff while encouraging women to boost creativity and implement innovations within their specialism. While the majority of ideas generated will not lead to a patent or implementation it is about the passion to make a difference, with the patient being the core focus for the innovation. Leaders that can develop a culture that supports all staff equally to generate ideas with optimal patient value and take moderate risks that will not in any way harm the patient are more likely to foster innovative behavior among staff.

Leaders need to recognize and appreciate the distinctive values that men and women bring to the organization and utilize those differences to bring a higher standard of innovations that will generate higher quality healthcare. Women innovators and entrepreneurs in healthcare are likely to experience gender bias. However, the more leaders encourage innovation and entrepreneurship equally among genders the more effective they will be at motivating staff to participate and develop viable innovations. Innovation and entrepreneurship should be deeply embedded in the culture of every healthcare organization. Creating a culture of diversity, equity and fairness, where every woman believes they have equal opportunity to contribute and are equally rewarded and encouraged in their entrepreneurial endeavors, will increase the number of viable innovations for the organization. Leaders that support, facilitate and empower women as leaders and role models will actively engage more women as innovators in healthcare. Furthermore, this will allow women to become significant influencers of innovations within their specialism and develop the path for more women to engage in innovation.

INCLUSIVITY IN HEALTHCARE ORGANIZATIONS

Gender balance is important for individuals, organizations, patients and society at large; substantial benefits can be gained from gender parity in healthcare. Healthcare organizations need to be inclusive to all staff and ensure diverse, inclusive leadership at all levels in healthcare organizations globally. There needs to be clear and respectful boundaries where there is a fair, consistent and equitable work and workload among men and women. Inclusive healthcare organizations must work to achieve the following:

- Rules, policies and procedures that are all-inclusive and represent all staff at all levels.
- Leadership styles that inspire and motivate staff to be their best, driving innovation and facilitating equal opportunities for career progression.
- Empowering all staff in their roles and supporting them to go beyond their role to contribute to shape the future of healthcare by utilizing their expertise and being innovative and entrepreneurial.
- A culture of equity, fairness and transparency where there is equal opportunity and respect for all staff, with zero tolerance for any bias or prejudice.
- Everyone has a voice and is listened to and heard with empathy, compassion and respect.
- A future-oriented mindset that embraces change that will lead the world to better health.

The majority of healthcare staff are women, yet the number of women obtaining senior leadership roles is significantly disproportionate. Healthcare is facing unprecedented challenges and there is a need for more healthcare professionals that can change the world of healthcare through their expertise and ability to engender innovation. Therefore, women cannot be left behind in obtaining senior leadership roles. While healthcare is always uncertain, the Covid-19 pandemic has escalated this uncertainty at an exponential level with a greater need for more transformational leadership, innovation and entrepreneurship to manage this turbulence. According to a study by Gipson et al.

(2017: 48) their "findings indicate that women leaders tend to be more likely to manifest a democratic style and elements of transformational leadership than their male peers." The leadership gap for women holding senior roles is evident and can be addressed by engaging the transformational leadership attributes and innovations that women can bring to senior leadership roles that can lead healthcare into the future.

Globally across the field of healthcare the culture needs to change by developing a clear roadmap for the career development and advancement of women to ensure a more equitable representation of women in leadership roles. The current healthcare challenges can be better addressed through inclusivity and gender diversity by increasing the number of women in senior leadership roles which can further support the development of innovation and entrepreneurship to provide a significant impact that can further work to generate greater patient care.

SUMMARY

The field of healthcare needs to focus on equity, fairness and transparency for the most talented leaders and those with the highest potential to hold the most senior leadership roles. Gender diversity provides greater opportunity for healthcare staff and the healthcare organization to achieve its potential. Gender disparity in leadership, innovation and entrepreneurial opportunities is not serving healthcare and has to change. It is time to break down barriers and lead the way forward for women to have equal opportunities in leadership, innovation and entrepreneurship in healthcare. The Covid-19 pandemic shows us what healthcare globally can achieve when faced with an unprecedented crisis; there is an opportunity to maintain this momentum and stimulate innovative ideas that can address the challenges and transform healthcare.

The impostor phenomenon among healthcare professionals, particularly women, also needs to be addressed. Leaders need to work with their team to help them develop confidence in their competencies and reduce the risk of impostor phenomenon and the negative implications it has on the individual, their work performance, the organization and patients. This in turn should help more women challenge the status quo and push forward to engage in innovation and entrepreneurship within their specialism and, furthermore, break the glass ceiling to achieve equal opportunities in obtaining senior and board-level leadership roles in healthcare.

The question is how "healthy" are healthcare organizations? To be a healthcare provider they need to create a "healthy work environment" for all staff. This also requires a focus on encouraging staff to have self-compassion and self-care, which in turn allows individuals to provide better patient care. Strategies need to be developed in healthcare organizations to support women to advance to senior leadership roles and this mindset needs to be incorporated into the organizational culture. This is paramount to ensure a more equitable, innovative, entrepreneurial and sustainable future with excellence in patient care across all healthcare services. Furthermore, a more equitable gender balance at senior level allows greater unilization of the core competencies, diverse perspectives and expertise that can be critical to the development of innovation in healthcare.

REFERENCES

Aubeeluck, A., Stacey, G. and Stupple, E.J.N. (2016). Do graduate entry nursing students experience 'Impostor Phenomenon'?: an issue for debate. *Nurse Education in Practice* 19, 104–6.

Boniol, M., McIsaac, M., Xu, L., Wuliji, T., Diallo, K. and Campbell, J. (2019). Gender equity in the health workforce: analysis of 104 countries. Health Workforce Working Paper 1. Geneva: World Health Organization; 2019 (WHO/HIS/HWF/Gender/WP1/2019.1). Licence: CC BY-NC-SA 3.0 IGO.

Chamorro-Premuzic, T. and Gallop, C. (2020). 7 leadership lessons men can learn from women. *Harvard Business Review.* https://hbr.org/2020/04/7-leadership-lessons-men-can-learn-from-women.

Chisholm-Burns, M.A., Spivey, C.A., Hagemann, T. and Josephson, M.A. (2017). Women in leadership and the bewildering glass ceiling. *American Journal of Health-System Pharmacy* 74, 312–24.

Chyu, J., Peters, C.E., Nicholson, T.M., Dai, J.C., Taylor, J., Garg, T., Smith, A.B., Porten, S.P., Greene, K., Browning, N., Harris, E., Sutherland, S.E. and Psutka, S.P. (2021). Women in leadership in urology: the case for increasing diversity and equity. *Urology* 150, 16–24.

Exley, C. and Kessler, J. (2019). Why don't women self-promote as much as men? *Harvard Business Review.* December. https://hbr.org/2019/12/why-dont-women-self-promote-as-much-as-men.

Gipson, A.N., Pfaff, D.L., Mendelsohn, D.B., Catenacci, L.T. and Burke, W.W. (2017). Women and leadership: selection, development, leadership style, and performance. *Journal of Applied Behavioral Science* 53(1), 32–65.

Kalaitzi, S., Czabanowska, K., Azzopardi-Muscat, N., Cuschieri, L., Petelos, E., Papadakaki, M. and Babich, S. (2019). Women, healthcare leadership and societal culture: a qualitative study. *Journal of Healthcare Leadership* 11, 43–59.

OECD (2017). Gender equality: women make up most of the health sector workers but they are under-represented in high-skilled jobs. http://www.oecd.org/gender/data/women-make-up-most-of-the-health-sector-workers-but-they-are-under-represented-in-high-skilled-jobs.htm.

WHO [World Health Organization] (2017). Health employment and economic growth: an evidence base. https://www.who.int/hrh/resources/WHO-HLC-Report_web.pdf.

Suggested Reading

Armstrong, M.J. and Shulman, L.M. (2019). Tackling the impostor phenomenon to advance women in neurology. *Neurology Clinical Practice* 9(2), 155–9.

In this article, the authors' review highlights recent literature on gender differences in neurology, the definition of the impostor phenomenon, and research on the impostor phenomenon in academic medicine. Approaches for managing the impostor phenomenon are described including personal, mentoring and institutional strategies.

Kalaitzi, S., Czabanowska, K., Azzopardi-Muscat, N., Cuschieri, L., Petelos, E., Papadakaki, M., and Babich, S. (2019). Women, healthcare leadership and societal culture: A qualitative study. *Journal of Healthcare Leadership*, 11, 43–59. https://doi.org/10.2147/JHL.S194733

In this article, the authors aim to assess empirically gendered barriers to women's leadership in healthcare through the lens of sociocultural characteristics. The comparative study was conducted in Greece and Malta. Findings unveiled underlying interactions among gender, leadership and countries' sociocultural contexts, which may elucidate the varying degrees of strength of norms and barriers embedded in a society's egalitarian practices.

Kalaitzi, S., Czabanowska, K., Fowler-Davis, S., and Brand, H. (2017). Women leadership barriers in healthcare, academia and business. *Equality, Diversity and Inclusion* 36(5), 457–74. https://doi.org/10.1108/EDI-03-2017-0058.

In this article, the authors map the barriers to women leadership across healthcare, academia and business, and identify barriers' prevalence across sectors. A barriers thematic map, with quantitative logic, and a prevalence chart have been developed, with the aim to uncover inequalities and provide orientation to develop inclusion and equal opportunity strategies within different work environments.

Moyer, C.A., Abedini, N.C., Youngblood, J., Talib, Z., Jayaraman, T., Manzoor, M., Larson, H.J., Garcia, P.J., Binagwaho, A., Burke, K.S. and Barry, M. (2018). Advancing women leaders in global health: getting to solutions. *Annals of Global Health* 84(4), 743–52. https://doi.org/10.9204/aogh.2384.

In this article, the authors aim to elucidate prevailing attitudes, perceptions, and beliefs of women and men regarding opportunities and barriers for women's career advancement, as well as what can be done to address barriers going forward. This is a convergent mixed-methods, cross-sectional, anonymous, online study of participants. 405 participants responded: 96.7 percent were female, 61.6 percent were aged 40 or under, and 64.0 percent were originally from high-income countries. Leading barriers are lack of mentorship, challenges of balancing work and home, gender bias, and lack of assertiveness/confidence.

Rajan, E. (2020). Women in innovation in endoscopy: pitfalls and tips for success. *Techniques and Innovations in Gastrointestinal Endoscopy*. https://doi.org/10.1016/j.tige.2020.11.002

In this article, the author discusses how disruptive innovation in gastrointestinal endoscopy pushes us to imagine beyond the bounds of possibilities. Strong and committed leadership is vital to building an environment that supports physician-innovators with specific strategies to boost creativity and implement new ideas. With increasing gender balance in medical schools and increasing female gastroenterology trainees, women will continue to be significant influencers on the practice of endoscopy. Empowering women of today as leaders and role models will engage more women as future innovators in gastrointestinal endoscopy.

Yount, K.M., Cheong, Y.F., Miedema, S.S., Chen, J.S., Menstell, E., Maxwell, L., Ramakrishnan, U., Clark, C.J., Rochat, R. and del Rio, C. (2020). Gender equality in global health leadership: cross-sectional survey of global health graduates. *Global Public Health* 15(6), 852–64. https://doi.org/10.1080/17441692.2019.1701057.

In this article, the authors survey graduates from one global health department. They compared women's and men's post-training career agency and global health employment and assessed whether gender gaps in training accounted for gender gaps in career outcomes. Master-of-Public-Health and mid-career-fellow alumni since 2010 received a 31-question online survey. Using logistic regression, the authors tested gender gaps in training satisfaction, career agency, and global health employment, unadjusted and adjusted for training received.

9. Human capital and the future impact of innovation and entrepreneurship on key stakeholders

QUESTIONS

Innovations in healthcare have exceeded our expectations; what future innovations in healthcare are most likely? What is the impact of human capital on innovation and entrepreneurship in future healthcare initiatives? What is the organizational culture to drive future innovations in healthcare organizations? What is the impact of innovation and entrepreneurship in healthcare on patients, clinicians and healthcare professionals, healthcare organizations and government? What actions do healthcare organizations need to undertake to ensure cybersecurity becomes an essential part of protecting the delivery of healthcare and patient data?

INTRODUCTION

In healthcare it is paramount to develop innovations that generate the greatest patient value and maintain the health of society. Healthcare has a direct impact on individuals' quality of life and well-being, through prevention or treatment of diseases or conditions. Major developments in new innovations have transformed the delivery of healthcare over the last few decades. The potential for new innovations in healthcare can take numerous forms including drug development, surgical advancement, new devices and diagnostics; additionally, new approaches to medical training and education, new approaches to patient education and engagement, and changes in the delivery of care represent infinite possibilities. However, at times, innovations resulting in major scientific advancements have been slow to be implemented by some healthcare organizations. Such scientifically proven medical advancements need to be embraced in order to increase efficiency and effectiveness in the delivery of high-quality patient care. While there are various reasons why some innovations are not implemented across certain healthcare organizations, healthcare professionals need to be objective in their evaluation of new innovations being brought forward within their specialism. Just because a certain drug, treatment, or diagnostic is effective does not mean that there cannot be other alternatives that are more effective.

The future of healthcare is upon us with major recent scientific advancements such as multiple Covid-19 vaccines and technological advancement in the growing field of digital healthcare technologies such as artificial intelligence (AI), virtual reality/augmented reality (VR/AR), 3D-printing, robotics, and genomic sequencing that can guide more personalized treatments. There is a continuous need for healthcare to develop and innovate to maintain the health and well-being of society. The future of healthcare will include further technological advancements, as technology is facilitating better patient engagement and ownership, and healthcare professionals need to embrace these technologies to stay ahead of their specialism now and in the future. Technology is revolutionizing the delivery of patient care. Such innovations need to incorporate greater security and protection for healthcare organizations and patients to minimize the risk of cyberattacks, something that is not always at the forefront of medical device innovation but is becoming a necessity due to cybercrime.

Medicine is continuing to advance and develop in many ways beyond what was imaginable just a few decades ago. The Covid-19 pandemic has put unprecedented demands on healthcare and in many cases stretched healthcare systems beyond capacity. However, the drive, motivation and urgent necessity has bought experts such as scientists, academics, healthcare professionals and pharmaceutical organizations to work at a pace never seen before to bring innovations in the form of multiple Covid-19 vaccines to market in record time. Healthcare has demonstrated resilience at a catastrophic time.

Innovation and entrepreneurship must continue beyond Covid-19 to address the challenges and the disruption to medicine and healthcare that will have implications for years to come. It is through healthcare innovations that we can have a healthcare system that provides the most reliable, timely and highest standard of quality and safety in the delivery of patient care. Healthcare organizations should aspire to achieve zero patient errors, and innovations should contribute to accelerating progress toward that fundamental goal.

The objective of this chapter is to examine human capital and the future impact and opportunities for innovation and entrepreneurship on key stakeholders in healthcare. The chapter commences with a discussion on the importance of human capital and the recruitment and retention of the right caliber of staff to ensure the delivery of the highest standard of care and drive innovation and entrepreneurship in healthcare into the future. A culture of innovation and entrepreneurship from the national and organizational perspectives is discussed and the benefits it generates for society. Following that, the interconnectivity and rapid global changes in the world of healthcare, the impact and opportunity for innovation and entrepreneurship on key stakeholders including patients, clinicians and healthcare professionals, healthcare organizations and governments is examined. In recognition of the vulnerability of healthcare systems and medical device innovations there is a discussion on innovation and cybersecurity in healthcare, with a focus on a more advanced and sophisticated security infrastructure to protect patients and society from the enormous risk and catastrophic disaster of such inhumane cyberattacks.

HUMAN CAPITAL: INNOVATION AND ENTREPRENEURSHIP

For the future sustainability of innovation and entrepreneurship in healthcare, the critical resource is *human capital*, because no healthcare organization can exist without the specialist, scientific and medical knowledge of its healthcare clinicians and scientists. Innovation and entrepreneurship cannot happen in any industry or sector without the expertise of people. Human capital can be defined as the "individual capabilities, knowledge, skill, and experience of the company's employees and managers, as they are relevant to the task at hand, as well as the capacity to add to this reservoir of knowledge, skills, and experience through individual learning" (Dess and Lumpkin, 2001: 26). The distinctiveness of human capital emerges from the fact that individuals cannot be separated from their core competencies and the values they bring to the organization. Human capital is unique to each healthcare organization and increases the organization's capabilities and reputation with the right caliber of staff. The knowledge within the organization resides in the human capital. Therefore human capital is invaluable to the field of healthcare with the expertise and competencies of the organization's human resources significantly contributing to generate greater patient value and desirable patient outcomes that are key to successful organizational performance and reputation.

The drive for innovation and entrepreneurship in healthcare is determined by how human capital is supported to embrace opportunities for innovation and entrepreneurship, and how successful the organization is in attracting and retaining high-caliber staff. Healthcare human capital is pivotal for innovation and entrepreneurship and needs to be able to think beyond the possible and advance, develop and implement innovations for the future of healthcare. Leaders that are transformational and entrepreneurial can effectively recruit and retain the right caliber of staff that will drive innovation throughout the organization. Healthcare organizations require effective leadership that can manage human capital in a way that facilitates opportunity exploration and exploitation to generate greater patient value. The challenge facing healthcare organizations today is dedicating time to recognizing the creative competencies of its human capital and supporting and facilitating those individuals and teams to explore and exploit these potential opportunities for the benefit of patients. Healthcare organizations generate patient value through their recruitment, selection, development and retention of human capital that can embrace innovation and entrepreneurship. Leaders need to recognize any gaps in human capital that need filling to facilitate greater innovations in healthcare. The development of human capital should be continuous to generate greater innovation and contribute new medical and scientific knowledge.

Recruitment and Retention of Human Capital

The recruitment and retention of the right caliber of clinicians and healthcare professionals that fits into the organizational culture is of critical importance for healthcare organizations. Human capital is a core asset for healthcare organizations to effectively treat and save patients' lives.

Absenteeism and staff turnover are very costly and have major implications on the quality and standard of patient care and satisfaction, and can inhibit organizational performance. The role and working conditions impact the level of individual job satisfaction that in turn can result in absenteeism, anxiety, stress, burnout and finally staff turnover. Even before the Covid-19 pandemic, clinician burnout was problematic and led to inferior patient care; the need to improve clinician well-being is a well-recognized problem. Since the Covid-19 pandemic, the risk of burnout is particularly problematic among healthcare professionals who have experienced the greatest challenges of their careers in their fight to treat and save lives. As a result, many are fatigued, stressed and experiencing burnout that could lead to them evaluating alternative career options. Healthcare organizations globally cannot afford to lose high-caliber expertise, particularly during and in the aftermath of a global pandemic. It is imperative that healthcare organizations sustain well-being and resilience among their workforce, and develop effective recruitment and retention processes in order to attract and retain the right caliber of healthcare staff that will emerge and grow within the organizational culture that is patient-centered, innovative and entrepreneurial.

There is no doubt that staff recruitment and retention will be a challenge for healthcare organizations today and into the future. Higher staff retention can be achieved by organizations that are focused on an entrepreneurial strategy compared to organizations that have a more conservative strategic approach (Haar and White, 2013). Therefore, when the healthcare organizational culture is focused on innovation and entrepreneurship, it creates a culture of cutting-edge medical and scientific advancements that should attract and retain staff, thus achieving competitiveness and a strong reputation in terms of delivery of best scientific patient care. This drives and motivates leaders and healthcare professionals to feel part of an organization that is making a difference and is contributing to the betterment of healthcare.

CULTURE OF INNOVATION AND ENTREPRENEURSHIP

A country's national culture significantly impacts the attitudes toward driving or stifling innovation and entrepreneurship. To change from conforming to creativity is challenging and requires long-term commitment and support to escalate innovation and entrepreneurship across all industries and in all forms of small, medium and large organizations. Governments need to show commitment and invest in innovation and entrepreneurship. Every country and culture is different and they have a different mindset and approach toward innovation and entrepreneurship that needs to be recognized by governments and policymakers to achieve growth and development. Successful healthcare innovations go beyond generating patient value to benefit healthcare professionals and providers in how they deliver care, to governments to provide more cost effective ways to diagnose and treat patients, to individuals that are supported in their innovative endeavors, and to society that benefits from excellence in healthcare. All of this is essential for the economic well-being of healthcare organizations and countries.

Innovation and entrepreneurship in healthcare organizations need to be embedded in the organizational culture. Developing and sustaining an innovative corporate culture is imperative for healthcare organizations to achieve long-term success in their delivery of care. Leaders must make every effort to create an innovative corporate culture that drives innovation and entrepreneurship into the future by engaging with internal and external collaborators and key stakeholders. There are some key elements that make a difference:

1. An inspirational and innovative vision driven by all leaders for high-quality delivery of patient care throughout the organization.
2. Translation of vision into realistic priorities that are patient-centered.
3. Alignment of goals at every level throughout the organization.
4. A culture of compassionate leadership behaviors that encourages staff to develop and implement new innovative ways of doing things for the betterment of patients.
5. Leaders need to create conditions that reinforce fundamental altruism and intrinsic motivation among healthcare staff.
6. Consistent style of leadership that drives innovation and entrepreneurship across the healthcare organization.
7. Leadership that is characterized by authenticity, openness, humility, compassion and appreciation, where everyone has a voice and innovation and entrepreneurship is encouraged at all levels.

There is a constant need for innovation in healthcare to be embedded in the organizational culture. Innovation needs to be incorporated at all levels from incremental to breakthrough as they all make an important contribution to advance and deliver the best patient outcome. We have seen how the development of single devices transforms patients' experience and the delivery of care, to more large-scale projects that transform treatment and the way in which treatment is delivered to patients. Healthcare leaders need to utilize their human capital and recruit and retain clinicians and healthcare professionals that will "fit" into the organizational culture, and strive to make healthcare better by creating a vision for innovation that will generate greater patient value. Innovation and entrepreneurship has a significant impact on key stakeholders that needs to be recognized as we strive to advance and develop the world of healthcare.

IMPACT AND OPPORTUNITY FOR INNOVATION AND ENTREPRENEURSHIP AMONG KEY STAKEHOLDERS

There are and will continue to be major demands on healthcare systems globally. Covid-19 has demonstrated the importance of revitalizing the healthcare system based on unpredictable healthcare needs that have placed most healthcare systems globally in a catastrophic situation. There are changes in demographics and epidemiological transition with additional pressure on hospital systems. The future of healthcare impacts everyone and there is a need to improve the quality and standard of care, accessibility to care, and ensure equity in the healthcare service. Globally, governments and public health leaders must focus on a patient-centered, needs-driven, innovative healthcare system that will lead the world to better health. Healthcare is not a luxury but a necessity that needs to be delivered to the highest standard.

Future innovation and entrepreneurship can continue to strengthen the global healthcare system and generate significant and sustained patient value. Innovation and entrepreneurship for sustainable development in the field of healthcare is paramount for key stakeholders and society at large. The continued exploration and exploitation of sustainable opportunities to advance the field of healthcare and succinctly address the needs of patients will continue to transform healthcare. Innovation in healthcare impacts everyone in one form or another at certain points in their lives and is therefore everyone's business.

Impact and Opportunity for Patients

Innovation is paramount for patients who are at their most vulnerable and in need of innovations in medicine and science that will provide greater chances of a cure or at least make their condition treatable and extend their quality of life. In any innovation in medicine it is important that the treatment is not worse than the disease, with severe and adverse side-effects that give a poor quality of life. Innovation in medicine and science needs to provide a higher quality of life and standard of care, ensuring better outcomes for patients. The more innovation there is in healthcare, the greater the competition between drugs, procedures and services; this in turn allows more options for clinicians in providing care to patients and most likely at a lower price.

Innovations in healthcare have the greatest impact on the end user who, in most situations, is the patient; for example, drug development, new vaccines, or wearable devices. Innovations in digital devices have been advanced to diagnose and treat illness and disease, support and facilitate the self-management of chronic diseases and conditions, and provide patients with control to monitor their functions and activities (Lupton, 2017). More than ever, patients are taking more control over their healthcare and are phenomenal influencers on the development of future innovations. Therefore the patient's experience can significantly contribute and drive innovation by revealing their experience, problems, concerns and side-effects that demand further advancements and new solutions.

The increase in internet accessibility among the population with smartphones, tablets and other electronic devices has opened up new ways for consultation between clinicians and patients. This allows patients to have virtual consultations in the safety, privacy and comfort of their own home or private space, without having to commute to the hospital or medical clinic or experience long waiting times.

In recent years, the internet of things (IoT) and, more specifically innovations in wearable devices, support and facilitate a more novel approach to monitor health conditions. Mobile electronic devices in healthcare such as smartphone applications have transformed the way clinicians and patients interact, and increases engagement through telemedicine. Both telemedicine and virtual appointments have escalated due to Covid-19 and are likely to continue beyond the pandemic as an effective way to address patient needs in a less onerous manner. Proactive healthcare professionals, healthcare providers and participative patients will engage together through telemedicine and virtual consultations. This new way of doing things will further contribute to the next generation of healthcare. Technological advancement will continue to shape the future of healthcare and empower patients to take more ownership of their care. Healthcare is now at a point where patients decide whether or not they will accept proposed treatments or procedures. This new source of empowerment has significant implications on patients, healthcare providers and governments.

Impact and Opportunity for Clinicians and Healthcare Professionals

For clinicians and healthcare professionals, key innovations have been trans-formational, making the delivery of care more efficient, effective, accurate and timely, resulting in better patient outcomes that have saved patients' lives. Yet more innovation is needed to support clinicians in the turbulent and unpredictable world of healthcare. The current healthcare system prior to Covid-19 was not sustainable due to growing aging populations with increasing long-term conditions, a rise in unmet medical needs, increases in rare and unknown conditions, higher healthcare costs and an increasing demand for healthcare services. To totally challenge the healthcare system beyond its capacity Covid-19 emerged as a global pandemic with no vaccine available for the first year. Healthcare professionals globally have achieved more than could have been anticipated due to medical and scientific innovations, but this is not sustainable for their own personal health and well-being. There needs to be a greater balance between the needs of patients and the capacity for healthcare professionals to realistically meet those needs without being stretched beyond their own capability.

To manage the growing needs of patients in this uncertain world, healthcare professionals need to continue to develop innovations that further advance healthcare in the assessment, diagnosis and treatment of patients. Clinicians are presented with problems on a daily basis and are well placed to generate innovative ideas; however, many do not consider themselves to be innovators and do not have time to commit to innovation. Clinicians and healthcare professionals that are front and center in the delivery of healthcare are best placed to be innovative and entrepreneurial, and need to be supported in their endeavors. They can play a crucial role in developing sustainable innovations for the present and future of healthcare. They have the core competencies to effectively collaborate internally and externally with other professionals expanding the multidisciplinary team in order to develop new innovations and solutions to address unmet problems specific to the healthcare context of which they have first-hand experience. Effective utilization of core expertise achieves synergy and maximizes the opportunity for successful innovations, thus positively impacting clinicians and healthcare professionals in the delivery of care.

Impact and Opportunity for Healthcare Organizations

Over the last two decades there have been major changes in the delivery of healthcare that have impacted healthcare organizations. The extent of such changes and the challenges they can bring should be recognized in the development of future innovations so the organization learns from its experience and is prepared to embrace new innovations.

Innovation and entrepreneurship is a viable way to enhance the performance of healthcare organizations and increase patient satisfaction. However, within healthcare organizations, there are challenges in the execution of viable innovations with a diverse group of stakeholders. The field of healthcare is complex, uncertain and ambiguous, and healthcare systems globally are challenged. Covid-19 has escalated those challenges in ways that were unimaginable prior to the global pandemic. More than ever, healthcare organizations need to look beyond their own specific organization to develop innovation into the future. Healthcare organizations need to leverage the knowledge, skills and expertise of individuals across relevant disciplines within and outside of their organization. By going beyond the organization boundaries they can tap into more diverse knowledge and expertise on a broader global scale. These individuals include patients, clinicians, healthcare professionals, scientists, researchers, academics, technologists, engineers, inventors, governments and other key stakeholders and experts, as appropriate. Academics and universities focus on scholarship and research can play a central role in the development of scientific innovations. Geographic distance should not cause any boundary in today's technologically advanced world where we can connect anywhere in the world remotely. The Internet, through for example Skype, Zoom and MS Teams, has created major opportunities that healthcare can utilize to bring key individuals together in real-time, collaborative environments to share and facilitate borderless creativity and innovation that will develop healthcare into the future. This enables healthcare to come together to undertake innovation and entrepreneurship that can be breakthrough, technological or incremental in terms of product, service or process development.

While innovations may need to be modified for different culture settings in different contexts, there is phenomenal scope to engage, collaborate and more effectively synergize across different geographic locations. Building a shared understanding among heterogeneous stakeholders can achieve greater synergy as they explore new opportunities to develop viable innovations that can be utilized globally. The three core areas are inputs, process and outputs (Figure 9.1).

While individual healthcare professionals may be motivated to engage in innovations that generate greater patient experience and outcomes, they need to be part of a supportive environment that aspires to achieve the highest standards of patient care. Leaders at all levels play a key role in developing such an environment. Leaders that drive innovation and an entrepreneurial mindset from top management teams are important throughout healthcare organizations. Leaders need to support internal and external engagement and collaboration in their drive for innovation. Engagement and collaboration can achieve deeper insights into problems and the development of innovative solutions that will transform the delivery of healthcare. Such collaborations must be nurtured and built on trust, respect and a shared goal to generate greater patient value.

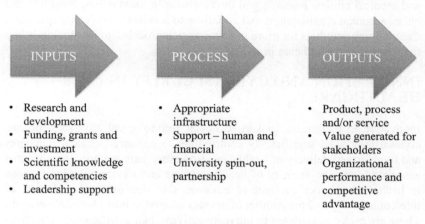

INPUTS	PROCESS	OUTPUTS
• Research and development • Funding, grants and investment • Scientific knowledge and competencies • Leadership support	• Appropriate infrastructure • Support – human and financial • University spin-out, partnership	• Product, process and/or service • Value generated for stakeholders • Organizational performance and competitive advantage

Figure 9.1   The input–output innovation model

Impact and Opportunity for Government

Innovation in healthcare provides a greater standard and quality of patient care. Furthermore, innovation generates economic growth, prosperity and job creation. It is in the best interest of every government to develop policies and create an environment that supports and facilitates innovation and entrepreneurial activities. This is particularly important to healthcare that generally is allocated the largest budget. According to the WHO (2019), health expenditure accounts for 10 percent of global gross domestic product (GDP). Spending on health comes from government expenditure, individuals paying for their own treatment and care, and private health insurance. The level of government spending is influenced by, for example, national income, changes in demographics, aging population, inflation, technological advancement and development, and structural reforms. On average, government spending accounts for 51 percent of health costs and over 35 percent comes from individuals paying for their own care (WHO, 2019).

Governments need to continue to drive innovation in healthcare as part of their long-term strategies. As we work to emerge from this global Covid-19 pandemic, they need to actively support innovation across healthcare systems – this will be imperative for the recovery and transformation of healthcare that will improve patient outcomes. By stimulating innovation in healthcare, governments will bring about better healthcare systems that will attract and retain high-caliber healthcare professionals that have the passion to make a difference. This support should be inclusive for small- and medium-sized entrepreneurial ventures, corporate entrepreneurial initiatives as part of hospitals and medical clinics, research and development in universities, hospitals and pharmaceutical organizations and initiatives to accelerate university spin-outs. Creating opportunities for more collaborative approaches to innovation is key for the future of healthcare in society.

INNOVATION AND CYBERSECURITY IN HEALTHCARE

Innovation in healthcare, and in particular technological advancement, has come a long way, significantly contributing to enhanced clinical outcomes and transformed delivery of healthcare. However, there are growing concerns associated with the security of healthcare data and devices. As innovations in healthcare devices continue to advance, this also increases the level of interconnectivity and the number of devices integrated into a hospital network. There are major advantages to interconnectivity such as efficiency, effectiveness, error reduction, and remote monitoring that allows clinicians to monitor and adjust implanted devices remotely. However, more interconnection brings higher risk of cyberattack; therefore there is a need for more sophisticated cybersecurity that protects the delivery of care and patients.

Medical devices such as X-ray machines, MRI scanners, insulin pumps, defibrillators and life-support equipment are critical to healthcare; however, such devices can be subject to cybersecurity threats that could result in the loss of functioning of critical equipment that could be detrimental to patients. In addition to the complex challenges due to the Covid-19 pandemic, healthcare systems globally are increasingly experiencing cybersecurity threats and are a high-risk sector. In recent times such attacks have occurred in Ireland, the United Kingdom, the United States, New Zealand, and the Middle East.

Medical innovations are designed for a specific medical purpose to address patient needs; however, they are vulnerable to cyberattacks, for example cardiac pacemakers or radiotherapy (both highly technology-dependent), in addition to other medical devices and treatments that are connected to the Internet and vulnerable to the same risk as a computer system. While these medical devices may not store patient data, they are a target due to the lack of security and can be used to launch an attack on the server that holds confidential patient information. Healthcare organizations hold an extensive amount of patient data, as well as a significant network of connected medical devices. If there is any level of compromise on any one device, the network becomes vulnerable to hacking of medical devices and data breaches. All medical devices need to have security measures that prevent such attacks to ensure patient safety. Future innovations must incorporate security measures into the design of the medical device from the outset.

Despite major medical technological innovations, the security and protection of such devices has not kept pace. Many healthcare systems are not adequately investing in security measures and the technology is outdated. Insufficient investment in cybersecurity exposes healthcare organizations to the risk of a cyberattack, particularly during a pandemic. Patient information is in high demand, making healthcare attractive to hackers who attempt to use malware or other forms of cyberattack as ransomware, demanding financial payment in return for reversing their coding attack to allow normal access to data. A cyberattack can compromise an organization in minutes by shutting down devices, servers or the whole network; however, it can take weeks or possibly months to recover from such an attack. The impact can be inhuman and devastate the healthcare system with hackers taking over and preventing healthcare organizations accessing patient data, interrupting clinical services and patient diagnoses, inhibiting the delivery of life-saving treatment to patients, interrupting imaging and surgical procedures, and potentially risking patients' lives. It is critical that every healthcare system globally is protected to the highest standard to ensure the protection of patient data and the continued delivery of care. This requires the highest level of security on network devices and to take the next step in the development of innovations to ensure they are secure to minimize the risk of hackers accessing the healthcare network through unsecured medical devices. There is a need for substantial investment in up-to-date IT infrastructure with appropriate malware protection, as the short-term costs generate significant long-term benefits. Additionally, all staff must be aware and updated and trained on likely cyberattacks including the use and regular changing of strong passwords, firewall protection, and avoiding the opening of unknown emails and links. Healthcare organizations need to be meticulous in who can access the system, both onsite and remotely, and monitor accessibility. While the cost of high security is substantial, the damage caused by cyberattacks is too high to risk, most specifically when it puts patient treatment and care in jeopardy. The continuous delivery of patient care and the protection of patient data requires healthcare organizations to have in place rigorous and secure systems.

Covid-19 has significantly impacted healthcare systems globally and its impact is likely to continue into the future. In the global drive to develop new innovations in the form of multiple Covid-19 vaccines, among other medical and scientific innovations, healthcare organizations must not lose sight of the importance of cybersecurity. The threat of cybercrime can immobilize entire systems and, most significantly, put patients' lives at risk. Patient care is a priority and cybersecurity must be invested in so the system is safe, adaptable and patients are protected at all times.

SUMMARY

Innovation in healthcare is significant and healthcare organizations must innovate faster than ever before to keep pace with the needed changes and developments. There have been unprecedented demands on healthcare systems globally due to Covid-19; however, the global response has demonstrated vast innovations and strong resilience which can lead the way to future developments in healthcare.

The innovations that have emerged are likely to transform the future of healthcare delivery and the continued advancement in innovation and entrepreneurship, which could not happen without the brilliant minds of people with the necessary expertise and passion to make a difference. Healthcare leaders need to recognize the value of human capital and staff retention in leading the world to better health. Without a talented workforce an organization's ability to innovate is minimal. Leaders need to drive this momentum and evaluate their organization's innovativeness and ability to further develop and grow this entrepreneurial culture within their organization.

Innovation and entrepreneurship has a major impact on key stakeholders and provides opportunities for future innovations that can further advance the world of healthcare. Patients, clinicians and healthcare professionals, healthcare organizations and governments are all impacted and have the opportunity to direct future innovations in healthcare. We have seen out of urgent necessity how efficiently and effectively multiple pharmaceutical organizations and scientists worked relentlessly to develop Covid-19 vaccines in record-breaking time. Major digital technological innovations have led to new ways of treating and empowering patients to manage their own health in the comfort of their own home and communicate their needs. Digital innovations are also providing the opportunity for healthcare to reach more people. While these innovations can be life changing and life saving, it is paramount that medical devices and technological advancements incorporate security measures in their design and development to protect healthcare from the huge cybercrime events that many have experienced in recent times.

REFERENCES

Dess, G.G. and Lumpkin, G.T. (2001). Emerging issues in strategy process research. In M.A. Hitt, R.E. Freeman and J.S. Harrison (eds.), *Handbook of Strategic Management*, pp. 3–34. Oxford: Blackwell Publishers.

Haar, J.M. and White, B.J. (2013). Corporate entrepreneurship and information technology towards employee retention: a study of New Zealand firms. *Human Resource Management Journal* 23(1), 109–25.

Lupton D. (2017). Digital health now and in the future: findings from a participatory design stakeholder workshop. *Digital Health*, 3, 1–17.

WHO (2019). Countries are spending more on health, but people are still paying too much out of their own pockets. https://www.who.int/news/item/20-02-2019 -countries-are-spending-more-on-health-but-people-are-still-paying-too-much-out -of-their-own-pockets.

Suggested Reading

Andrews, R., Greasley, S., Knight, S., Sireau, S., Jordan, A., Bell, A. and White, P. (2020). Collaboration for clinical innovation: a nursing and engineering alliance for better patient care. *Journal of Research in Nursing* 25(3), 291–304. https://doi.org/ 10.1177/1744987120918263.

In this article, the authors aim to present a collaborative approach to innovation between clinicians and engineers, using two nursing case studies as examples. An engineering design process was applied to develop novel medical devices in response to unmet clinical needs identified by nurses. Both projects resulted in novel medical devices being put into clinical use safely and effectively. Collaboration between nurses and engineers facilitates rapid iteration of novel solutions to unmet clinical needs. Both professions have similar approaches to problem-solving, complemented by specialist knowledge in their contrasting areas of expertise, making for a highly capable multidisciplinary team.

Brodtkorb, K., Skaar, R. and Slettebø, Å. (2019). The importance of leadership in innovation processes in nursing homes: an integrative review. *Nordic Journal of Nursing Research* 39(3), 127–36. https://doi.org/10.1177/2057158519828140.

In this article, the authors provide a comprehensive overview of the current state of evidence for the importance of leadership in innovation processes in nursing homes. A systematic search was conducted. The innovations described in the included studies transform the underlying values of organizational culture. The review shows that participative, involving and innovative leadership is the key to success in innovation processes.

Brimhall, K.C. (2019). Inclusion is important ... But how do I include? Examining the effects of leader engagement on inclusion, innovation, job satisfaction, and perceived quality of care in a diverse nonprofit healthcare organization. *Nonprofit and Voluntary Sector Quarterly* 48(4), 716–37. https://doi.org/10.1177/0899764019829834.

In this article, the author examines the relationships among leader engagement, inclusion, innovation, job satisfaction, and perceived quality of care in a diverse nonprofit health care organization. Data was collected at three points at six-monthly intervals from a U.S. nonprofit hospital. Multilevel path analysis indicated significant direct associations between leader engagement, inclusion, and innovation. Innovation was directly linked to improved job satisfaction and perceived quality of care. Findings suggest that nonprofit leaders who engage others in critical organizational processes can help foster an inclusive climate that leads to increased innovation, employee job satisfaction and perceived quality of care.

Busch-Casler, J., Haubner, S. and Pinkwart, A. (2021). Employee involvement in inno-
vation activities in hospitals: how perception matters. *Health Services Management Research* 34(2), 70–79. https://doi.org/10.1177/0951484820943600.

In this article, the authors address the following research questions: "How do different employee groups perceive their involvement in the innovation process in hospitals and how do their actual involvement levels differ?" and (2) "How do different employee groups perceive their interaction with other employee groups in the innovation process and how do their actual interactions differ?" The findings reveal that while all groups of employees are involved in innovation activities, perception of their involvement in innovation activities differs widely. There is a gap between perception and actual involvement, particularly for lower level employees such as nurses.

Lawton Smith, H., Bagchi-Sen, S. and Edmunds, L. (2018). Innovation cycles and geog-
raphies of innovation: a study of healthcare innovation in Europe. *European Urban and Regional Studies* 25(4), 405–22. https://doi.org/10.1177/0969776417716220.

In this article, the authors examine place-specific factors affecting geographies of innovation, that is, the transfer of research from the laboratory to bedside in the healthcare sector in four European bioscience regions. These regions are Medical Delta (MD; Leiden, Rotterdam and Delft, Netherlands) Oxford and the Thames Valley (OTV; UK), Biocat (Catalonia, Spain) and Life Science Zurich (LSZ; Switzerland). The paper shows that each region represents different positions within international value chains of innovation in the healthcare sector. They range from the highly research intensive but with relatively less in the way of commercial exploitation location (OTV) to the less research intensive but with more commercialization (LSZ).

Muthuppalaniappan, M. and Stevenson, K. (2021). Healthcare cyber-attacks and the
COVID-19 pandemic: an urgent threat to global health. *International Journal for Quality in Health Care*, 33(1), 1–4. https://doi.org/10.1093/intqhc/mzaa117.

In this article, the authors outline key Covid-19 cybersecurity principles for both healthcare organizations and academic institutions. International and national regulatory bodies have stressed the urgent need for healthcare providers and universities to protect themselves against cyberattacks during Covid-19, recognizing that a growing number of cybercriminals are seeking to capitalize on the vulnerabilities of the healthcare sector during this period. This includes a desire to steal intellectual property such as data relating to Covid-19 vaccine development, modeling and experimental therapeutics. It is therefore essential that healthcare providers and universities ensure they are informed, protected and prepared to respond to any cyberthreat.

10. The future of innovation and entrepreneurship in healthcare

QUESTIONS

What are the most recent innovations in healthcare? How are these innovations impacting the field of healthcare? How have innovations in healthcare changed in recent years? What are the likely healthcare innovations of the future? What is blockchain in healthcare? What is the future leadership approach to escalate innovation and entrepreneurship in healthcare?

INTRODUCTION

The exploration, discovery, adoption and diffusion of innovation in healthcare are intense and time-consuming processes that may require scientific evidence. While much has been achieved there is more to do to further advance and develop the field of healthcare with innovations that are life changing. Significant innovations and research in science have changed and will continue to change the practice of medicine. Scientists are continuously developing drugs, medicines and therapeutics that address the growing needs of society. Science is a necessity to address the growing and unpredictable needs of people globally.

Millions of patients worldwide are benefitting from the discovery, development and delivery of innovative drugs, medicines and therapeutics to treat chronic diseases. Additionally, healthcare is being transformed by innovations including genomics and precision medicine, the growth and development of machine learning, AI, digital technologies, big data, drugs and devices that are driving innovation in healthcare into the future. The acceleration of change is driven by innovation and technological advancements that are core and critical to the field of healthcare. This is just the beginning as we could not have anticipated two decades ago the advancement that we see today. Future innovations and research and development in medicine will continue to advance the field of healthcare beyond our expectations in the coming decades. Such advancements are significantly changing the outcome for people with conditions that previously were untreatable or incurable. The future of healthcare is changing globally and the challenges and opportunities need to be embraced. For innovations to succeed and change the field of healthcare we need to understand the current healthcare system and its existing gaps and limitations together with recognition of the needs of patients, healthcare professionals, stakeholders and society at large.

Covid-19 has brought about major change to all industries and sectors and has significantly impacted healthcare and the delivery of patient care in both Covid-19-related and non-Covid-19 related diseases, conditions and treatments. There is major transformation in how we work with telemedicine and virtual appointments are becoming the norm. Patients need to be front and center of healthcare innovations today and in the future. What will the future of healthcare look like post-Covid-19? What change has been accelerated as a result of Covid-19? As we strive toward future innovations in medicine and healthcare we need to learn from the past and the present to make a truly innovative and entrepreneurial difference that will allow our healthcare system to excel and flourish.

The purpose of this chapter is to provide an understanding of past, present and likely future innovations and entrepreneurship in the field of healthcare and the leadership approach for such innovations in the future. This chapter commences by providing an understanding of past and present innovations and their influence on the development of future innovations in healthcare; in doing so, scientific innovations, big data and exceptional current and likely future innovations are examined. Following a discussion on blockchain technology and its benefits for healthcare, the future of innovation and entrepreneurship in healthcare is examined. Leading healthcare into the future is discussed, with specific focus on the leadership approach for future innovations in healthcare.

UNDERSTANDING PAST AND PRESENT TO DEVELOP INNOVATIONS FOR THE FUTURE

The development of innovation in medicine can be highly complex and challenging, particularly with science-based innovations such as drug development and vaccines that are subject to scrutiny of evidence and regulatory approval. The delivery of healthcare is risky and each individual patient is unique and may have a different outcome depending on the treatment and delivery of care; for example, timeliness of assessment and diagnoses, accuracy of assessment and treatment plan, and quality and clarity of interaction between clinician and patient. It is paramount to understand the patient and their unique circumstances, recognizing that past innovation does not always generate future success and we need to constantly engage in the innovation process to develop more precise innovations to address specific patient needs.

Today's healthcare requires leading innovators with an entrepreneurial mindset that can work toward developing "state of the art" innovations that can better diagnose and treat patients. There are aging populations globally with an increasing number of people living with long-term morbidity and possibly multiple comorbidities requiring continuous medical treatment. This puts major pressure on any healthcare system globally. However, people do not have a choice when they become patients and require life changing treatment and care – it is through necessity that they require such treatment. For innovations to be successful they need to be monitored and evaluated to ensure that they are effective. No innovation should be implemented without clear evaluation plans to ensure it is achieving the desired results. Past, present and future innovations are imperative in making a difference to the delivery of patient care now and in the future, and transform the field of healthcare.

Healthcare has demonstrated exceptionally rich science-based innovations that are life changing. It is through scientific evidence that the best course of treatment can be determined, for example in determining the best diagnostic strategies, treatment plan, surgery, and medications. For the continued development of innovations into the future there is a need to more effectively utilize this scientific knowledge beyond its current level. We can see the global need to create safe and effective vaccines, which has resulted in scientists in the world's leading pharmaceutical organizations quickly and effectively responding to the urgent need for a life-changing vaccine for Covid-19. Within just one year, thirteen vaccines (e.g., Comirnaty (Pfizer, BioNTech – multinational), Moderna Covid-19 Vaccine (Moderna, Barda – USA), AstraZeneca (Barda Ows – UK), Sputnik V (Gamaleya Research Institute – Russia), Vaccine Janssen (Johnson & Johnson – The Netherlands, USA), CoronaVac (Sinovac – China)) have received regulatory approval in a number of countries, of which four were approved in the European Union. An additional fifty-five vaccines are in process ranging from pre-clinical to phase 3 stage of development. There are many more preclinical vaccines under active investigation. It validates what can be done out of "necessity" and what can be done post-Covid-19 out of "opportunity" through the effective utilization of scientific knowledge.

Limited utilization of scientific knowledge is harmful and extremely costly. Such limitations result in doing the same things that are not working leading to inefficient and ineffective care that lacks science-based innovations to enhance the healthcare system. The implementation of major innovations is challenging but invaluable to healthcare globally. On this premise we need to move from the healthcare we have to the healthcare we could have to ensure we deliver the best and highest standard of safe care that is innovative and entrepreneurial, and invaluable to patients.

Scientific Innovations

Scientists are focused on innovations that meet the diverse needs of society. Essential elements in reaching this goal include leveraging technologies, advanced data and analytics to ensure the best possible discoveries, and development and delivery of innovative medicines and treatments. Scientists need to identify potential projects that meet societal needs, that can be successfully completed, and ensure that objectives and milestones are clearly defined to monitor and evaluate progress. Healthcare and the standard of care impact everyone at some point in their life. Significant innovations have been made in drug development, therapeutics and technologies including ICT-integrated biotechnology-efficient disease prevention and well-being programs, precision medicine, genome editing, organ production, and stem-cell therapy. There have been exceptional developments in genomics and supporting technologies that can change the field of healthcare. Genomic testing has brought about a revolution in medicine. Innovative genomics can include the following: next-generation sequencing (NGS); single cell sequencing studies; pharmacogenomics; and cell-free DNA blood-based testing. Genomics' technological breakthrough innovations are driving healthcare into the area of more personalized care through prevention, diagnoses and precision medicine, so there is the right therapy for the right patient at the right time. All of this will contribute to support the health challenges brought about by aging populations worldwide. Life expectancy is increasing and has further accelerated over the last one hundred years. The means the health requirements of aging populations and the increase in chronic diseases are more challenging and complex. However, challenges can also provide more opportunities as we strive to do better, thus escalating the exploration, exploitation, evaluation and dissemination of viable innovations.

Future trends and innovations are influenced by:

- Environmental uncertainty;
- Aging populations with more diverse conditions and chronic diseases that need to be treated;
- Financial pressures on governments to provide high-cost medications;
- Technological advancements;
- Innovations in genetics, biotechnology, material sciences and bioinformatics;
- Public attitudes and expectations.

Precision medicine is also known as personalized medicine with the objective of providing the correct treatment to the correct person at the correct time. Pharmacogenomics is a new discipline that aims to determine how a patient's genetic profile affects their reaction to specific medicines. The objective is to identify which genetic profiles will benefit from a given medicine. Over the last decade there have been numerous data-intensive approaches to diagnosis and treatment with the core goal to divert from the traditional "one-size-fits-all" approach and develop more patient-centered strategies. This development aims to focus on the specific needs of patients and ensure they receive treatments best suited to their conditions, genetic composition and specific health characteristics. According to Amgen, pharmacogenics has already changed the clinical trial process. Furthermore, biotechnology is radically changing the diagnosis of diseases that are a result of genetic factors. Tests can now identify changes in the DNA sequence of genes connected with the risk of disease and the likelihood of patients developing a disease.

As technological advancement makes individual genome sequencing more realistic and biology becomes more advanced, opportunities are generated in disease prediction, diagnosis, prevention and treatment (Friend and Ideker, 2011); the earlier the detection, the better for curing or slowing the progression of the disease with appropriate treatment. For more effective individualized healthcare, DNA technological advances are fundamental for pharmacogenomics and personalized medicine. Medicine is aiming to personalize healthcare to meet the specific needs of individuals. Precision medicine allows clinicians an opportunity to differentiate between healthy and unhealthy individuals, and stratify them across stages of disease progression. This requires sophisticated screening technologies that are extremely costly and, as a result, many parts of the world are unable to avail of such medical advances.

Big Data in Healthcare

Big data has gained great interest over the last two decades and can develop the field of healthcare. Big data is defined as the "Information asset characterized by such a High Volume, Velocity and Variety to require specific Technology and Analytical Methods for its transformation into Value" (De Mauro et al., 2016: 122). Big data requires technologically advanced applications and software. Today, big data combined with advanced analytical approaches that include, for example, artificial intelligence (AI), can potentially enhance patient outcomes. The primary healthcare objective is to prevent, assess, diagnose and treat patients with health issues. Healthcare professionals hold confidential patient information regarding their personal medical history and medical data. With technological advancement, healthcare has transformed beyond the typed and/or handwritten notes to more efficient, effective, reliable and timely systems. In healthcare, big data can include hospital records, electronic medical records, medical examination results, and devices that are a part of the internet of things (IoT). Medical IoT devices are either attached to the patient's body or remotely monitor the patient, all of which creates a substantial amount of data. It is now more cost effective to generate, process, evaluate and share (with patients' permission) data from electronic medical records and other smart devices, to improve healthcare services. The use of electronic medical records has created more efficient and effective approaches to obtaining healthcare information, permitting patients to access and view their medical records and actively participate in their treatment. Records need to be accurate, concise and timely with full up to date information on, for example, all test results, medications and referrals. Patient confidentiality must be of the highest standard and protected at all times. With an increase in internet access and smartphones more patients across all age groups are using mobile apps to support their health needs. In this new online era these devices can also integrate with telemedicine. Such devices and mobile apps can support, for example, fitness, tracking of symptoms, care management, health and well-being.

Exceptional Current and Future Innovations

Exceptional innovations in healthcare have provided life saving and life changing treatment to patients, and include antibiotics, vaccinations, aspirin, statins, analgesia, antihypertensives, immunosuppressants, chemotherapy, transfusion medicine, surgery and anaesthesia. From where we have come to where we are now with the continued development of exceptional innovations, the future of medicine is unimaginable. Outstanding innovations are being introduced into medicine and healthcare at a fast pace. Innovations such as *mind-reading exoskeletons*, *digital tattoos* and *3D printed drugs* give us a taste of the infinite future opportunities of medicine and healthcare. Technology has significantly contributed to innovations in medicine and most notably technological advancements and developments in device technology have revolutionized surgery, making it less invasive.

Augmented, virtual and mixed reality technologies are opening new avenues in the field of medicine.

- Augmented reality (AR) is a major technology trend that is readily available, and allows users to see the real environment by projecting digital information. In medicine and healthcare, AR creates new opportunities to enhance clinical practice. AR can be used in areas such as diagnostics, surgery (including preoperative and intraoperative support) and rehabilitation; for example, neurosurgeons can use an AR projection of a 3D brain to support them in surgical procedures.
- Virtual reality (VR) provides a full simulation that can be used, for example, in medical education, pain management, psychiatry and rehabil-

itation. This can include using VR to educate patients and prevent disease, to explore ways to help reduce stress and anxiety, and in psychiatry to treat phobias. VR is already used in many applications; for example, in 2019, Case Western in collaboration with the Cleveland Clinic opened a health education campus where students use VR rather than cadavers to study anatomy.

- Mixed reality (MR) combines the real world with the virtual world in ways that were previously unimaginable. MR is used in areas such as medical education and preoperative planning. MR provides more timely diagnoses and facilitates personalization and better outcomes.

The world of healthcare delivery is changing and the global Covid-19 pandemic has further escalated these changes. Educators are finding new innovative ways to teach medical students through 3D, providing a more vivid learning experience. Healthcare providers need to find new ways to address patient needs, particularly when there is restricted access to face-to-face medical appointments. AR, VR and MR tools offer major potential and can be further developed in healthcare to increase accuracy, efficiency and effectiveness, and to reduce the risk of medical error thus ensuring more precise care and treatment of patients now and into the future.

Other innovations in medical technology have positively impacted individual lives. While it is important that patients are actively involved in their own healthcare, the devices used must be accurate and timely to provide value to patients and ensure their well-being. Examples of more recent medical technology devices include:

- AliverCor's Kardia and Apple Watch: The accurate detection of atrial fibrillation which is a leading cause of stroke by KardiaBand for Apple Watch, as asserted in a study undertaken by the Cleveland Clinic.
- WIWE: A smartphone powered, handheld ECG device that features a pulse oximeter. As heart disease is a leading cause of death, more mobile ECG devices have been developed for personal use.
- CliniCloud, EKO Core and eKuore Pro: Have all transformed the analog stethoscope into a digital one, measuring heart and lung sounds.
- Omron: Blood pressure monitors are used worldwide. The Omron blood pressure smartwatch aims to decrease the risk of stroke and provide a detailed overview of the condition of the user's heart.
- AliveCor and Omron: A strategic alliance integrating Alivecor's mobile device ECG technology with Omron's wireless blood pressure monitoring technology to provide a system for remote patient cardiovascular monitoring.

- Barostim Neo System: A pacemaker-like device to treat heart failure. It uses a pulse generator to send electrical signals to the heart and blood vessels to improve heart failure symptoms. The FDA approved the device in 2019, giving it Breakthrough Device designation.

Other medical innovations that are life changing include cochlear and retinal implants. Brain implant therapies for individuals paralyzed due to spinal cord injuries are also available, facilitating some movement and communication. In 2015, the FDA approved Spritam, a drug for epilepsy that is made by 3D printers. This highlights the opportunity for further innovations in drug development and composition through the use of 3D printers.

There are many diseases and conditions that are challenging to treat and many that cannot be cured or have no suitable current treatment, with limited life expectancy for certain patients. These include, for example, conditions and diseases such as metastatic cancers; advanced lung, heart, kidney and liver disease; cystic fibrosis; dementia, including Alzheimer's disease; strokes and other neurological diseases, including motor neuron disease and multiple sclerosis; and spinal injuries. All of these and many more have a significant impact on the lives of patients globally, and years of future research to improve outcomes and find appropriate treatment and potential cures. With continued research and commitment to develop appropriate innovations we have seen major clinical improvements in patients with conditions that were previously untreatable and the potential for new innovations in areas that are currently untreatable provides a potential promise for patients in the future.

Future innovations will also be required to address potentially unknown issues that can be caused by some technological advancements, for example the impact of excessive use of video games and the risk of epilepsy, and how excessive use of smart phones and tablets can affect individuals' vision or cause neck pain and hand strain.

BLOCKCHAIN TECHNOLOGY IN HEALTHCARE

Blockchain technology was initially introduced through Bitcoin and has received much attention across many sectors including healthcare and pharmaceuticals. Blockchain has many important uses across the field of healthcare, including electronic medical records, drugs and pharmaceutical supply chain management, biomedical research and education, remote patient monitoring, and health data analytics (Agbo et al., 2019). Blockchain in healthcare can be defined as "a new type of digital architecture, consisting of a shared, immutable ledger that can better ensure the resilience, provenance, traceability, and management of health data" (Mackey et al., 2019: 2).

The significant growth of digitization in healthcare has resulted in extensive electronic patient records that are subject to data protection legislation. The advancement of blockchain technology is an effective approach to store data by providing new ways to address major data breaches in privacy, security, sharing and storage in healthcare. Furthermore, a patient-centered approach is paramount in healthcare and blockchain technology gives patients a greater level of access, control and security over their health data. Blockchain technology can address challenges in patient engagement, patient consent, privacy and security through a platform that ensures secure exchange of data. The sharing and accessibility of patients' health data is subject to privacy, legal and regulatory requirements. With General Data Protection Regulation (GDPR) throughout the EU and appropriate privacy laws in other jurisdictions, the effective and secure management of patients' health data is paramount.

Blockchain technology is a major revolution and brings significant change to healthcare, allowing the accurate, efficient and effective exchange of information between two parties that is safe and secure. Such information would include, for example, electronic patient health records that could be shared between the healthcare provider and the patient across different hospitals and locations as appropriately agreed by the patient for the delivery of care. Patients can allow consent to permit or prevent access to their data, giving them clarity about who sees their health records. Blockchain can provide greater security for patients' healthcare records and clinical trials, and ensure compliance with all regulations. Blockchain technology in healthcare is positively impacting patient outcomes, patient data and compliance, through the sharing of healthcare data without the risk of breaching patients' privacy and security. This in turn can contribute to enhancing the quality and safety of healthcare services and the patients' experience.

Blockchain in healthcare can provide great benefit to many individuals through the accurate and timely dissemination of data with high levels of security and privacy. A systematic review by Agbo et al. (2019) clearly articulates the benefits of blockchain to healthcare applications (Table 10.1).

Table 10.1   Benefits of blockchain to healthcare applications

Decentralization	The very nature of healthcare, in which there are distributed stakeholders, requires a decentralized management system. Blockchain can become that decentralized health data management backbone from where all the stakeholders can have controlled access to the same health records, without any one playing the role of a central authority over the global health data.
Improved data security and privacy	The immutability property of blockchain greatly improves the security of the health data stored on it, since the data, once saved to the blockchain cannot be corrupted, altered or retrieved. All the health data on blockchain are encrypted, time-stamped and appended in a chronological order. Additionally, health data are saved on blockchain using cryptographic keys which help to protect the identity or the privacy of the patients.
Health data ownership	Patients need to own their data and be in control of how their data is used. Patients need the assurance that their health data are not misused by other stakeholders and should have a means to detect when such misuse occurs. Blockchain helps to meet these requirements through strong cryptographic protocols and well-defined smart contracts.
Availability/robustness	Since the records on blockchain are replicated in multiple nodes, the availability of the health data stored on blockchain is guaranteed as the system is robust and resilient against data losses, data corruption and some security attacks on data availability.
Transparency and trust	Blockchain, through its open and transparent nature, creates an atmosphere of trust around distributed healthcare applications. This facilitates the acceptance of such applications by the healthcare stakeholders.
Data verifiability	Even without accessing the plaintext of the records stored on blockchain, the integrity and validity of those records can be verified. This feature is very useful in areas of healthcare where verification of records is a requirement, such as pharmaceutical supply chain management and insurance claim processing.

Source: Agbo, Mahmoud and Eklund (2019: 7).

THE FUTURE OF INNOVATION AND ENTREPRENEURSHIP IN HEALTHCARE

The greatest danger in times of rapid change is to continue to do the same thing and expect different results. We need to be ahead in our innovative mindset and look for tomorrow's innovations today! While breakthrough innovations in healthcare can dramatically change the healthcare landscape and bring about change, it is key that for all innovations from breakthrough to incremental the patient is front and center.

Healthcare is changing and those changes bring about more opportunities for innovation and entrepreneurship. There is greater openness for new ideas and technological advancements in healthcare, with a greater emphasis on the patient as a consumer. Technology is changing the field of healthcare. Innovations in healthcare technology (e.g., wearable technologies and fitness apps) are providing supportive measures for patients once they meet regulatory standards and are quality assured.

Healthcare needs to focus on "prevention rather than cure" and keep patients healthy with timely diagnoses, assessments, treatment and care. Prevention of illness is paramount with global aging populations where healthcare requirements are greater than the timely availability of care.

Innovation and entrepreneurship is developing healthcare into the future. Major areas for innovation and entrepreneurship, as discussed above, include, for example, personalized medicine/health, big data/analytics, medical devices, patient/consumer experience, and wellness/lifestyle medicine. Furthermore, innovation and entrepreneurship is growing in the area of biotechnology which is important for scientists, physicians, consultants and other healthcare professionals, bioengineers and technologists. Wellness and preventative care are other major areas for growth and development in the area of nutrition, wearable technologies and home fitness. Innovators, whether part of a large public or private hospital, pharmaceutical organization, or the start-up entrepreneur, need to have the passion to bring their idea forward, a vision that drives, motivates and inspires others, and focuses on lifelong learning so they can gain knowledge and acquire expertise in areas in which they are not qualified. It is important for all innovators and entrepreneurs to "know what they know" and "know what they do not know" and discover what the "unknowns" are by being open and objective in gaining advice, insight and guidance from others. They need to have persistence and perseverance (especially during product development and testing processes), an effective leadership style and teamwork ethos, and demonstrate engagement and flexibility.

Innovation and entrepreneurship in healthcare today and in the future is complex and challenging, yet it is a necessity. We can see with the Covid-19 pandemic how significant funding was invested into multiple pharmaceutical organizations globally to develop a breakthrough vaccine at record speed. The innovation and entrepreneurial mindset of the scientists developing those vaccines (now approved by their respective regulatory bodies) can save lives, restore our healthcare systems back to full capacity for non-Covid-19 patients and give people the opportunity to live life again.

Entrepreneurial start-ups in healthcare can develop innovations that revolutionize the delivery of future patient care. Therefore, these start-ups need to be nurtured and supported with greater clarity and guidance from governments and the healthcare system on *available funding, rules, regulations, policies, procedures, intellectual property, scalability* and *procurement.* Innovation and entrepreneurship in healthcare will help each country deliver better healthcare to society.

LEADING INNOVATION IN HEALTHCARE INTO THE FUTURE

Innovation can develop and flourish in some parts of an organization but not in others. There can be challenges diffusing innovation throughout an organization, and on a broader national, international and global scale. This creates a concern across the field of healthcare where there is an opportunity to be more innovative and generate greater patient value. Leadership is paramount for innovation to truly flourish and diffuse throughout the organization and, where appropriate, across the healthcare system. Leaders that champion innovation must demonstrate an innovative mindset that embraces opportunities in order to get their team on board. Leading innovation is challenging but rewarding as it gives leaders the chance to explore and utilize the untapped creative mindset of their team; a leadership approach that is supportive and motivates teamwork, utilizing core competencies to contribute to the success of a shared goal for the benefit of patients.

Today's patients are more actively involved in their own healthcare treatment and decision-making. Too much healthcare expenditure is unnecessarily wasted, this needs to change at a time when demand continuously exceeds capacity. There are many preventable medical errors due to failings in systems involving the giving and not giving of timely and appropriate care. Excessive staff pressure and the risk of burnout is concerning and has an impact on the individual healthcare professional, the patient and the healthcare system. Patients need to have more timely access to care, and clear and concise communication with their healthcare professional, and be assured of a safe and high standard of care that will provide the best patient outcomes. In doing so, the delivery of patient care must be caring and compassionate. Leaders need to be responsive to those needs and drive innovation so that every step is taken to consistently deliver the highest standard of care to each and every patient with empathy and compassion.

Leaders need to be able to lead through uncertainty so they can effectively transform their environment. At times the healthcare environment can be so overwhelmed and pressured that healthcare professionals are unable to find time to focus and identify the key issues in front of them. Despite the relentless and unprecedented challenges facing healthcare, leaders need to keep focused and have a heightened sense of awareness of the key issues surrounding them. Leaders need to be open and objective in their mindset, with clear awareness of current issues and their likely future impact on the healthcare system in order to strive to make a difference to the quality and standard of care.

Leaders need to use their transformational leadership skills and expertise, and reflect on past and current innovations to be able to anticipate and focus on future innovations in healthcare in order to be successful. Having a future-oriented mindset and a sense of foresight allows leaders to prepare and focus on the future by anticipating trends and their consequences. The future of healthcare needs to be different – the need to demonstrate courage, commitment and perseverance is at an all-time high. Leaders need to understand and drive innovation, encourage its diffusion beyond their own organization, and effectively collaborate and engage with others internally and externally.

SUMMARY

We have seen outstanding advancements in innovation in medicine and healthcare, and in many areas technology, such as AI, big data and IoT, has significantly contributed to those advancements. It is anticipated that blockchain technology will further develop and contribute to the healthcare ecosystem. This will provide higher quality and safer care, greater transparency, and more secure processes at a lower cost. However, there is a need to continue to develop innovations that advance medicine and deliver the highest standard of patient care. Medicine and healthcare does not stand still and in many ways it is unpredictable, and demand often exceeds capacity. There is a growing burden on the healthcare system with aging global populations, increases in chronic diseases and multiple comorbidities, and delays in diagnoses and treatment due to long waiting lists that have reached an all-time high in many areas of specialism across healthcare globally due to Covid-19. Innovation is an integral part of addressing healthcare problems and ensuring better patient outcomes.

The future of healthcare requires leaders that are willing to take appropriate risks and drive the development, nurturing and promotion of innovation that is forward-looking, patient-focused and generates greater patient value to manage and overcome current issues and challenges in healthcare.

We are living in an era where innovation and entrepreneurship in healthcare can achieve outstanding results if healthcare leaders and healthcare professionals are willing to:

- Lead as you would like to be led;
- Treat patients in the way you or your loved one would want to be treated as a patient;
- Put patients at the heart of everything you do;
- Communicate with clarity, integrity and respect;
- Demonstrate empathy, kindness, humanity and compassion;
- Be passionate and compassionate in what you do and how you do it.

The future of healthcare is here and needs healthcare professionals who are inspired and motivated to make the impossible possible in their pursuit of delivering innovative, entrepreneurial excellence that will lead the world to better health!

Together, let us make a positive impact!

REFERENCES

Agbo, C.C., Mahmoud, Q.H. and Eklund, J.M. (2019). Blockchain technology in healthcare: a systematic review. *Healthcare* 7(2), 56.

De Mauro, A., Greco, M. and Grimaldi, M. (2016). A formal definition of Big Data based on its essential features. *Library Review* 65(3), 122–35.

Friend, S.H. and Ideker, T. (2011). Biomedical technology and the clinic of the future. *Nature Biotechnology* 29(3), 215.

Mackey, T.K., Kuo, T.T., Gummadi, B., Clauson, K.A., Church, G., Grishin, D., Obbad, K., Barkovich, R. and Palombini, M. (2019). 'Fit-for-purpose?' – challenges and opportunities for applications of blockchain technology in the future of health-care. *BMC Medicine* 17(68), 1–17.

Suggested Reading

Car, J., Sheikh, A., Wicks, P. and Williams, M.S. (2019). Beyond the hype of big data and artificial intelligence: building foundations for knowledge and wisdom. *BMC Medicine* 17, 143. https://doi.org/10.1186/s12916-019-1382-x.

In this article, the authors provide concrete examples of how "big data" can be used to advance healthcare and discuss some of the limitations and challenges encountered with this type of research. It primarily focuses on real-world data, such as electronic medical records and genomic medicine, considers new developments in AI and digital health, and discusses ethical considerations and issues related to data sharing.

Cho, N., Squair, J.W., Bloch, J. and Courtine, G. (2019). Neurorestorative inter-ventions involving bioelectronic implants after spinal cord injury. *Bioelectronic Medicine* 5(10). https://doi.org/10.1186/s42234-019-0027-x.

In this article, the authors highlight multiple neuromodulation therapies that target circuits located in the brain, midbrain, or spinal cord have been able to improve motor and autonomic functions. The authors summarize the impend-ing arrival of bioelectronic medicine in the field of spinal cord injury (SCI). They also discuss the new role of functional neurosurgeons in neurorestorative interventional medicine, a new discipline at the intersection of neurosurgery, neuro-engineering, and neurorehabilitation.

Denis, J.L. and van Gestel, N. (2016). Medical doctors in healthcare leadership: theoretical and practical challenges. *BMC Health Services Research* 16(Supplement 1), 158, 45–56. https://doi.org/10.1186/s12913-016-1392-8.

In this article, the authors examine recent government and organizational policies in two different health systems that aim to develop clinical leadership among the medical profession. Different institutional contexts have different policy experiences regarding the engagement and leadership of medical doctors but seem to face similar policy challenges. Achieving alignment between soft (trust, collaboration) and hard (financial incentives) levers may require facilitative conditions at the level of the health system, like clarity and stability of broad policy orientations and openness to local experimentation.

Lee, S.Y. and Lee, K. (2018). Factors that influence an individual's intention to adopt a wearable healthcare device: the case of a wearable fitness tracker. *Technological Forecasting and Social Change*, 129, 154–63. https://doi.org/10.1016/j.techfore .2018.01.002.

In this article, the authors examine factors that influence an individual's intention to adopt a wearable fitness tracker, which is a type of wearable healthcare device. Analyzing data collected from 616 respondents, they found that the intention to adopt was stronger among respondents who were aware of wearable fitness trackers than it was among those who were not aware. Results of ordered logistic regressions indicate that in both groups of respondents, consumer attitudes, personal innovativeness, and health interests had statistically significant and positive associations with the intention to adopt a wearable fitness tracker.

Mackey, T.K., Kuo, TT., Gummadi, B., Clauson, K.A., Church, G., Grishin, D., Obbad, K., Barkovich, R. and Palombini, M. (2019). 'Fit-for-purpose?' – challenges and opportunities for applications of blockchain technology in the future of healthcare. *BMC Medicine*, 17(68), 1-17. https://doi.org/10.1186/s12916-019-1296-7

In this article, the authors discuss blockchain in healthcare and answering the real needs of healthcare stakeholders, blockchain approaches must also be responsive to the unique challenges faced in healthcare compared to other sectors of the economy. In this sense, ensuring that a health blockchain is 'fit-for-purpose' is pivotal. This concept forms the basis for this article, where the authors' share views from a multidisciplinary group of practitioners at the forefront of blockchain conceptualization, development, and deployment.

Wu, J., Li, H., Cheng, S. and Lin, Z. (2016). The promising future of healthcare services: when big data analytics meets wearable technology. *Information and Management* 53(8), 1020–33. https://doi.org/10.1016/j.im.2016.07.003.

In this article, the authors discuss how the thriving development of healthcare-wearable technology is creating great opportunities and posing a remarkable future for healthcare services. The authors' findings provide practical guidance to wearable device manufacturers on optimizing competition strategies and offer insights to social planners on potential policymaking to promote better healthcare services.

Index